SPIRITUAL WARRIOR

Beyond Fanaticism, Terrorism, and War: Discover the Peace Solution

B.T. SWAMI

HARI
NAMA
PRESS

Hari-Nama Press gratefully acknowledges the BBT for the use of verses and purports from Srila Prabhupada's books. All such verses and purports are © Bhaktivedanta Book Trust International, Inc.

The publisher gratefully acknowledges the kind permission of Goloka Books in allowing us the use of their artwork for incorporation into our cover design.

First printing 2005

Cover and interior design by Subala dasa / Ecstatic Creations
Cover artwork by Philip Malpass / Goloka Books

Printed in the United States of America

ISBN: 1-885414-18-8

Library of Congress Control Number: 2005924130

Persons interested in the subject matter of this book are invited to correspond with the publisher:

Hari-Nama Press
PO Box 76451, Capitol Hill, Washington, DC 20013

www.ifast.net/hnp

SPIRITUAL WARRIOR VI

Beyond Fanaticism, Terrorism, and War:
Discover the Peace Solution

Works by B.T. Swami (Swami Krishnapada)

Leadership for an Age of Higher Consciousness I
Administration from a Metaphysical Perspective

Leadership for an Age of Higher Consciousness II
Ancient Wisdom for Modern Times

Spiritual Warrior I
Uncovering Spiritual Truths in Psychic Phenomena

Spiritual Warrior II
Transforming Lust into Love

Spiritual Warrior III
Solace for the Heart in Difficult Times

Spiritual Warrior IV
Conquering the Enemies of the Mind

Spiritual Warrior V
Making the Mind Your Best Friend

Spiritual Warrior VI
Beyond Fanaticism, Terrorism, and War: Discover the Peace Solution

Reflections on Sacred Teachings I
Sri Siksastaka

Reflections on Sacred Teachings II
Madhurya-Kadambini

Reflections on Sacred Teachings III
Harinama Cintamani

Reflections on Sacred Teachings IV
Sri Isopanisad

Reflections on Sacred Teachings V
Srila Bhaktisiddhanta's Sixty-four Principles for Community

The Beggar I
Meditations and Prayers on the Supreme Lord

The Beggar II
Crying Out for the Mercy

The Beggar III
False Ego: The Greatest Enemy of the Spiritual Leader

The Beggar IV
Die Before Dying

Check our web site at **www.ifast.net/hnp** for information on braille and international versions.

Dedication

To the leaders of the Mauritian Government, who have consistently worked so hard in maintaining unity in one of the most diversified countries in the world.

Contents

Acknowledgements

I would sincerely like to thank Lauren Kossis for the editing of the book; Adam Kenney and Stewart Cannon for layout and cover design; and Krista Oliver for final editing. I would also like to thank Lisa Webb and Makeda Cannon for proofreading; Jambavan Dasa for Sanskrit editing; Prentiss Alter for scriptural editing; and Jo Ann Noble for her assistance with the research. I would also like to thank the Ewing family for financing the printing of *Spiritual Warrior VI*. You are all wonderful spiritual warriors who are ready to embrace the culture of peace in the fight against fanaticism, sectarianism, terrorism, and war.

Foreword

I'm flattered to be able to share a few thoughts with such an important international audience. Today, we live in an age of modernity, with hi-tech communication tools and technology that defies the speed of light. We are in fact already in post-modernity! We can use our mobile phone to uplink onto any website, download any information, and chat with anyone on earth, but does that mean effective communication?

We don't have time to share with anyone. The usual courtesy, basic manners, have given way in the name of workload. We don't have time to talk to our parents and friends except when we need them to serve us! New "scriptures" have been written in this era, and a new world order established!

"Indulge yourself in the material world to the fullest. Welcome to Kali-yuga—the age of quarrel, confusion, and war!" Young people my age do many things. Rarely do they want to fight for a cause, give their time to others, or help this

3

world become a better place. This selfish and egoistic attitude is quickly spreading everywhere. We have to wake up and realize that if this goes on, it is the beginning of the end.

Things are so simple; we complicate everything. Recently, the world has been shaken by the unscrupulous deeds of terrorists who fight a deadly war in the name of peace. The winners call themselves heroes.... of what exactly, no one knows. Many small economies are paying the price of globalization. Only the fittest will survive. Strategies are devised and implemented in this quest for acquiring market share often unethically and immorally. Instead of loving and helping each other out, we are breeding skepticism and hatred. We divide, sub-divide, and invent causes leading to fanaticism and sectarianism.

Leaders, this has to stop. Go out and tell them that they are wrong—that the medals they polish bear the scars of wars that feed the rich and bury the poor. The peace solution is not an illusion. It can be easily reached. We are all citizens of one world. Our differences enrich our potential. We complete each other, like the flowers that make up our beautiful garden, that of humanity.

I am blessed to live in Mauritius, a land where all the cultures meet in utmost trust and respect. Unity in diversity is our motto and nation-building our renewed mission. This is the theme of this wonderful and most needed book. Allow me to invite you to share this ideal worldwide.

—OM Shanti, Shanti, Shanti
Hon Ravi Raj Yerrigadoo
Minister of Youths and Sports
Mauritius

Editor's Preface

The *Spiritual Warrior* series consists of lectures given by His Holiness Bhakti Tirtha Swami (Swami Krishnapada) to a wide variety of live radio and television audiences around the world, over a period of several years. Since the topics were originally presented in spoken form, the style is conversational and informal. In the editing process, we have modified the text to enhance readability, yet sought to preserve some of the verbal nuances that would maintain the mood of the original presentations. By so doing, we hope to create an atmosphere that literally makes you part of the audience so that you can experience the powerful presence of the speaker as he shares essential nourishment for the soul.

We would like to mention several other stylistic considerations. In the course of his discussions, B.T. Swami includes perspectives from many different spiritual philosophies; however, because his audiences are composed mainly of people in the Christian and Vedic traditions, he makes the most extensive references to these scriptures. At times, he uses Sanskrit terminology from the Vedas, a vast body of ancient scriptures originating from the area of the world known today as India. We have endeavored to keep many of these terms and have tried to explain them within the context of the discussion. When coming upon such terms, if you need additional information and clarification, we invite you to consult the glossary. However, there are some terms we would like to initially clarify:

• When His Holiness B.T. Swami refers to the one God that we all know of, he uses different terminologies. Sometimes he says the Supreme Lord, the Supreme Personality of Godhead, Mother-Father God, or Krishna.

• He often uses the word "devotees." He is drawing attention to those spiritualists who are connected to the Vedic tradition as well as to all aspiring spiritualists who are embarking on the spiritual journey.

• He also uses the term "nine-fold process," which refers to various activities that a person engages in during his or her spiritual practices of devotion to God, such as hearing about the Lord, speaking about Him, remembering Him, praying to Him, serving Him, fully surrendering, and so on.

The end of each chapter includes many of the questions and answers exchanged during the original lectures. We hope that these will respond to some of the concerns that may arise in the course of your reading. These discussions between B.T. Swami and the audience may also give you different angles from which to view the topics presented.

This book is the sixth volume in our *Spiritual Warrior* series. The first five volumes, *Spiritual Warrior I: Uncovering Spiritual Truths in Psychic Phenomena*, *Spiritual Warrior II: Transforming Lust into Love*, *Spiritual Warrior III: Solace for the Heart in Difficult Times*, *Spiritual Warrior IV: Conquering the Enemies of the Mind*, and *Spiritual Warrior V: Making the Mind Your Best Friend* are already in print and have been translated into several different languages, along with His Holiness' other works. The information presented in these pages is extremely rare, and we hope you will make the most of the knowledge they contain. If you take these teachings seriously, they can transform your life into a most sublime, loving adventure.

Introduction

I met His Holiness Bhakti Tirtha Swami through a synchronistic meeting with one of his devoted students on a street of Cape Town, South Africa very soon after taking up a position with the Center for Conflict Resolution (CCR). In the usual indomitable way that comes from a deep conviction and I daresay another faculty of knowing, the devotee talked about conflict and peace and the work of his teacher Bhakti Tirtha Swami who was scheduled to visit the upcoming week. I was searching for ways to infuse my work and the field of peacemaking with a base of values. I was personally challenged in my work to find a way to create a learning circle that contributed to animating parliamentarians and decision-makers in foreign affairs, and to help extend defense ministries from southern and central Africa from being just adept negotiators to peacemakers. The answer lay I thought in the crucial factor of leadership. The meeting on the street presented me with the opportunity to work with Swami, a "light worker" or in his terms a "spiritual warrior."

Since 2001, Swami has contributed to the work of CCR through his role as a resource person on the Senior Government Project at CCR. And in his annual visit with staff at CCR, he has assisted us to understand what it means to lead and build communities as we grappled with the organizational journey work of dealing with the conflict that comes with organizational and societal change. Yes, even in conflict resolution and peace organizations as in all organizations and societal groupings, the potential for us to respond destructively exists. This is where the work of B.T. Swami is so relevant and empowering.

Drawing on ancient Vedic teachings, he gives us an extended understanding of time and purpose. The view espoused is rooted in the views of the life of the soul. Each lifetime we spend on earth or in the material realm brings with it specific lessons for the soul to learn, and each person in our circle in this Age of Existence known as Kali-yuga has a lesson to offer our soul's learning. In this age, he reminds us that personal transformation is a prerequisite for societal transformation; that personal transformation requires more than a pragmatic morality; and that discernment is a spiritual muscle we need to exercise in order to become "spiritual warriors."

The robustness of the term "warrior" is a clear indicator that the ever increasing gross human rights violations and the misspent inventiveness of the cruelty of people towards each other requires a response of "spiritual warfare." Spiritual warriors, who sense the danger presented by impious and destructive forces and who actively engage in waging love and peace, fighting the war on the battlefield of consciousness, are activists with a keen spirituality. We must take notice of the very important point that we need a proactive role as peacemakers and leaders. Leadership has a rich source in the spirituality embedded in the ancient texts of world religions. Swami promotes a respectful engagement with these texts as a means to unmask all forms of religious fanaticism and its opportunistic use of the affective response religious identity generates. Through his teachings of the *Bhagavad-gita*, he dispels the obfuscation created by religious fanatics who promote the idea of a physical "just or righteous war" while exhibiting a decidedly cold lack of love for humanity.

The *Spiritual Warrior* series is a welcome addition to the growing literature that promotes the holistic response to the challenges of the human condition and its societal systems. For me, this new text humanizes political science and conflict studies, reminding us that systems without soul or spirituality will mutate to engender dangerous, narrow systems of control. If we do not recognize that the dual need for interconnectedness between people and between person and God is a deep hunger, those who may start their struggles in response to valid grievances will very quickly be usurped by the seduction of the economies of greed, manipulation, and repression: the economy of war.

The insight stimulated by this text that I take into my personal tool kit is that while the forces of inhumanity do exist and thrive, there is a spirituality of hope, compassion, and communion that is growing in legions, leading to a critical mass of spiritual warriors ready to make the change that will connect us to God and Love. What's even more wonderful is that there is an open invitation for all to participate!

—Alison Lazarus
    The Director of International Solidarity and Peace-
    building Institute: Center for Conflict Resolution
    Cape Town, South Africa

"So in everything, do to others as you would have them do to you, for this sums up the Law and the Prophets."

Matthew 7:12 (Christianity)

Chapter 1

The Phenomena of Evil

What Is Evil?

When we hear the word "evil," many images come to our minds. For instance, we might think of the terrorist attacks in America on September 11th that took almost 3,000 lives. We might think of a serial killer who heinously kills dozens of people. Sometimes we think of a child abuser preying on innocent children, or the death camps in former Yugoslavia. We think about the tremendous impoverishment and war in Sudan, Liberia, Sierra Leone, and Somalia. Perhaps we think about the starvation in Ethiopia and the events causing young children and elderly women to meet their deaths by the millions. We think of people such as Saddam Hussein, who used torture freely, or Adolf Hitler, who was responsible for the murder of millions of Jews. We think of Idi Amin, who delighted in killing, sometimes eating the organs of his enemies, or Emperor Nero, who killed countless of his own citizens including his wife and mother. We think of Joseph Stalin, who probably killed more of his own countrymen than any other leader in history. We think of the murder of millions of American Indians by the settlers. We think of the millions of African slaves brought to the West from their native land, most of whom did not even survive the passage across the sea. As we think of the many current holocausts, we may think of the major companies and corporations polluting cities and countries without considering the long-term effects of their actions. We might even think of the satanic rituals performed by so-called elite and powerful personalities in various countries. As we reflect on all this, we might wonder how God can be all-merciful when we see such devastating events.

Is there a devil, who makes people commit these vicious acts of violence? Are people just trying to find some scapegoat as they express their animalistic tendencies? Is the demonic superior to the divine? We now see more sinful activities becoming a part of the "normal" structure of society and people are accepting them. If we examine most communities in the world, we will find that the negative is increasingly dominating over the activities of liberation. Have the soldiers of righteousness lost the battle, and should they surrender to more kinds of incarceration? Let us examine some of these questions. We want to address the phenomena of evil because we can understand more about the phenomena of goodness, righteousness, and divinity by recognizing its opposite. This understanding will also help us recognize how evil creeps in and contaminates our consciousness.

The Propensity for Evil Within Us

We all have a lower self and a higher self. The Vedic scriptures tell us that there was a time when evil and righteousness could not co-exist within the same universe. Later, there came a time when evil and righteousness not only existed within the same universe but within the same planet. As humankind moved farther away from the original spiritual culture created by God and moved closer to excessive pursuits of commodities and materialism, then evil and righteousness began to co-exist powerfully even within the same individual. This means that there is a godly and a demonic side to each of us at this state of evolution. When we find one polarity in the material world, we will always find its opposite: we reside in the realm of relativity and duality. The Native American Indians believe that we all have two dogs fighting inside of us—one bad and one good. When asked which one wins the fight, they affirm that the one who gets fed the most wins. The aspect of ourselves to which we give the most energy will dominate and defeat the other.

Don't think that there is just a devil outside, because the propensity for evil is within. It is not that there is only one devil; there are many devils. It is not that there is one type of sin; there are many types of sin and different combinations of sinful activities. There are divine, pious entities as well as highly empowered negative beings. There are extraterrestrial beings from other realms who are godly and others who are devilish. If we read the Bible, the Koran, the Torah, or the Vedas, we will find that all of these scriptures tell us about extraordinary personalities and demonic entities of different calibers.

Disembodied thought forms can also enter into a person's consciousness and influence him or her. Thoughts are sources of energy, which, once released into the atmosphere, can have a life of their own and seriously impact upon the environment. However, they primarily influence people who are receptive. For this reason, mind control is one of the biggest problems in the 21st century. As technology and science become more subtle, there are more ways to harness people's mental energy without their awareness. Many people would be outraged to find out how much mind control, for instance, is being used by the CIA, FBI, and in military and secret police units around the world. It is being used even more prevalently in major advertising campaigns. As we build up our spiritual strength and understand more about our real identity, we will have greater protection from those influences that are negative.

There are even some people who talk about the devil in terms of race and gender. For instance, there are those who say that white people are devils, and others who say that black people are devils. There are people who say all men are devils, and there are men who say that all women are witches and devils. For people to even utter such nonsense shows that they have already been devilishly affected. People should be evaluated not by race or gender, but by consciousness, understanding, and perception. Racism and sexism pits man against woman, race against race, nation against nation, and tribe against tribe, and this can only continue to bring increasing fragmentation, conflicts, and sufferings.

How to Recognize Destructive Behavior

We can make a further analysis of evil by looking at its results. If an activity or behavior is righteous, it will produce more righteousness if the majority of people accept the same activity. However, if it is wicked, it will produce more degradation if the majority follow suit. We can make an evaluation using this barometer. If the majority of people take up a certain behavior, will it lead to the growth of human civilization or to its destruction? If everyone engaged in abortion, would we have a future? If everyone took to crime, would we have a future? If everyone propagated genocide, would any of us still exist? If everyone took to chauvinism, racism, nationalism, or tribalism, would we have a viable planet? No, beloved. If everyone took to some kind of sectarian religious lifestyle, could we ever reach any sense of unity with diversity? If everyone felt that they had the only answer, would there be any means of communication? If a massive number of people accepted any of these mentalities and lifestyles, would it promote a higher good?

Healthy ancient cultures addressed deviations naturally by having deviant people embarrassed and shamed out of the community. Now, practically the most successful people are those known to be the most duplicitous and manipulative. These days, especially in many of the urban communities, the people who have the greatest assets of wealth are those involved in some kind of illegal or dehumanizing activity. This is another reason why the drug business has become so intense. The drug dealers often have the best houses, cars, and girlfriends or boyfriends, which make them more popular and admired. However, when people decide that they will not accept this kind of cultural expression, the deviants will lose their ability to function in the community because they will noticeably stand out. This invokes the culture of love—a culture in which we have an actual future. Sometimes we do not know or realize how much we are saturated by an environment of sin; that is, a culture of degradation.

A Culture of Fragmentation and Relativity

We have a tendency to create such fragmentation, which moves us away from developing higher consciousness. Basically, active negative forces in the world are trying to fragment everything so that we will not be left with anything but anarchy. Some people in the United States feel that, in our lifetime, we may see so much anarchy that there will no longer be a strong federal system. Governors and mayors may simply refuse to accommodate the system. Some feel that the constant exposure of the leaders' discrepancies by the media is part of a plan to minimize the citizens' trust and support in their leaders. Those with the demoniac mindset are expert in trying to destabilize societies.

Two major polarities have always existed—the pious versus the impious, or the godly versus the atheistic. These types of wars have raged since before we came into these universes and will continue after we leave. The demonic agenda is to try to keep people away from deeper levels of understanding so that they will not have the weaponry to protect themselves from devastations.

Healthy culture minimizes or keeps the demonic influences out. As we look at evil from a subtle perspective, we see that relative situations also create evil. Modern day cultures influence people to think that everything is relative. It encourages people to do what they want, when they want, and how they want. There are many books and teachings on the market now telling us to own our feelings by doing whatever we feel without inhibitions. Such a mentality borders on animal life, which functions solely based on instincts. Many psychiatrists and psychotherapists are encouraging their patients to abandon any feelings of compunction or regret about their sinful life.

They encourage people to do whatever they want and to feel comfortable with it. If a person feels guilt, then they seek treatment and give their money to a person who in many cases has more problems than the patient. Many people enter into such professions in the first place due to certain dysfunctional patterns in their own lives. It is often like the sick being treated by the sick.

Material culture practically forces people to accept relative considerations that disregard any understanding of an absolute. If we look at wholesome ancient systems, we will undoubtedly find expressions of universal truths. For instance, Islam has the sheikh, Judaism has the rabbi, Christianity has the priest, Eastern systems have *guru*, and African systems have a king or chief. What did these people do? They were to be protectors of the sacred and mediums for divinity. When they did not act as mediums, an assembly of overseers, which also included priests or *brahmanas*, would check them to ensure that they properly executed their duty. Genuine kings or chiefs were not ruthless or cruel dictators. They were to serve as the doorway for blessings to come from the ancestors, demigods, and ultimately from the Supreme Personality of Godhead.

When we function only on relative considerations, we do what we want and constantly fight those who get in our way because we have lost a sense of honoring divinity, communalism, and of really acting as our brother's and sister's keeper. As we become more and more cultureless, we throw out all of these traditions because our new systems view them as archaic and even exploitive due to misuse by dictators. This movement towards relativity has allowed millions of people to accept abortion and even call it freedom. In just three weeks after conception, the embryo develops a heartbeat, and in seven weeks, the brain functions. At this early stage of development, all the chromosomes are there that will determine eye color, skin color, and hair color, along with all the other traits that distinguish a human being as an individual. Regardless, leaders, presidents, ministers, and so on are afraid to address the problem because they might lose their position or election. Women, who are blessed to act as caretakers for some particular soul, now engage in murder, and our society accepts it as okay. The majority will even look at those who speak against abortion as if something is wrong with them.

Many souls are trying to come into this world to make it a better place, but we are losing all understanding about the science of sexuality. Now sex simply becomes a matter of lust in which bodies rub together. Sex is, in reality, also connected with the consciousness of a man and woman when they have union. Their consciousness will invite a particular type of soul into this world. There are spiritual practices to engage in before the act, while in the act, and after the act. However, since we are cultureless, we are too much caught up in the culture of Hollywood. If you want to follow that culture, then look at their relationships and decide if you consider them to be successful. I guarantee you, beloved, that those are not the kinds of role models that you want to follow. They are surely inimical to the path of the spiritual warrior.

As you evaluate relativity, run away from anything and anyone who tells you to just do your own thing. It is about doing God's thing. It is about your involvement in family, community, and society. The materialistic paradigm says that, as individuals, we should kick, push, or shove anyone hindering the fulfillment of our sense gratification. That is evil. In wholesome cultures, a person finds fulfillment when they can add value to community. Much of modern day materialistic thought says, "I think, therefore, I am." However, an intelligent person knows that the mere ability to think is not the most significant factor; rather, the quality of a person's thoughts is most important. Existence is meaningful because we are part of a community, part of a cosmos, and part of a holistic scheme that we are accountable to. This relative consideration makes us less and less accountable to others.

A Cultureless Society

Basically, our current society lacks healthy culture. The more the world becomes materialistic, individualistic, and egocentric, the more we continue to obscure a sense of wholesome culture. Real culture is an expression of humankind's pursuit for higher goals, and it involves the activities we engage in during that pursuit. Therefore, any culture which is not a culture of liberation becomes a culture of stagnation. In much of the modern world, we do not have a healthy culture. We have forgotten how to respect parents and elders. We have lost our fear and reverence towards God. We have lost our understanding of how to contact angles, demigods, etc. We have lost our ability to perform *yajnas* or sacrifices that have the potency to bring divine intervention. We normally do not practice valuable *samskaras* or rights of passage. With the loss of our healthy culture, we have instead turned to money, prestige, and commodities as a substitute. We are now accepting transitory pleasures or *capala-sukha* in our search for that substantive lifestyle.

Wholesome culture helps us express our personalities and individual creativity to our highest potential. We ultimately access healthy culture through spirituality. Although we have a material body, if we know how to access our higher nature, we can become metaphysically endowed and spiritually competent. If we look particularly at wholesome ancient cultures, we will normally find a spiritual nucleus. There existed a conception of motherhood and fatherhood that allowed a communal or extended family situation to exist. However, we have now lost the understanding of how to function side by side with each other in the march towards liberation. Most people do not even understand what liberation is. It is not just a matter of reform, which basically means replacing one material system with another. It is not a matter of replacing one nation with another or one race with another; liberation is a matter of understanding our purpose here. We are all in this particular universe because we have work to do. That work will bring us back to a state of consciousness in which we are free of limitations, and where we can reside in the higher realms spoken about in all major religious systems.

We are all working to find ways to function in a world that is hostile toward our basic existence, but there are ways to reach a higher state of evolution. We can reach that goal through the culture of spirituality, which will bring out more of the natural quality of the soul. Spiritual warfare is the science of creating and invoking auspiciousness. Anyone involved in spiritual warriorship understands that it is not just a matter of what you do, but it is also a matter of being sensitive to other's needs, perceptions, and activities. It is not just a matter of living as an island, but it is a matter of understanding what aggregates to make up our environment.

There is an attempt throughout the planet to take away healthy culture, theism, and people's ability to realize that they actually have a future. It is manifesting in gross and subtle attempts to lead people more into a culture of confusion. It is allowing people to involve themselves in activities detrimental to individual and collective growth. People are involving themselves with great eagerness without understanding that they are involved in activities of spiritual suicide.

Develop Inner Strength

Some of the greatest problems are problems that we have to deal with inside ourselves. They involve raising our own consciousness. If I allow you to excessively bother me mentally, it means that my own consciousness is low; otherwise, your actions or words could not disturb my mind. Whatever your position may be, if you bother me, it is because I stand on insecure ground. We must avoid a mood of always seeing others as the full problem. We must avoid letting people's nonsense turn us into nonsense. If we fall prey to weakness, it is because we do not have sufficient strength.

If we have determination, we can make a difference by raising better families, addressing our own situations, and looking at our own consciousness. The mind can be the greatest enemy of any person, but a mind harnessed for higher achievements and for knowledge of spiritual truths cannot be held down.

uddhared atmanatmanam
natmanam avasadayet
atmaiva hy atmano bandhur
atmaiva ripur atmanah

One must deliver himself with the help
of his mind, and not degrade himself.
The mind is the friend of the conditioned
soul, and his enemy as well.
Bhagavad-gita 6.5

We are getting help from higher beings in the universe, but there is also a tremendous influx of influence from lower entities. These lower entities are constantly devising new ways to pollute our minds. For instance, the lyrics of songs are infused with such negativity that they can make people suicidal. Don't think that these are just accidents. Even the movies and the subliminal influences in advertising assist in bringing human-kind to a state in which they are ready for any kind of support, even if it is completely demonic.

Many of the topics we are discussing in this *Spiritual Warrior* series will determine how many people will survive in the 21st century. Many things that currently give us a sense of security will not always be so accessible. People will break down economically, socially, and psychologically if they do not find a way to fortify themselves and understand more about the sources and manifestations of evil. If a soldier goes out to fight and does not know the location of the enemy, he or she will end up fighting in the dark while the enemy laughs and waits to launch an attack. We don't want to fight and waste energy in the dark. We want to know what we have to deal with and then deal with it so we can be victorious.

Evil activities often give us immediate rewards and stimulation in a flamboyant or intoxicating way, but they later produce all types of problems. Divine ambitions might begin with a struggle or some investment of austerity, but they ulti-mately produce genuine and lasting results.

yat tad agre visam iva
pariname 'mrtopamam
tat sukham sattvikam proktam
atma-buddhi-prasada-jam
visayendriya-samyogad
yat tad agre 'mrtopamam
pariname visam iva
tat sukham rajas am smrtam

> That which in the beginning may be
> just like poison but at the end is just like
> nectar and which awakens one to self-
> realization is said to be happiness in
> the mode of goodness. That happiness
> which is derived from contact of the
> senses with their objects and which
> appears like nectar at first but poison
> at the end is said to be of the nature of
> passion.
>
> *Bhagavad-gita* 18.37-38

Cheaters want the results without paying the price. Manip-ulators and crooks want to get as much as they can without paying any price, and they even want to take what belongs to others. When we pursue life as cheaters, we might get quick solutions, but they will only be cosmetic, as inauspiciousness will inevitably catch up with us.

A Change in Heart

By looking into the life of Valmiki Muni, who authored the great epic known as the *Ramayana*, we can easily recognize the detrimental effects of sin and evil. Valmiki had once been a hunter named Ratnakara, who lived in the forest and maintained his family by robbing and even killing travelers as they passed through the woods. He would bring his bounties home for his family daily just to go out again the next day. One day, he came across a saintly person known as Narada Muni and prepared to viciously attack this saint. However, when Ratnakara told the saint to give him all of his wealth, Narada remained equipoised and undisturbed. He then asked the hunter, "You are robbing to maintain your family, but don't you realize that you will have to suffer the consequences due to *karma*?" Every action produces a corresponding reaction. Narada continued by asking, "Will your family members who share the wealth that you earn also share the sins that you are earning as well?"

The rogue had never thought of the matter in that way and decided to approach his family. After all, if he had to take the responsibility for all of his activities, he at least wanted to spread the *karma* between those for whom he stole. He went home and asked his wife and children, "Everyday I rob travelers and then bring back all kinds of wealth, property, jewels, and money. I have given so much opulence to all of you. A saint talked to me today and informed me that I will have to be accountable for all of my crimes. I want to know if you are willing to share in some of the burden that I will have to accept?" Both the wife and children refused, replying, "You have decided to maintain us in this way. We never asked you to commit sins for the purpose of maintaining us. You will have to bear the consequences alone." The father had imposed his lifestyle on the family without really being a loving or genuine father. In complete devastation, he left and ran out to find that saint. He realized how much he had been preoccupied in sinful activities even though they produced some immediate results. The long-term results were not worth the short-term pleasures.

Combat Evil with Love and Righteousness

Love extinguishes evil. The more that we understand what we can attain through righteousness and purity, the more we will want to escape ignorance and confusion by running towards higher goals. If we have sufficient love, we will have sufficient protection. Don't think that love is just some lusty drama portrayed on soap operas. Love is the greatest weapon that we will ever have. However, many of the most evil attacks confuse the world's citizens about the actual meaning of love.

People live together for years in a so-called romantic relationship without ever having a chance to express any genuine symptoms of love towards each other. It is all a matter of utilitarianism. People come together in order to find an extension to their own sense gratification. For this same reason, we also see an increase in incest. People just do not know what love means. In some cases, when a person gets raped, she might explain the situation by saying that the man made love with her. The rapist didn't make love—he made war. So many people equate love with sex. Consequently, they are missing the chance to enjoy life on a higher level and become the divine personalities that they are meant to be.

Keep in mind that we have a lower self and a higher self, meaning that each person has within themselves a godly and a demonic aspect. Some of those things that influence or stimulate the lower self are relative and temporary. They come to us fast but have no sense of permanence and allow us to think that life revolves solely around the satisfaction of the senses. They cause us to minimize family, community, or gender. They cause us to put one religion, tribe, gender, or race against another. All of these mentalities are a part of the culture of destruction and evil.

Real Strength Develops from Love

We want to appreciate that real power comes from love and

wisdom—not from data or information processing. However, we have to become natural to acquire that wisdom. Since we involve ourselves in so many superfluous things, we have forgotten how to be natural. We have to begin to work on ourselves by acting naturally because such actions will automatically bring about auspiciousness and will connect us with the higher realms. We encourage you to pursue more wholesome cultural investigations as you go deeper into philosophy, religion, and spirituality. You will begin to come to certain universal conclusions. Any person who honestly makes a deep investigation into any science will begin to arrive at similar conclusions. It is only those stuck at a superficial level who resort to sectarianism. Religion against religion stems from that kind of consideration. However, people who develop a deeper understanding will be able to maintain their sense of individuality, but, at the same time, appreciate the pursuits of other people. When they see a difference, it will help them become more inspired to take their own path seriously.

Remember that none of us are residents of this place. The bodies we have are simply costumes given to us according to our state of evolution. People from authentic spiritual cultures who have actual wisdom understand that there are higher aspects of existence which can help us become more aware of the past and able to even touch into the future. We should not cheat ourselves by accepting limitations. Let us not get caught up in other types of relativities, and other in-groups and out-groups. Let us get involved in higher consciousness as we move on and march as spiritual warriors committed to producing a better planet. If we maintain weapons of love and compassion, evil will be disappointed at every turn.

Questions and Answers

Question: Do the bombardments of superficial information distract us from being reflective, pious, and transcendental?

Answer: Yes, this information age is making us more mechanical. We do not really need to think so deeply; we just need to know how to push some buttons or work machines. But where does it lead? It takes away from our ability to connect with the Divine. Even scientists know with their present understanding of the human condition that humankind uses less than ten percent of their normal faculties. This means that even with our present knowledge, we can recognize that there is much more available for us to cultivate. However, as long as we remain distracted by superficial distractions and avoid introspection and meditation, we will not be able to bring out that higher consciousness.

Not only should we practice processes of meditation and calling on the names of God, but sometimes we also just have to get out of these chaotic city environments and take a walk in the park or forest. You will see the difference in your consciousness when the bombardments are minimized. We do not realize the heavy influences coming from computers, cell phones, microwaves, and even from the electrical wires. Many aspects of modernity assault our minds and devastate our bodies physically, leading to cancer and other unhealthy diseases. Leaving those environments, even temporarily, can take us away from some of the ongoing attacks. Furthermore, removing ourselves from the daily mechanical scheme and going into a state of reflection could amaze us as we see how the Lord in the heart comes forth to supply knowledge and insight.

Question: Is there actually an entity who we sometimes refer to as Satan? Could you discuss this entity? You explain that nothing in the universe is greater than God; therefore, why wouldn't God prevent such a hostile personality from entering this realm?

Answer: We always have the ability to choose evil or righteousness. There cannot be real love without freedom. Making a choice means we have options. We have an opportunity to access our lower or higher self. We have an opportunity to say yes to the Lord, but we also have an opportunity to procrastinate. Saying no to the Lord does not mean that we make Him disappear. Denying His love doesn't mean that the Supreme stops loving us. It just means that we temporarily turn our backs on Him while we preoccupy ourselves with this temporary realm. The Lord arranged a place for those people who temporarily want to turn their backs on His eternal pastimes and associates. The material bodies and universes are literally arenas in which we can have the opportunity to play God. Once we are finished playing, then we can finally access our real divinity in the association of God.

While we are in this state of separation, the Lord sends His agents to test our current position. Are we ready to give up our insanity and return to the spiritual world or do we still want the separation? We might compare Satan or *maya* to a teacher who gives the students various tests. The teacher does not want to simply fail the student, but the teacher has to present a certain type of test in order to determine the student's level of mastery over the subject matter. Satan or *maya* is in fact under the jurisdiction of God. If Satan were not under God's control, it would mean that God is not absolute. However, Satan is under God and has a particular type of work to execute. Satan or *maya* is there to determine whether or not we still want false proprietor-ship and separation from God. We must face different tempta-tions in order to determine if we have given up our insanity.

Most people still hang onto the insanity because external influences cause them to think that their insanity is normal. When you have a mass of insane people, they have an inter-esting way of reinforcing themselves. For this reason, when the great servants of God come into these realms, the insane people attack or even assassinate them. However, the Lord continues to send them anyway even though He knows He is sending them into an insane environment.

Question: If, in this age, we all have within us both divine and demonic aspects, how can we ever trust anyone, including ourselves? Can we ever subdue or overcome the demonic side to a point in which it can never again dominate?

Answer: People who are not serious about controlling their senses should actually not be fully trusted, including ourselves. People who are not ethical or principle-centered, and who lack integrity prove from their actions that they are not trustworthy.

When someone is addicted to some substance, for their well-being and for others, he or she should not be fully trusted. If we trust such a person too much, we can reinforce his or her bad habits or give the person opportunities to deviate. Humans are, by nature, under the influence of *kama* or lust, which leads to *ahankara* or the false ego of identifying with the material body.

As a result of this addiction, we are subjected to four prominent defects. We are sure to commit mistakes (*bhrama*); are invariably illusioned (*pramada*); have the tendency to cheat others (*vipralipsa*); and we are limited by imperfect senses (*karanapatava*). In spite of these weaknesses, we can increase our propensity to trust ourselves and other addicts by keeping the environment free of overwhelming temptations that may appear irresistible. Also, through a healthy environment, good association, sufficient knowledge, and guidance, we can gain the strength to access higher aspirations, enabling us to become fully trustworthy.

This is the sum of duty: Do naught to others which would cause you pain if done to you.

Mahabharata 5.5.7 (Hinduism)

.

Chapter 2

Why Do We Suffer?

The Question of Suffering

Coming to the platform of love of God is a process, and the Lord has no favorites. As He tells us in *Bhagavad-gita* 9.29:

> *samo 'ham sarva-bhutesu*
> *na me dvesyo 'sti na priyah*
> *ye bhajanti tu mam bhaktya*
> *mayi te tesu capy aham*

> I envy no one, nor am I partial to anyone. I am equal to all. But whoever renders service unto Me in devotion is a friend, is in Me, and I am also a friend to him.

Just as the Supreme Lord is equal to all, the different agents of the Lord are also kind and equal to everyone. At the same time, when we see and experience so much suffering in the world, we may wonder about the nature of God's kindness and doubt the kindness of His representatives. All of us question the reason for suffering at different times. Why does Krishna or God, who is controlling everything, allow His topmost servants to undergo so many hardships, inconveniences, and attacks? After all, if a Vaisnava or a servant of God must undergo extensive suffering, why should people even serve the Lord? In fact, we sometimes see that those who worship demigods experience more material prosperity and less suffering than the devotees of the Supreme Lord. We may begin to think, "Why should I go through all of these austerities, just to suffer intensely as a servant of God?"

We should really think about this topic from time to time; otherwise, when we go through difficulties without understanding their deeper purpose, we can lose faith and decide to renounce the service of God. We might then resort to temporary and unhealthy shelters. We might even feel that the price we have to pay to reach the goal is not worth the ultimate result.

Suffering Has a Reason

The *Bhagavad-gita* explains that this material world is in fact very difficult to overcome and is full of misery, but the Lord can help us if we surrender to His help:

> *a-brahma-bhuvanal lokah*
> *punar avartino 'rjuna*
> *mam upetya tu kaunteya*
> *punar janma na vidyate*

> From the highest planet in the material
> world down to the lowest, all are places
> of misery wherein repeated birth and
> death take place. But one who attains
> to My abode, O son of Kunti, never
> takes birth again.
>
> *Bhagavad-gita* 8.16

Basically, we want to make the best of a bad bargain by using every situation for our growth. Of course, in spite of our endeavor to serve the Lord, we must still deal with the material energy. Nevertheless, we can eventually transcend the misery.

Since our material bodies are not yet fully spiritualized, we carry particular burdens and *karma*. Sometimes due to different types of *karma*, we experience suffering. We might have karmic reactions chasing us that will later cause some disturbances even if we have given up our previous sinful activities and now follow a religious lifestyle. Suffering also develops from *aparadhas* or offenses. We might be engaged in devotional activities, but, due to some improper activities such as offenses to the devotees (*vaisnava-aparadha*), to the spiritual teachers (*guru-aparadha*), to the holy places (*dhama-aparadha*), while chanting the holy name of God (*nama-aparadha*), or during service (*seva-aparadha*), we might suffer from imbalances and stagnations that can cause intense suffering. Therefore, when we are suffering, we can look to see if perhaps we have committed offenses, or whether it stems from the natural process of spiritual maturation. This material world is full of misery.

Most importantly, the difficulties do not always have to have a negative effect. The challenges on the spiritual path can function as catalysts to help us increase our meditation on

Krishna or God. As we struggle and suffer, we especially want to use the suffering as a means for growth and purification. Sometimes a devotee will suffer because the Lord is giving them mercy. They might have to go through specific challenges that God sends in rapid succession so that they can overcome an obstacle and move on. There are times in people's lives when they just have a series of difficulties. Actually, we can see it as a special blessing when the Supreme Lord sends so many tests. He sees our sincerity in wanting to move faster toward the goal; therefore, He arranges events that can help us burn up negative *karma* from the past and move forward faster. Sometimes we are acting properly, and it is this proper activity that is creating some of the challenges. It might appear to be suffering, but the Lord is letting it come upon us so that we can once and for all put it behind us. Sometimes the difficulties allow us to shine even more.

No one has to undergo as many challenges and so-called setbacks as the pure representatives of the Lord because their entire existence is anti-material. They go against the current of material energy. For instance, Haridasa Thakura, a great devotee of the Lord in Vaisnava history, was flogged in many marketplaces by government officials who could not tolerate his intense devotional practices. However, he literally felt ecstasy during the incident due to his love of God. In spite of the physical torture, he did not feel the pain. There are times when great devotees of the Lord experience what might seem to be problems, but, due to their absorption in love of God, they are happy to make sacrifices on behalf of the Lord. An event that would give an ordinary person suffering and pain stimulates their consciousness and causes them to experience great expressions of love and devotion.

In other cases, some of the *acaryas* were attacked by

impersonalists or by *smarta-brahmanas* (impotent priests) who were often arrogant and self-righteous fundamentalists. We see such attacks in the life of Bhaktivinoda Thakura, a great Vaisnava devotee of the Lord who lived in India from 1838 to 1915. Since he was exposing the hypocrisy among the cheaters, a cheating person who had some mystic powers tried to curse the whole family and destroy them. We see that for a while the attacks became effective. Bhaktivinoda's son was viciously attacked.

God never says that if we serve Him, we will not experience any difficulty, or that our lives will unfold very expediently. But Krishna does say that His devotees shall never perish. He lets us know that ultimately He will protect the devotees, and always receive their love and service. Even in the case of Arjuna, Krishna was personally present with him, but he still had to undergo an intense challenge and make life and death decisions. He had to deal with adversarial conditions in spite of the Lord's personal presence. We are to exhibit tolerance, with the understanding that every situation is a part of the devotional experience, and to try to be less distracted by the material energy. We understand that we often grow the fastest from our challenges and suffering. When we are suffering, we really begin to think deeply about our lives.

It is often when we suffer the most that we cry out to the Lord. Sometimes the Lord places us in a situation so that we cry out more and increase our ability to receive more. It helps us to not take for granted what we do have, and it can make our love stronger if we do have a foundation of love. When we have faith and understanding, these will also get stronger. In the process, we try to access even more understanding so that we can go deeper and deeper. God has many ways to make Himself available, show His mercy, and show the amazing power of His devotees. In spite of what might appear to be obstacles, His devotees become glorious. It is amazing that the Lord allows the atheists to become so powerful that even the demigods fear them. At the same time, we see the ultimate outcome.

We also have to be careful that we maintain our spiritual practices and avoid what could be detrimental to our spiritual lives. We have to be aware that *maya* is waiting for us to weaken. She is enticing us to participate in her allurements, and, as soon as we make that little step, a whole avenue of arrangements and complexities begin to come down on us.

Looking to the Great Devotees for Guidance

The Lord also puts His servants in difficulties to glorify them. We see this pattern occur in the lives of many great teachers throughout the various theologies of the world. For instance, the fact that Muhammad was illiterate made his ability to present his theology to the world even more glorious. Furthermore, as Muhammad began to spread his teachings, the rulers at that time persecuted him and even tried to assassinate him. However, he never wavered from his beliefs in spite of all the difficulties. The life of Jesus also exemplifies this in a very dynamic way. He too faced many trials and challenges, each of which only increased his fame. For instance, the various temptations presented to him exhibited his deep faith in God and his steadfastness. He could not be swayed by any negative influence. Even his death and resurrection, the ultimate trial, increased his glories rather than diminished them. It is, in part, because of his extraordinary life and death that his teachings have endured throughout the centuries.

The great Vaisnava teacher and founder of the International

Society for Krishna Consciousness (ISKCON), His Divine Grace A.C. Bhaktivedanta Swami Prabhupada, similarly had to confront one difficulty after another, but they only magnified his glorious position. His feats would not have shown through to the same extent had he been a multi-millionaire or a huge industrialist who already had businesses all over the world. In such a case, a person could easily use their contacts and money in different parts of the world to start a spiritual commission. It makes it even more dynamic that he seemingly had nothing material, but Krishna gave him practically the entire world in which to preach love of God. When Srila Prabhupada was leaving the planet, we could understand that his sickness partly resulted from the sins of his disciples.

Furthermore, the fact that Srila Prabhupada came to America at such a late age makes his life even more unique. He came with only a handful of coins and hardly knew anyone. In spite of all the material difficulties, he was able to initiate a worldwide mission. Srila Prabhupada also had to endure so many difficulties while trying to fulfill his spiritual master's desires by spreading his mission. He suffered heart attacks on the trip to America, and later had essential items stolen which he needed for his mission.

As we look at some of the lives of the great Vaisnavas and saints in all traditions, we may wonder why they must suffer so much, but it helps us appreciate the possibilities for something greater. As these great souls overcame so many obstacles, the Lord arranged for them to have distinct guides. Their actions and words are important because they give us a better idea of what we are to do in similar situations and how it is to be done. As we look at the pure servants of God, we can understand how much they are suffering on our behalf. We can see how the Lord is using them in these amazing dramas to help us have a deeper understanding of how to return back to Him. We see how God is using them to show even more dynamically how good ultimately triumphs over evil, and to show the importance of strong faith and perseverance.

We see in these amazing pastimes that when the devotees of the Lord are suffering, the Lord is always caring for them, and ultimately they are trying to carry out the Lord's desire in spite of obstacles or even attacks. However, the servants of the Lord expect opposition in this material realm; they realize that *maya* will always try to find some way to attack. We see in the pastime of Lord Rama as narrated in the *Ramayana* that Laksmana drew a circle around Sita to protect her, which is very significant. We should all have a circle of security in which we maintain proper boundaries and understand the tricks initiated by *maya*. We should realize that this material world is full of danger, and that we unnecessarily suffer more when we become captured by sense gratification.

Our Rightful Claim

Sridhara Maharaja, a great *acarya* in the Vaisnava line, comments on a verse in the *Srimad-Bhagavatam* 10.14.8, which presents the idea of *daya-bhak*:

> *tat te 'nukampam su-samiksamano*
> *bhunjana evatma-krtam vipakam*
> *hrd-vag-vapurbhir vidadhan namas te*
> *jiveta yo mukti-pade sa daya-bhak*

My dear Lord, one who earnestly waits for You to bestow Your causeless

mercy upon him, all the while patiently
suffering the reactions of his past
misdeeds and offering You respectful
obeisances with his heart, words and
body, is surely eligible for liberation,
for it has become his rightful claim.

He explains that a person might be suffering intensely due
to sins and *karma* from previous lives, but the devotee should
continue offering obeisances to the Lord and serving with
dedication, knowing that in time he or she will be freed from
the reactions of improper activities. In time, the person will
become eligible to inherit the Kingdom of God.

How does a son inherit the property of the father? If the
father has a will and leaves his wealth to his son, how does the
son acquire the inheritance? The son simply has to stay alive.
If the son is living, he will naturally inherit the property after
his father's death. Therefore, if we remain alive, active, and
pure in spiritual life, it becomes our rightful claim to inherit
the Kingdom of God. When we do experience some pain
from karmic reactions, we might develop doubts and fears
according to the problem. We might perceive the spiritual path
as insurmountable. However, by remaining fixed on the path of
devotional service, it becomes our rightful claim to inherit the
Kingdom of God.

The Supreme Lord has many different ways of glorifying
His devotees as well as ways of purifying them. He has so many
arrangements to help us understand that the material world is
problematic and full of misery. Consequently, it increases our
eagerness to become free of that misery. In the midst of all of
these different factors, Krishna tells us in the *Bhagavad-gita*
9.31, *kaunteya pratijanihi na me bhaktah pranasyati*: "O son

of Kunti, declare it boldly that My devotee never perishes." If we remain focused and alive, we can inherit so much. Staying alive means that we do not let the weeds and obstacles that inevitably occur in spiritual life dominate to such an extent that they pull us backwards. We can be happy when we see the suffering as a part of the maturation process.

The Struggle Will Make Us Strong

One day a man found the cocoon of a butterfly. Over a period of time, the caterpillar gradually turned into a butterfly and began its attempt to break open the cocoon. However, it seemed as if the butterfly could not get out alone even though it had broken a small hole. It would struggle, but then stop due to fatigue. The man, out of his compassion, thought that he could help the butterfly by cutting the cocoon open, thus enabling the butterfly to emerge much quicker. However, once it emerged in this artificial way, it simply fell down. It flapped its wings but could not fly which shocked the man. It could not fly because it was removed from its natural process of growth. The struggle to break open the cocoon helps a butterfly develop the necessary muscles and dexterity to fly. Since the man interfered with the natural process, it did not have the capability to fly.

Sometimes our suffering is literally an arrangement from God so that we can develop a certain level of strength, which will then help us break through the modes of material nature. In some cases, the suffering is specifically meant to help us develop deeper levels of consciousness. It will help us deepen our cries and prayers through the process of introspection. If we do not have the growing pains, we might not go through the normal phases of maturation and growth. Under these circumstances, it may seem that God leaves us alone and lets us suffer when in fact He is doing the exact opposite. He might be allowing us to develop the necessary intensity of consciousness that comes from the learning experiences.

Let us reflect on another story which can help illustrate this point. There was once a ship filled with many travelers taking a long voyage across the sea. At one point during its journey, a tumultuous storm destroyed the ship, killing the captain and all of the passengers—except one man. This man was a good swimmer and consequently made it to the shore of an island. Upon reaching land, he felt most fortunate considering that the ship and all of the other people met their demise. However, his journey had just begun.

He was alone and had to find some means to survive until someone discovered him. He built a very simple hut and would go out daily looking for eatables. After many days, which turned into weeks and later into months, he began to feel that maybe he was the one who was more unfortunate than the other passengers who died very quickly. Due to his isolation and austere life, he was suffering so much mentally and sometimes physically, causing him to think that it would have been better if he had died with the other passengers and crew.

One day while looking for food, he saw a huge cloud of smoke in the direction of his hut. As he began to return home, he was feeling extremely depressed because he had not seen any humans or ships since his own ship had sunk. He was beginning to accept that he would simply die without anyone ever coming to his rescue. While thinking such demoralizing thoughts, he approached his hut only to discover that it had caught on fire. As he started running towards the hut to watch it burn, he felt like committing suicide. Not only had he been left to slowly die on the island, but now his little shelter was up in flames. He was just on the verge of cursing God and perhaps committing suicide when all of a sudden he began to see a ship in the distance heading straight towards the island.

He remained stunned, unsure of himself. Was he hallucinating, had he gone mad, or was he having some kind of death experience? As he tried to reflect on his predicament, the ship came closer, until it finally docked on the island. Surprisingly, the captain stepped off the ship and walked directly towards the man. Choked up with tears, the man cried out, "Have you come to rescue me? So many months I have been here alone, suffering intensely, and today my suffering climaxed. How did you know that I was here?" The captain replied, "I saw from far away your smoke signal." The man began to cry in great joy.

The man's faith in God was restored. He realized that the Lord does things in His own time because He knows what is best for everyone. In his own case, the Lord allowed his hut to catch on fire at the exact time when the ship sailed by. This story provides another way of understanding suffering. Sometimes we suffer because we do not or cannot see the bigger picture. We are impatient with different situations in our lives, and we forget that the Lord will make arrangements for our well-being at the most auspicious time.

Srila Prabhupada and many great saints went through all of these seemingly challenging experiences to show us how to remain steady in spite of all kinds of adversities. However, it should not let us doubt the Lord; rather, we should persevere and expect God's mercy as our rightful inheritance. We just have to follow through on our promise to serve Him, and the Lord will follow through on His. We can gain our rightful inheritance as we endure some of the fallout from our previous karmic activities. As those reactions are gradually burned up and fully extinguished, we will become fully God conscious.

We don't want to slow down; we want to speed up. We should pray to the Supreme, "Whatever I need to experience to come to You faster, please let those things happen so that I can once and for all be free. And whatever is interfering with my spiritual life that I need to have taken away, please remove it from my life. For so many lifetimes I have functioned on my intelligence and it has only brought me to another body in the material world. I know what I want, but You know what I need. Therefore, I place myself before You and ask You to arrange whatever I need."

Questions and Answers

Question: I have found that suffering can function as a deep lesson of compassion because we cannot always understand the predicament of someone else until we experience the same difficulty. Then we can genuinely empathize without any tinges of condescension, which might otherwise make us look down on another person while attempting to sympathize. However, how do we develop a deep and genuine compassion for another person's struggle if we have never had the same experience or personally felt the depth of their suffering?

Answer: In the healing professions, people who are often the most caring and the most effective are those who have personally undergone similar difficulties as those who they are trying to help. For instance, especially in natural health care, many of those who aid others have gone through life threatening situations themselves. Since they have healed, they have full empathy and knowledge about how to help others. Nevertheless, even if we have not had the same suffering experience as other people, if we have deep and genuine love for them, we will be able to understand their predicament. In Sanskrit we call this *para-duhkha-duhkhi*, which means that a person feels the happiness of another as well as their sadness. This naturally happens when people are highly connected or affectionate towards each other. Of course, this level of compassion will not develop as easily when the individuals do not have a deep connection or deep affection.

Just as no sane person wants to suffer and will try their best to eliminate their own suffering, similarly a deeply compassionate person will do everything in their means to eliminate the suffering of those they love. Wherever there is rich spiritual consciousness, which is the position of a genuine spiritual warrior, there will concomitantly be a display of superhuman compassion. Spiritual warriors see themselves in connection with others and see everyone in connection with the same God. Many people with good intentions can sympathize, but few people can really have genuine empathy unless they have opened their own consciousness to the God-centered platform of compassion, service, and love.

Question: What is suffering? Is it just a matter of perception?

Answer: Suffering is real, but it is also fully associated with perception. A person can experience physical pain, emotional pain, or both simultaneously which is even worse. Often, the emotional pain brings on the physical pain. Some doctors suggest that as much as seventy-five percent of all physical sicknesses are connected to stress and mental anxieties. Some holistic practitioners even write and teach that every physical sickness is connected to a certain emotional state. Of the two, emotional pain and suffering is actually the worst.

For instance, when a person is in physical pain, it becomes much more unbearable when the mind is also having difficulties understanding or accepting the physical challenges. When people have a strong mental and spiritual constitution, it helps them cope with their chronic pain or handicap, and sometimes even brings about spontaneous remission. However, if the deeper suffering is not addressed, the relief is still superficial. The deeper suffering is often connected with a person's perceptions and understandings. Overall, perception plays an extremely significant role since it affects the physical and most importantly, the emotional and psychological existence.

Question: You describe various causes of suffering; however, when we are submerged in a difficult experience, we are not always able to philosophize and recognize the Lord's mercy as easily. It is easy to look at suffering neutrally when we are feeling good. How can we maintain our composure in difficult situations that often send our minds reeling?

Answer: It is true that when we are personally confronted with great difficulties, it is harder to philosophize and recognize it as the Lord's mercy. This ability to remain equipoised does not usually come overnight; as in any other process, it requires training and practice. By practicing this kind of thinking and allowing ourselves to reflect more on different events from the past in relationship to others and ourselves, we will be in better shape to appreciate the different ways in which the Lord's mercy permeates throughout our lives. Take the example of an outstanding sportsman or musician. Normally, they did not acquire their skills overnight. Rather, they underwent intense practice and developed skills that now help them face new challenges. In many cases, they have also learned how to get help and guidance from their mentors.

Probably the most difficult type of suffering occurs when a person is suffering both physically and mentally but does not understand the reason for their suffering. It is meaningless suffering that is the worst, and it is especially overwhelming when a person has nothing to look forward to. For this reason, higher philosophical understandings are most important because they can help a person understand that no one can fully avoid some type of suffering in this material world. In the background, some of the main reasons that people suffer are simply due to the material world and the material body, which are both unnatural. It is like being in prison. A prisoner can do so many things to minimize or distract him or herself from the difficulty of being in confinement, but the distractions will not fully take away the reality of the situation. No entity in the material world can completely avoid suffering because each conditioned soul is limited and restricted due to our separation from our natural state of self-realization and unalloyed devotional service in the higher spiritual realms.

By taking birth in the material world, all living entities will find themselves dealing with the three miseries of material existence regardless of how successful or secure they may seem to be. The three miseries include *adhyatmika* or suffering caused by our own minds; *adhidaivika* or misery caused by the demigods who officiate the workings of nature, especially environmental conditions such as hurricanes, tornadoes, storms, etc.; and *adhibautika* or misery caused by other living entities. Suffering cannot be fully avoided, but as we have a stronger mental understanding and greater spiritual culture, we will not be overly distracted by the difficulties. We will be able to use our encounters with suffering to become deeper spiritualists who develop higher realizations and greater empathy and compassion.

Question: Do the pure devotees of the Lord who fully realize their identity as separate from the material body feel physical pain? Is it that they no longer feel the pain, or do they feel the pain but it cannot disturb them anymore?

Answer: The pure devotees of the Lord have the greatest compassion and empathy for everyone, so how can they not feel pain when they see people intensely and foolishly suffering all around them? For them, associating with humanity is similar to associating with people confined to a mental institution. They see so many people around them who are deeply entrenched in the illusions and who are so bewildered, sad, and constantly torturing themselves. For this reason, such pure devotees go out of their way and agitate their minds about how to help others. Of course, this is why the pure devotees are so often misunderstood, attacked, and sometimes even killed because people who are chronically insane may lack the ability to appreciate those who try to help. They may even see the helpers as the enemy.

It is a great undertaking for such pure devotees to continue to try to help such insane people who sometimes even attack them in different ways and at different times. Furthermore, the pure devotee such as the authentic *guru* suffers from the sinful actions of his disciples. Since the disciples are connected very deeply with him, it is like that of the mother or father—they naturally bathe in happiness with the success of their children, and they go through great anguish when they are confronted with their children's deviations, failures, and sufferings. Of course, the pure devotees of the Lord are protected by Him and are under His personal guidance, but, due to their great happiness and satisfaction stemming from their intense connection with the Godhead, they selflessly want others to experience the great boons, satisfaction, happiness, and love that they themselves feel. They are the well-wishers of everyone. It is quite esoteric and contradictory. Although they are undisturbed in their faith, dedication, and love, in another sense they are the most disturbed because they are the most aware of the pain of other living entities. Actually, they are the most eager to make sacrifices in order to make an auspicious difference.

In the material world, we can ironically say that no one is as happy and as full of joy as the pure servants of the Lord, but, at the same time, no one is as disturbed and sad about the pain that the living entities in these material worlds constantly experience. Therefore, they are on a powerful mission to help the global population to once and for all be freed from the incarcerations, illusions, and confusions permanently connected with material existence. They remind us of the extraordinary mercy of the Supreme Personality of Godhead.

Just as the shipwrecked man was helped at the right time by the Lord through the captain, the pure devotees who are sent by the Lord constantly act as envoys to search out and rescue those souls who are crying out in despair. And as we can understand from the example of the butterfly, there are times when the Lord allows us to undergo challenges and suffering as a way to prepare us for great work and accomplishments in the future. Some of the greatest mercy comes when the Lord allows a person to undergo what seems to be personal suffering as a way to prepare him or her to act as a special envoy or pure spiritual warrior who will be specially empowered to come into the material universes to relieve hundreds, thousands, and even millions from their excruciating pain and suffering. We pray that the discussions in this *Spiritual Warrior* series will prepare and produce an army of spiritual warriors who are focused on rescuing souls from their ongoing despair, depression, gloom, and helplessness.

Do not do to others what you would not like yourself. Then there will be no resentment against you, either in the family or in the state.

Analects 12:2 (Confucianism)

Chapter 3

Heaven and Religious Fanaticism

In the Name of God

Religion and God are on trial. People are doing many inauspicious things under the guise of religion, and the inhumanities are intensifying. Religion is supposed to elevate us and help us cultivate higher qualities, allowing us to become deep lovers of humanity and God—the ultimate source of love. Many people are using their theology and even God to justify behaviors that in many cases diametrically oppose the essence of religion.

Even in the midst of all this negativity, we still see people increasingly turning to religious pursuits. For instance, the American Association of Publishers reported that, in America, the sale of religious books increased significantly in 2003 in comparison to the previous year. Furthermore, self-help and spiritual books are now the second most popular category of books. Through this interesting revolution, there are people who are trying to improve the quality of their lives as well as the lives of their friends and relatives. On the other hand, we simultaneously see great inhumanities manifesting as terrorism and fanaticism, which have developed from so-called religious sentiment.

This violence and aggression is not a new phenomenon, although it has certainly been amplified at the start of the 21st century. During the time of the crusades under the Christian influence, numerous people were viciously tortured, abused and killed. Under the Islamic influence over the centuries, *jihads* or holy wars have taken hundreds of thousands of lives. In Europe and America during the 17th century, people who supposedly represented Christianity hunted and burned suspected witches. Many innocent people lost their lives due to this fanaticism. The concept of ethnic cleansing has also lead to innumerable deaths. Basically, someone from a particular ethnic group and religious orientation becomes the enemy of those with a different religious and ethnic affiliation, and the better armed of the two groups becomes determined to wipe the other group from the face of the earth. These examples only represent a small fraction of the crimes committed in the name of God over the centuries.

The events of September 11, 2001 exposed some of the rituals the terrorists underwent before their acts of violence. They believed that their suicides would ensure them a place in paradise. Interestingly, many of their victims also hoped to attain heaven or paradise as they faced death. Although many people are undergoing intense suffering as a result of these acts, the suicide bombers considered their crime to be a religious act, which would bring the highest rewards. Sometimes ardent enemies on the same battlefield both consider their cause to be justified, and both think they will attain heaven as a result.

What does it mean when both groups think that they will

attain heaven if they destroy the enemy? What if they are both right and they meet in the afterlife? What kind of God would honor their presence in the same place? What kind of God would allow people to viciously annihilate and abuse others as the means to achieve His blessings? What kind of God would bring them all together after they viciously destroyed each other with such intense hatred? What genuinely intelligent person would worship a God who sanctions such abuse, awarding such exploitation with eternal blessings? It is a very strange conception of God and His system of justice. However, some people are so obsessed with their own righteousness that they are ready to act in horrendous ways while expecting auspicious consequences. They must have a myopic conception of God, considering Him limited to their religion or group of people. They consider that their scriptures provide the only way to His mercy and association.

Descriptions of Heaven and the Kingdom of God

A *Newsweek* poll in 2002 reported that 76 percent of Americans believe in heaven, and of those who do believe, 71 percent think of it as an actual physical place. Out of that 71 percent, 19 percent think heaven looks like a garden, 13 percent think it looks like a city, and 17 percent just don't know. Despite all the fighting, Jews, Christians, and Muslims share some common conceptions. They believe that God resides in heaven and He is merciful. They all also believe that His judgment will determine whether a person goes to heaven or hell. They accept that heaven is the perfect place for the righteous and hell is intended for the condemned and sinful.[1]

The Vaisnava teachings, which focus on the worship of a personal God as described in the Vedas, give insight into these concepts. Do Vaisnavas accept heaven as the place where God resides? Not really. The Vaisnava paradigm accepts that within just one universe, there are many planets ranging from the lower planetary systems to the higher. Within the many heavenly planets, the servants of the Lord reside and manage the affairs of the material world. The Vedic scriptures describe many different entities that inhabit these realms such as demigods and more refined entities. Vaisnavas believe that these personalities are associated with the heavenly planets, and that the true residence of God is elsewhere. In Christianity and Judaism, the Bible explains that God created the heavens and the earth, which means that He existed somewhere before creating these realms. From this perspective, we should naturally inquire, "Where did God exist before he created those environments?"

Furthermore, in the Judeo-Christian tradition, the Lord says in the Bible in Genesis, "Let us make man in our image." Who is the Lord talking to? Some followers of the Vedas contend that this is a discussion between demigods rather than God since the Supreme Lord would not say let *us* make man in *our* image. It appears that the demigods have some involvement in the secondary creation.

The place described as heaven in the Judaic, Christian, and Muslim scriptures is normally described in the Vedic scriptures as Svarloka or the higher planetary systems. Brahmaloka, the highest material planet in Svarloka, is governed by Lord Brahma who, for many, would appear to be the Supreme Lord. However, it is understood from the *Brahma-samhita* and other great texts that Brahma works on behalf of the Supreme. Lord Brahma declares:

isvarah paramah krsnah
sac-cid-ananda-vigrahah
anadir adir govindah
sarva-karana-karanam

Krishna who is known as Govinda
is the Supreme Godhead. He has an
eternal blissful spiritual body. He is the
origin of all. He has no other origin and
He is the prime cause of all causes.

Brahma-samhita 5.1

Lord Brahma understands that there are many controllers
like himself, but there is one Supreme Controller responsible
for his existence and all of creation. The Supreme Personality of Godhead also confirms this truth about Himself in
Bhagavad-gita 10.8:

aham sarvasya prabhavo
mattah sarvam pravartate
iti matva bhajante mam
budha bhava-samanvitah

I am the source of all spiritual and
material worlds. Everything emanates
from Me. The wise who perfectly know
this engage in My devotional service
and worship Me with all their hearts.

The Lord states that all that exists ultimately comes from
Him, but, at the same time, He is outside of His own creation.
Vaisnavas have a very detailed explanation of creation in the

Srimad-Bhagavatam. This great text describes the lower, middle, and higher planetary systems, and offers a description of the Kingdom of God where the Lord Himself resides. It even discusses in detail what happens to the soul at the time of death. The Judaic, Christian, and Muslim traditions view heaven as a perfect place where one lives forever. The Vedic scriptures contend that a transition will eventually take place for even the residents of heaven, since the soul has not yet found its actual home. The scriptures further explain that the Kingdom of God is beyond the heavenly kingdoms and is an eternal abode.

Sanatana Gosvami, the most senior of the *gosvamis* (ascetic spiritual leaders) of Vrndavana, India, gave us the book, *Sri Brhad-bhagavatamrta*, a book expanding on the essential meaning of the *Srimad-Bhagavatam.* In this narration, the main character, Gopa Kumara, gives us tremendous insight into phenomenal aspects of the universe, creation, transcendence, and God realization. In this adventure, he makes connections with the residents of the heavenly planets such as Lord Brahma and Lord Siva and he makes a connection with the *brahma-jyoti* or the impersonal bodily effulgence emanating from the Supreme Lord, but then he goes beyond this effulgence in order to reach the Vaikuntha planets where everyone has characteristics and potencies similar to the Lord. In this realm, the Supreme Lord is worshipped with pomp and reverence.

While on this journey, Gopa Kumara helps us to understand that there is even an abode beyond heaven and beyond the Vaikuntha planets where one can associate with God in different types of relationships. In the higher abode known as Goloka Vrndavana, the *Bhagavatamrta* explains that we can worship and associate with God eternally in different relationships either as a servant, a friend, a parent, or even a lover. This is the ultimate position of the soul in its most natural and highest connection with the Supreme Lord.

Judgment and Hell

Is God just? If God possesses the highest expression of all opulences, He must also possess the ultimate expressions of mercy and righteousness. In terms of judgment, Judaism, Christianity, and Islam propound that judgment will occur at the time of death, allowing God to make an evaluation. The Vaisnava scriptures also explain this phenomenon of judgment at the time of death, which will determine what body the soul will have to accept in the next life.

Many religious traditions view hell as the place where sinful souls will suffer eternally. However, some modern day Christians understand hell to be any place where the soul is separated from God rather than just a place to burn forever. The Vaisnava scriptures also give insight into this topic. In the Fifth Canto of *Srimad-Bhagavatam*, we find descriptions of different hellish conditions and punishments that a soul might have to undergo due to sinful activities. It also describes places known as the subterranean heavenly planets that offer exorbitant sense gratification, but, due to separation from God, life there will still lead to ultimate suffering. Even though these planets offer massive enjoyment, they are still considered hellish since they distract the soul from associating with and serving God.

Heaven as a Manipulative Tool

The emphasis on attaining heaven and avoiding hell has been used by religions as a tool to manipulate ignorant followers. A person might end up fantasizing about a heavenly abode to the point that any means appears to justify the end. Since the reward will come in the afterlife, the person may not take his or her present situation seriously. It also keeps people in a sectarian mood because they believe that only a specific religious path will lead to the ultimate reward. They see themselves as special, and this justifies their abuse and misuse of other people from different traditions. Some people are suffering so much that they only focus on the future promise of heaven without accessing the possibilities in the present. For those who believe in eternal damnation, the conception of hell negates the mercy of God. It can also cause people to act out of fear rather than out of love, consequently preventing them from connecting deeper with their spiritual nature.

These conceptions relate to some of the growing fanaticism that will continue to increase in the next decade. We want to look at more perspectives of heaven and war from different traditions and time periods because it is important to know what motivates people to think, act, and justify their actions according to their theology. We know that religion and theology are powerful. They have some of the most powerful influences on humanity, which have frequently led to and will continue to lead to some of the most devastating abuse and exploitation.

In our recent history, we have witnessed many examples of how this conception of heaven led to exploitation and suffering. For example, David Koresh, who established a group of followers in Waco, Texas, told his followers that they would go to heaven if they died with him. A similar theme pervaded the Jonestown tragedy in 1978. In both cases, people committed suicide with the idea that they would receive blessings and an auspicious afterlife.

In the eleventh century and later, Christian warriors known as the Crusaders were told by the Pope himself that if they were killed in battle, they would go to heaven. Some of the Popes even blessed those warriors in their attempt to recapture the holy land from the Muslims. In the sixteenth century, Protestants involved in the reformation were also told that their cause was so righteous that if they were killed while abusing and even killing others, they would go to heaven.

In Islam, the Sahih Bukhari Hadith 1:2:35 says that whoever engages in *jihad* will either attain a reward in this life if he survives, or will attain paradise if he dies as a martyr. The Koran describes paradise in greater detail in Sura 55, which is devoted to a description of the heavenly realm. It explains that such a person who reaches paradise will have many houris or virgins to enjoy, numerous servants, every type of fruit, an abundant supply of fresh water, green pastures, and gardens. Some Muslims even specify 70 or 72 as the number of virgins each man will have for his own pleasure. Without being offensive to the Islamic doctrine, some people will feel that these teachings are chauvinistic when one considers the position of the women and many virgins who will seem to eternally remain slaves in that situation. Furthermore, some of the Islamic scholars even say that there will be many palaces in paradise. They give a detailed description of the lovely furniture and other opulences, which might appear to some as a preoccupation with opulence from a material paradigm.

One can imagine how these descriptions may appeal to people suffering economically and socially on a day-to-day basis, and living under so much sexual repression. Some people are so economically deprived that they can easily become swayed by this conception of heaven. In the West Bank, young men and women have seen death all their lives, and live in constant fear of bombs and fighting. This promise of paradise seriously appeals to many. Even as we write this, thousands of people are being trained to die in *jihad*. Their greatest desire in life is to kill others in the process of so-called religious justification with the belief that they will receive blessings from God and go to heaven eternally. It is almost like a new type of human entity is being created who is so intensely absorbed in misdirected God consciousness in a fanatical way that they are simply fixed on taking the lives of others. It is a very dangerous time.

However, there is a verse in the Koran that says, "If you kill one innocent person, it is as if you kill all of humanity."[2] All the bona fide scriptures such as the Bible, Torah, Koran, Vedas, and so on present some aspect of God consciousness, but if we do not approach them in the spirit of love along with the proper guidance from spiritual teachers, the same scriptures can justify massive exploitation. In this sense, people are hijacking religion and using it for their own purposes. While we have more people interested in religious connections, reading more spiritual books, and trying to connect more with a God conscious lifestyle, we simultaneously have this powerful current sweeping the planet, stirring people to religious fanaticism.

Srila Bhaktivinoda Thakura can help us as we examine these different theologies. He explains the concept of *adhunika-vada* in which we make a careful evaluation of religion from a modern perspective in order to avoid changing the essence of what God has given. One should want to understand what God and His great servants have really given humankind in contrast to what has been added due to modern or past needs, desires, and frustrations. Much of what people consider religion relates extensively to present-day frustrations and anxieties that get converted into religious doctrines and shape our conception of the Godhead.

This happens in all theologies including Hinduism, Christianity, Buddhism, Islam, Judaism, and so on when people try to approach divinity with their contaminated senses and material desires. Consequently, something as powerful as religion can be abused in such a sectarian way that it brings down humanity and justifies all kinds of exploitation.

Removing Unnecessary Layers of Consciousness

We want to look closer at the nature of the soul and the process of transmigration. In our current human existence, we experience tremendous anxiety, gloom, and frustration. We are practically in a dead state because we are not giving nourishment to the soul. We might compare our consciousness to an onion, which has many layers. Many people simply remain on the outside of the onion due to the false ego that acts as a tyrant. It constantly tries to keep us on the outside. At any given time, the *atma* or soul is having many different levels of experiences in different realms of reality, but the dominant ego causes us to tune into just the outer layer. Consequently, we feel anxiety and pain while existing on that outer layer because no one can be happy when they feel incomplete. We have potential to experience the higher realities, but since we are not consciously experiencing it, we feel miserable.

We have so many scientists telling us that life comes from matter, but the scriptures explain just the opposite. Consciousness creates all forms, all experiences, all matter, all relationships, and all activities. A person with a high level of consciousness will have many more inclusive experiences. Those with an intermediate or low consciousness will only have limited experiences and realizations. Low consciousness compares to remaining on the outer layer of the onion.

Furthermore, our individual and collective environments are all based on individual and collective consciousness. The change of body at the time of death and entrance into another expression of existence has to do with the aggregate as well as individual consciousness. This determines what happens to an individual at the time of death. The consciousness of each family and civilization will determine what entities are brought together into those associations.

Death and Beyond

At the time of death, so many things take place. It is more variegated than our experience in this life. What we call life is more like death because, in the material worlds and material bodies, the soul experiences many limitations. Srila Bhakti-vinoda Thakura implies that hell is allegorical. At the same time, the *Srimad-Bhagavatam* tells us that they are actual places. How do we deal with the seeming contradiction? Is there really a heaven and hell? Are they just figments of imagination? Yes and no, simultaneously. What actually happens when we die? It is tremendously variegated.

First of all, a person's culture, perception, and theology can influence his or her experiences and interpretations. Everything is connected to a mental construct. There is nothing material that is totally solid. Every experience is associated with a mental construct. Therefore, when someone dies, there are absolute situations and experiences along with relative situations that can differ. It is not always that the Hindu, Buddhist, Christian, Muslim, and so on will have the exact same experiences at the time of death, for everything is connected with *karma*. Even individuals in the same tradition can and will have different experiences and destinations according to their individual *karma*.

We know from the *Srimad-Bhagavatam* that the Yamadutas and Visnudutas are two categories of entities who help the soul at death. The Visnudutas come for those who have reached perfection and the Yamadutas come for the rest. There are also all kinds of helpers and environments that we will experience according to the mental construct. If someone leaves the body in strong alignment with Christianity, their helpers can appear in a Christian manifestation. A Muslim can have helpers come in an Islamic manifestation. A person who did not believe in the afterlife or in God might not understand that they died. Their helpers might have to meet them as a friend to help them gradually understand the next stage of their existence.

When some people meet death, they will immediately take on a new body due to high levels of elevation and due to their mission. They simply move on to their next situation to continue their purpose and work. In some cases, due to their attachment to the physical world, they immediately take another physical body in circumstances designed just for them. Other souls might have to go through centuries of training and preparation before they can enter another physical body. Sometimes they meet with entities who have been guiding them for many lifetimes, and who will help them enter their next experience. In some cases, they initially experience gardens or cities they consider to be heaven. And the most successful can return back to rejoin the Supreme Lord in His abode, never having to encounter *samsara*, the cycle of repeated birth and death, again. Bhaktivinoda Thakura, for various reasons, explains that this may be allegorical based on the mental anticipation and according to what the entity experienced in their immediate past life. Of course, some experiences will manifest according to the person's specific *karma*.

Awake while Asleep

There are many special entities that help us prepare for the transition while sleeping. We may have no conscious awareness because dreams are such dynamic experiences, and the dream state can actually be more real than the physical experience we now call life. In the physical realm, we are often farther away from the cognizance of the soul. In the dream state, we often go back to the past, experience the future, and even experience deeper states of consciousness. Psychologists study dreams extensively, but they cannot record the level at which the soul interacts and has experiences, sometimes outside of the body. As Srila Prabhupada describes in the purport of *Srimad-Bhagavatam* 4.12.18, "One can experience the distinction between the subtle and gross bodies even daily; in a dream, one's gross body is lying on the bed while the subtle body carries the soul, the living entity, to another atmosphere. But because the gross body has to be continued, the subtle body comes back and settles in the present gross body."[3]

Dreams are so powerful that we can even change our present physical experiences by what we do in the dreams. We also find in the purport of *Srimad-Bhagavatam* 8.4.15 that the spiritual master sometimes has to suffer bad dreams due to the sinful disciples. All of us have experienced many things in a dream so that we do not have to experience it in the physical realm. However, many things that we have experienced in dreams later have some way of spilling over into the physical.

As we try to go to sleep in a more meditative and spiritual mood, we can have a direct influence on what we will experience in our day-to-day activities and relationships. In other words, we can change our physical reality based on some of the associations and experiences that go on in a dream. Keep in mind that in the dream, we can penetrate the deeper layers of the onion. We are unfolding the layers consciously as well as unconsciously. At almost any given time, we are experiencing all of those layers without a conscious awareness.

In the dream states and in these more subtle states, we are not restricted to geographical situations. Unfortunately, when we come out of the sleep state, we may interpret what we remember from the dream based on the ego, or we simply forget any deeper experiences on the level of the soul. It is like we die daily. When death comes, we will have tremendous opportunities after we have left the physical body. Often in dreams and even at death, we meet up with entities that we have possibly associated with in other lifetimes. We meet many entities from so many different realms and levels. The soul, however, is *sac-cid-ananda* or eternal, full of knowledge, and full of bliss, which means that our full consciousness understands all the layers of the onion. We have locked ourselves into certain mindsets by thinking that nothing exists beyond our current experiences.

We often describe leaving the physical bodies as if we go to a different place—yes and no. Leaving the body and having phenomenal experiences can happen in the middle of one's own room. Our normal conceptions of space and time are actually a misnomer. In the higher sense, there is no such thing as space and time. It is just a matter of mental expressions. In other words, our ego causes us to minimize and cover our real identity as an eternal soul and causes us to suffer while we are dealing with all of these limitations. What we call space and time in many cases is also a matter of different levels of mental awareness.

If we analyze this concept deeper, we realize that all knowledge and experience is available for us according to our

experience. The Vedic scriptures explain that the whole material world fits into just one corner of the spiritual world and is
covered over by what is called the *maha-tattva*. The spiritual
world is actually all that exists! It is the mind that determines
what we perceive. Understand that the mind has created this
prison for us through its activities of accepting and rejecting.
Self-realization simply means pulling off the layers of the
onion or removing the coverings of illusion. Developing the
inner senses and minimizing the false ego is most important for
experiencing and connecting with the Kingdom of God—our
true eternal home.

The Reality of Pretending

This leads us to the importance of practice or pretending in
a certain way until the full unfoldment takes place. In one sense,
this is *sadhana-bhakti*, which involves following the rules and
regulations of devotional service. We do not necessarily have
the realization or the full taste for spiritual activities, but we
are to act properly until we develop full taste and appreciation.
It is through proper practice that we become competent. All
matter, what we normally call reality, is just symbolism. For
instance, when we read a newspaper, we are reading letters of
the alphabet, but these letters create a realm of different mean-
ings and experiences. This is the entirety of what is happening
in our day-to-day involvement. Different phenomena that seem
to be the total reality are just constructs within the mind that act
as catalysts for our thoughts or experiences.

Whatever we experience is based on some stimulation that
the mind receives, which it then interprets in particular ways.
It means that we have the power to experience everything on

a much deeper level. We know that the mind can act as the greatest friend or the greatest enemy. When the false ego no longer captures the mind, we will be able to experience our eternal relationship in the spiritual kingdom.

When we look at the Deity form of the Lord in the temple, the false ego can tell us that it is a marble statue, or we can go deeper by realizing that the Deity is acting as a catalyst to help remind us of our position as servants of the Lord. Our original position is to always be in the service of the Lord. However, since we are simply residing on the surface of the onion, we do not realize that we are now in the spiritual world in the midst of pure divine beings. As we realize that essential truth, we allow our senses to transcend the limits of their normal perception so that we can connect deeper with the Supreme Godhead. We begin to anticipate the experiences so that we can break out of the misery of limited experiences.

For this reason, *sravanam* (hearing) and *kirtanam* (chanting) about the Lord are so important. We want to hear about the Lord as a way to constantly remind ourselves that we have a limited material body due to our unhealthy previous thoughts. Such thoughts have added up to produce our current situation and environment. At every moment, our thoughts are influencing the physical body and environment. By thinking in this way, we realize that the idea of time and space is a misnomer. We can realize that we are deader now than when we seemingly die because when we die, we will be exposed to all kinds of supernatural experiences. We might witness our actions from previous lifetimes or encounter realms that we can prepare for in the future. However, we might have to take another material body, which lacks this great sensitivity. In that dullness, there are all kinds of miserable experiences because our real selves are longing for our real home.

Even from our intellectual understanding, we can recognize that we are eternal spiritual entities temporarily limited to this body. We are eternal parts and parcels of the Supreme Personality of Godhead, but different in quantity. Our connection with the Lord radiates far beyond every aspect of these molecules and cells that we call the body. As we reflect on these realities, we begin to sharpen our internal senses and reclaim our actual identity as the soul. Instead of suffering the limitations of our material senses, we will gain spiritual senses, which are interchangeable. For instance, with spiritual senses one can see through the ears, hear through the eyes, or feel through the heart. Such experiences are the natural attributes of life—not the death we now experience. No wonder people suffer from so many anxieties and problems. No wonder so many people want to go to heaven, even when it is presented in a perverted sense. A part of them understands that existence involves greater experiences, but, due to their confusion, they are missing the essence. We understand that death is an opportunity for real life, but our individual experiences are based on our mental constructs.

We want to avoid *pasyann api na pasyati* which means to see but not see. Due to false ego, we basically remain on the surface and these layers distract us from the core. Our goal, on the other hand, is to experience all that is available which means full liberation and association with the Supreme Lord in the spiritual world. Remember these experiences are already part of us, but we have to remove the coverings. We start the process by having greater internal investigations and reflections. In our daily life, we should constantly reflect while eating, reading, working, and so on. We should appreciate that our current experiences are only symbols of what we can experience on a much deeper level. Our whole experience of so-called reality involves symbols and stimulations that should increase our hunger for the deeper reality. Otherwise, our hunger will turn into depression, lust, anger and fanaticism. A hunger that is not being properly addressed will lead people to abuse religion by using it to control, exploit and even harm others. On a lesser level, people will simply be captured by the basic problems of daily life, which is more like death. These problems will distract us from the loving connections and mental reflections available, causing us to stay on the surface of the onion. We will suffer peacefully or sometimes not so peacefully. However, the suffering will intensify. It is the duty of the spiritual warriors to show others how to penetrate the layers of the onion in order to experience the deeper blissful realities.

Questions and Answers

Question: You have thousands of people who you encounter as you travel and teach around the world who want to break away from their current mental images and experience a higher consciousness. Is the difficulty in our inability to recognize those images, our lack of faith to change, or simply the need for the Lord's mercy before we can change? What are the biggest restraints stopping us from just changing our images?

Answer: Before we accepted our particular body, each of us had some involvement in choosing what body and experiences we would have in this lifetime. Some of it has to do with why we chose such a situation. This again is connected to the free will that has been given to us by God. Due to certain desires, we make various choices that will then bring forth corresponding reactions because we have some involvement in the decision. Furthermore, the ego has convinced us for so long that the false world is real, so we have to start convincing ourselves of what is actually real. Since we firmly accept the authenticity of the false reality, it will require that same intensity to recondition ourselves. We have to put that same kind of energy into pretending that we are not that and engage more in activities that nourish the soul. Doing so will help us realize our real identity.

A devotee once asked his teacher if he should offer obeisances even if he doesn't genuinely feel like it. The spiritual master replied that he should continue to do the act because the proper action will gradually lead to the proper consciousness. We have pretended for so long to have various limitations; therefore, we cannot simply change by going to a few seminars. The mind will continue to reject the reality. We have to put the same energy into pretending to be different. For example, if someone walks into the room and you pretend that the person loves you deeply, you will in turn radiate a very positive mood towards that person. Actually, we are beautiful, we are loved, and we are protected. The soul has all of these qualities in its relationship with God. When we maintain a negative internal dialogue and pretend to accept our false selves, we will only increase our incarceration. However, we can use that same level of intensity to pretend ourselves into our ultimate reality.

For instance, a Vaisnava who wants to attain association with Krishna or God in the spiritual world has to realize what is available and then pretend to have that. It is not sahajiyaism or offensive behavior if one is not absorbed in sinful life and if one is under proper guidance; it is a part of *mana-seva* or worship within the mind. One may pretend that they really love Krishna and that they are in the spiritual world. One may pretend that they hear Krishna's flute because, in one sense, all of these experiences are already going on—only our egos have blocked the reception. When we interact in spiritual communities, we realize that our external senses are only picking up a small portion of the reality whereas our internal senses are tuning into the entire reality. We have pretended long enough to be separate from the reality, but now we want to pretend that we are in perfect harmony, fully surrendered to the Lord. We discuss this topic in more detail in *Spiritual Warrior V*. If we engage ourselves in this selfless practice, in time we will fully imbibe this nature. After awhile, the falseness will fall to the side and the internal senses will become more dominant until we integrate the internal reality into all of our experiences.

As we walk around, our minds might tell us that we are in Australia, France, India, America, Africa, Croatia, Russia and so on, but we are actually in the Kingdom of God now. As we chant the holy names of God and purify ourselves through proper discipline, we will be able to see and associate with the Supreme. Our minds and false egos tell us that it cannot happen, but since it is a reality, as we reflect on the genuine possibility and reality awaiting us, we will speed up our ability to experience it. As we accelerate, the false illusions will have less of an impact on us.

We have played a role in choosing our current experiences. Now the mind has created such powerful limitations, and we continue to hold onto them. It is like a person who keeps putting his hand in the fire, constantly burning himself and then complaining without accepting his own involvement in causing the pain. Our whole conception of reality is completely warped because we see good and evil or time and space according to our limited vision. However, reality has to do with Krishna and the soul. Everything outside of the reality is a part of the illusion.

For instance, before we go to sleep and enter the dream state, try to reflect on what we want to experience at the higher levels and we may then reflect on that in the dream. In many cases, we can experience deeper connections in the dream that will later become a part of our waking reality. However, as long as we think that it is beyond our means to change our situation, we will not only have this conception in this lifetime, but we will maintain it lifetime after lifetime. However, the Supreme Lord does not want us to suffer; He wants us to become happy. What is interfering with that reality? The whole process of self-realization involves minimizing the interferences that block our connection with reality. We might think it is easier said than done, but it is only our constant negative pretending that makes it hard. That is the madness of the material world.

For this reason, people and communities incarnate together due to the similar *karma* and madness. If we look at other planets and universes described in the *Srimad-Bhagavatam*, we see other types of madness. Our consciousness will lead us to the type of body and existence we will accept in the future. Our mindset will determine if we go to the spiritual kingdom or if we have to take another material body in these hells. We can gradually determine what we will experience and how we will unfold. Keep in mind that matter did not produce life; consciousness produced every aspect of matter. Everything that happens in the physical realm has to do distinctly with the consciousness of individuals, and it may not happen the way we expect. Every day we walk around thinking that we are alive when we are really partly dead, and when we go to sleep, we often have a greater chance to be really alive.

Question: I have been stumbling with your use of the word pretending, but I just translated it to practice.

Answer: Pretending can be defined as an inauthentic activity, but we are not using the word in this context, which would imply artificiality. We are talking about engaging in an intensity of practice even before the deeper devotional sentiments have fully blossomed. There is a difference. It is in fact improper if devotees enter into something without the proper *adhikara* or qualification because instead of healthy pretending or practice, they prematurely try to jump to a higher level. On the other hand, we might fully pretend to be humble for instance although we might not yet have that quality, but we genuinely and sincerely pretend. The difference is that we act authentically before we have fully reached that level by doing what is necessary to attain that goal permanently.

I use the word pretend in reference to healthy practice since it later becomes naturally incorporated into one's culture and becomes totally realized. I do not mean that we should be artificial or inauthentic. It means acting authentically, realizing that such actions relate to our essence even though we are presently covered over. We want to act in a way that will help us accept the truth so that one day we can fully accept our identity again. It means that we have to take on the mindset that will give us the ability to ultimately involve ourselves in unconditional, loving service to God. My main purpose in using the word pretending is to emphasize that we are currently acting or pretending to be different from our real self. Now we have to take that same intensity to accept our real identity.

Question: You mentioned that sometimes religiosity can be used to provoke genocide. How are we supposed to understand the *Bhagavad-gita* in this regard?

Answer: Yes, religion when abused can do the exact opposite of its intended purpose. In the *Bhagavad-gita*, we see war and adversarial situations. It also gives instructions about the eternality of the soul and about the pastimes of God. When the Lord comes in and out of universes, what does He do? He comes to enliven and inspire devotion in the people of this world by giving them a chance to hear about Him and change their mental constructs. At the same time, He takes steps to remove the blocks that cause some people to not think about Him. In some cases, He annihilates the demons; encourages the eradication of voidism, materialism, and impersonalism; and even destroys some physical bodies. All of this happens in the *Bhagavad-gita* for the benefit of humankind.

Question: The *Mahabharata* explains that a soldier who dies in battle will also obtain heaven. How do we understand this in relation to the discussion today because it seems to give some validity to this idea that a warrior can attain heaven?

Answer: We know that someone can obtain heaven if they die in war. They can obtain heaven if they die in a swimming pool. They can obtain heaven if they die in their beds. Their destination depends on how they have lived; what level of consciousness they have developed, and what mercy is bestowed upon them. The destination of a soul after death does not just depend on geographical environments or physical activities. It is not that a person can go to heaven simply by killing another person.

One could argue that priests in Vedic times would take the life of an animal—an act of violence—which would give the animal a higher birth in the next life. However, this type of violence involves the proper rituals according to the scripture. It involved taking an entity out of that body and immediately giving it a higher body. However, Lord Buddha stopped such sacrifice because acts that have such potency can cause great problems when abused. Therefore, the scriptures help us understand what God will accept from us, and the spiritual teachers and saints help us understand how to properly apply it.

In one sense, we can see that religion can cause a mess because it can be used to justify anything. It can produce the greatest inhumanity to humankind when followers turn to fanaticism. Especially when we think religion is all about dogma and rituals, it can create hell on Earth. Religion is really meant to develop love of God and uncover the soul. It is to help us accept the reality of our eternal identity so that we can move beyond the illusion, false ego, and the three modes of material nature. Religion really means to accept God's love and presence, and lovingly follow His laws.

Question: Can you clarify the sleep state for me because I have read that sleep is nescience?

Answer: Yes, a certain aspect of sleep, especially for the less evolved is nescience. There are many different aspects of sleep since the sleep state is potentially more variegated than the waking experience. Some aspects of sleep are defined by brain waves and consciousness. At times in our dreams, we just experience some sense gratification, depression, anxieties, or some crazy combination of activities. These are usually expressions of nescience. We also know that sleep has some basic biological functions such as rejuvenating the body, a machine that needs a certain amount of rest. However, we are addressing a deeper aspect of sleep. The psychologists can at least detect a state know as REM or rapid eye movement in which people begin to dream. They can measure this stage by brain waves.

However, there are levels that they cannot measure with the use of machines. It involves the soul or consciousness leaving the body and having experiences in various realms. The soul can have experiences of past, present, and future and interact with many great saints and spiritual teachers. This is often more accessible while the physical body is at rest.

When we are interacting with the external world, we are much more bound by the immediate senses, which constantly pick up stimulations from the environment. However, when we are at rest, the immediate senses are not so active. For instance, some devotees have had dreams in which the *guru* gives them instructions. Some might have met their spiritual master in a dream before they physically saw him. I have disciples who saw me in their dreams years before they saw me physically. In the dream state, when the sensory stimulation is not bombarding us, there is more of a chance for richer internal experiences. Especially when the pure devotees of the Lord sleep, they simply put the physical body to rest, but they are highly active in performing devotional service at this time.

Sleep could fall into the category of nescience if we take shelter of sleep to avoid work or to send the mind into an unhealthy space. The mind can go into some of our anxieties or sensual experiences, but the same sleep experience can also enrich the physical body and enrich our spiritual life. As we have deeper experiences in our dreams, they will also spill over into our present waking reality. Both states help each other. Just as the quality of our praying and chanting affects the quality of our service, the quality of our inner experiences in dreams can have even more of an impact on our waking state than our waking state has on our dream state. For this reason, the six *gosvamis* of Vrndavana, India slept so little because even when they seemingly slept, they were serving the Lord in different capacities. This can also help us understand how *yogis* can reside in caves for years because they have the ability to park their physical bodies while they have all kinds of experiences outside the body. It is just a matter of certain psychic technologies that can give a person particular *siddhis* or mystic powers.

When we realize what opportunities we have in the dream state, we can have more of an influence on what happens to us and even use our experiences in our waking state. In the waking state, if we have deeper internal experiences, we can then have deeper connections as we honor the soul and begin to revitalize who we really are. The abode of the Lord is awaiting all of us, but it cannot be obtained by religious fanaticism or material technologies. Rather, it can only be reached by the true culture of unalloyed devotion and service to the Godhead. Our souls are desperately longing to return to our homes.

Regard your neighbor's gain as your gain, and your neighbor's loss as your own loss.

Tai Shang Kan Yin P'ien (Taoism)

Chapter 4

Different Conceptions of Religion

In one sense, religions are like vehicles that people choose to ride in according to their nature. The vehicle is not as significant as its ability to carry you where you need to go. It is unfortunate when people want to push other drivers off the road or cannot appreciate another driver who has a different car. Of course, some vehicles just do not function properly at all, and others look very good but still have trouble because they are not kept up properly. However, if we have a good vehicle and continue to move along the road, we will progress towards the destination. All bona fide religious systems emphasize that one must righteously pursue God consciousness. Sectarianism is a creation of humankind. If people do not fix themselves on the pursuit of God consciousness and only maintain superficial connections, they will create more fragmentation and exploitation. Srila Bhaktivinoda Thakura elaborates on this point in his *Sri Caitanya Siksamrta*:

People in various countries on various continents have a wide variety of natures. Although their principal nature is only one, their secondary characteristics are many—you will not find any two people in the world who have identical secondary qualities. Since even twins born of the same womb have some difference in form and quality, can one expect that people born in different countries can ever have exactly the same qualities? Different countries have different water, air, mountains, forests, and different eatables and clothing. Because of this, the people of these places have naturally developed different physiques, complexions, customs, clothing and food. Similarly, people's mentalities differ. Thus various people's ideas of God, though being basically similar, will differ in secondary details... Considered objectively, there is no harm in secondary differences. If there is agreement concerning the essential nature of God and His worship, there should be no obstacle in attaining the same result. Thus Mahaprabhu has taught that we should instruct everyone to worship the pure form of the Lord, but at the same time we should not criticize others' modes of worship.[4]

Researching the Goal of a Theology

As we will see, there are many different religious traditions that have different conceptions of God and different practices. When we choose to follow a teaching, we want to find out if we do in fact feel comfortable with all aspects of the theology. Three initial questions can help us make a clear evaluation. First of all, *what is the ultimate goal of the system?* Many times people involve themselves in a religious system without even knowing the ultimate goal. If they really did their research, they might not feel comfortable with the goal. We all have free will, but we should be clear about what we want. Sometimes the ultimate accomplishment of a system is to kill all of one's enemies. For other systems, the ultimate goal is to capture someone and make them a lover. In other cases, the final goals are to attain *nirvana, samadhi*, cosmic consciousness, mystic power, heaven on earth, or the Kingdom of God.

Secondly, *what must we do to reach that goal?* Every system has various tenets that will lead to a particular goal. If someone introduces you to a religious system, but tells you that you do not need to do anything to attain that goal, you should run away very fast. No bona fide system will give higher realizations simply by waiting for them to happen. However, if we find out that a process requires us to sacrifice our first-born or do a gruesome ritual, we may decide against that path as well. Or if a process requires the followers to meditate twelve hours a day, we may not feel that we have the desire or stamina to execute those practices. We then decide to go elsewhere. On the other hand, if we are comfortable with the rituals, practices, and techniques of the system, then we can go to the third question.

Finally, *do we feel comfortable with what those who have*

authentically followed the goal obtained? If we feel comfortable with the process and like the goal, then we want to know
about the people who have succeeded on that specific path.
We want to find out if we are comfortable with what they are
experiencing since we can or will become like them. If we feel
comfortable after answering all of these three questions, then
we should use our free will to pursue that goal with great intensity and chastity.

Two Types of Religious Practitioners

Let us now examine some conceptions in relation to religious practices, beginning with those who follow those practices. According to Srila Bhaktivinoda, there are two types of
religious practitioners:

1. *Bharavahis—the external practitioner. Bharavahis* are
   those religionists who are fully caught up in the externals.
   They are more into the rituals, dress, dogma, etc. It is
   here where many of the fanatics are created. Often, such
   worshipers have trouble not only with other practitioners
   of other faiths, but even with those in their own faiths
   who do things different from them.

2. *Saragrahis—the internal practitioner.* These practitioners
   are focused on the essence of the religion and do not get
   distracted by the rituals, dress, dogma, details, etc. Such
   worshipers are chaste to their religion but not sectarian,
   and they are hungry to experience an even richer inner
   life. This spiritualist knows that one can follow rules
   and teachings superficially, or that one can go deeper to

understand the essence. They realize also that there are *mukhya*, or primary rules as well as *gauna*, or secondary rules. The *baravahis* normally confuse the secondary with the primary. These days the *baravahis* far outnumber the *saragrahis*, which obviously creates a tremendous problem for society.

Four Types of Motivated Worship (Bhajana-prayasera Cariti Karana)

There are four reasons why people engage in the worship of God—three types of motivated worship and one type of genuine worship. As long as people serve on a conditional basis, they can never access the purest expression of love because love is not a type of business exchange or utilitarianism. These conditional pursuits are all associated with the material realms.

1. *Bhaya: Worship Out of Fear*

   It means that people serve the Lord in order to avoid suffering in hell. They mostly follow a religious path because they believe they will suffer intensely if they do not worship God. This type of worship involves more fear than knowledge of the higher realities.

   Many years ago while meeting with the President of Ghana, I was asked by several of the President's cabinet officials if I would accept the offer to act as a consultant for their country. Some time later, after we sent some books to the President, we wondered from time to time if he had read them or taken advantage of the knowledge.

At one point when the country faced serious problems, the President summoned many of the religious leaders together. During the meeting, he made a very powerful statement directly related to the material in our books. He told the religious leaders that instead of just fearing God, he is learning to love God, and he felt that they should do the same. Some people viewed this statement as blasphemy since they interpreted it to mean that the President does not fear God. In a newspaper, they even published the headline, "The President Does Not Fear God."

He tried to offer them higher knowledge because serving the Supreme Lord only out of fear is not really so profound. For instance, if a child only acts properly when the parent threatens the child with punishment, the child will not act properly in the absence of the parent and the threat. However, when the child acts based on knowledge and love, then the parent who sets the rules will not have to directly oversee the child at all times since he or she will naturally want to act properly out of love. With this in mind, the President was trying to help them appreciate that they were worshipping out of fear, which was creating sectarianism. Due to fear, they only considered what would enhance their own organization, and many were not only selfish, but hypocritical as well.

2. Asa: Conditional Worship For Material Aspirations

Many times people only think about God when they want some material pleasure or commodity. Instead of trying to enter into a relationship in order to love and serve the Lord, they are mainly invoking the Lord's presence so that He can act as their servant. When people engage in their prayers and rituals, they often want the Lord to serve them by giving them good health, a better job, or a new car among other requests. Or they want the Lord to help their uncle, brother, sister, niece, father, cousin, etc. Although it sounds quite strange to view the Supreme Personality of Godhead as a servant, most people execute their rituals with this mindset. They simply invoke the Lord when they want sense gratification or need some obstacles removed from their lives.

Sometimes religionists do not have much interest in love, service, and realization, but they practice religion due to the frustration they have in their own lives. They hope that the metaphysical or spiritual connection will create some fulfillment in their lives and eliminate their obstacles. Such people do not really want to experience divine love; they mostly want to find a way to suffer more peacefully. Obviously, this is not a very high expression since it is motivated and conditional. Most people consider happiness to be a temporary cessation of the ongoing suffering, depression, and boredom, but how can we consider temporary relief from pain as happiness? Real happiness, love, and knowledge completely differ from temporary gratification.

3. *Kartavya-buddhi: Serving Out of Duty*

In this case, a person serves according to the rules and regulations propounded in the scriptures. The scriptures tell us what to do as well as what to avoid, regulations which one should follow until they rise to a more spontaneous level. Ultimately, rituals and rules are necessary to help the practitioner develop a deeper internal connection. If we disregard this essential foundation, we will not be able to make an organic connection that can take us to a higher level. Unfortunately, some people accept the rituals as the all in all, which is one of the difficulties of religious institutions. Sometimes people become more concerned with mechanical activities, politics, and externals rather than the philosophy and the goal. They then move farther and farther away from accessing the internal essence. We see this happen decade after decade.

4. *Raga: Worship Out of Genuine Attraction*
Love means that the lover goes out of his or her way for the beloved because he or she genuinely wants to honor the beloved's presence. When the knowledge and love is deep and the person has transcended the gross and subtle levels of alignment, the loving exchanges become spontaneous and exhilarating. The soul is *sac-cid-ananda-vigraha* or full of eternity, knowledge, and bliss. Self-realization does not mean that we have to learn who we are; rather, it means uncovering our actual identity by freeing ourselves of superfluous involvements in our lives. It involves removing the acculturation forced upon us by the material energy.

Differences Between Religious Traditions (Vibhinna-dharmera Pancavidha-bheda)

1. *Acaryabheda: A Difference In Teachers*
This addresses the fact that people of various faiths have particular saints, prophets, or *acaryas* whom they adore and abide by. Bhaktivinoda Thakura speaks of how the adoration of one's teacher is natural and important;

thus people of one faith should not try to impose the supremacy of their teacher upon another.

We honor the fact that there is ultimately one God. Whether we call God Allah, Yahweh, Jehovah, Krishna, or the Supreme Lord, we are ultimately addressing the same Supreme Person. However, we can appreciate that the same Lord sends different representatives according to *desa-kala-patra* or place, time, and circumstance. Sometimes these ambassadors have a very specific duty and have different qualities in terms of what they intend to give to the people. They are asked to present various levels of knowledge according to what the people need at a particular place.

For instance, three students might intend to graduate from a particular university, but the first student is in high school, the second student is in their first year of college, and the last student is in their final year of college. Obviously, the type of knowledge given to them will differ according to their specific level although they all intend to ultimately reach the same goal. The teachers might have the same level of knowledge, but they give according to the caliber of the student. Similarly, the representatives of the Lord might have a similar level of spiritual empowerment, but they have different tasks. However, some representatives do have different capacities.

When we look at the different proponents of the various religious traditions, we will find that they had similarities in what they knew, but in many cases they withheld knowledge from their followers. For instance, Jesus very emphatically said, "I have many other things to tell you, but you cannot grasp them now" (John 16:12). When Muhammad made his ascensions, he was given three calibers of knowledge. He was given knowledge that he was to keep for himself; knowledge to tell the people; and knowledge that he could share based on time and circumstance.[5] Buddha also said, "Many things I have not explained."[6]

These particular messengers shared some similarities, but they had specific assignments to complete. When we look at any bona fide messenger connected with the spiritual realm, we will find them emphasizing similar principles—love God with all your heart, love your neighbor as yourself, and this world is not your eternal home. They have variations on how they try to remind people of these basic truths. They try to guide people out of the incarceration of the three modes of material nature; try to stimulate them to develop more loving relationships amongst themselves; and ultimately want people to render loving service to God.

2. *Upasakera   manovrtti   o   bhajana-anubhava-bheda*: *Difference in the Worshipper's Mentality and Expression of Reverence.*

Here mentality refers to a psychological disposition, often infused by a person's culture or inherent to a particular religious tradition, which in many cases relates to the culture from which the tradition originated. Cultures carry certain patterns of mentality and mood.

This leads us to consider how our material condition is a part of our spiritual practice. Various people can be in line with the essence of a theology while extrinsically having differences. For instance, in my work with the International Society for Krishna Consciousness, I see a myriad of diversity—Chinese, African, German,

Indonesian, French, Mexican, Russian, Indian, American, Japanese, etc. There is an essential spiritual culture and philosophy while the idiosyncrasies carried by individual's cultures bring a variety of devotional expression. It is wonderful to see how the essential elements of devotion to Krishna are present, while the expression is so variegated. Of course, in cases where the devotees' understandings are shallow, I also see unfortunate quibbles over minor differences.

Furthermore, different systems have different ways of expressing their worship. A few years ago in Europe, I did a television program with the religious leaders of different traditions. They asked each of us to state which day we accept as our holy day and explain why. Some gave reasons why Friday is the best day to worship, someone said Saturday, and yet another group said Sunday. Another representative suggested that we have no need to have formal worship at all. When my turn came to speak, I simply asked, "Is there any day that is not a day of the Lord? Isn't everyday an opportunity to glorify the Lord? If only Friday, Saturday, or Sunday are the Lord's days, then to whom does the rest of the week belong?" Yes, it is true that our traditions may offer us different days in which we gather as a community, but we should focus on God's service every day. However, many people involve themselves in their religious systems with a superficial mindset. They do what will enhance their immediate sense gratification most of the time, but, one day a week or month, they try to involve themselves more deeply in spiritual matters. Again, love is not a flickering emotion that we turn on and off. When we genuinely love another, we try to honor and connect with the object of our love at all times.

Different systems also have different ways of approaching reincarnation. The Bible mentions that we reap what we sow (Matthew 26:52). As we look deeper into some of the esoteric aspects of the Bible, many expressions indicate that we have an existence beyond the physical body. Corinthians explains that we have a terrestrial body and a celestial body. While we reside in the physical body, we are away from God. The Koran 2: 28 says, "How disbelieve ye in Allah when ye were dead and He gave life to you! Then He will give you death, then life again, and then unto Him ye will return." This emphasizes the concept of *samsara* or repeated birth and death as found in the Vedic scriptures:

dehino 'smin yatha dehe
kaumaram yauvanam jara
tatha dehantara-praptir
dhiras tatra na muhyati

As the embodied soul continuously passes, in this body, from boyhood to youth to old age, the soul similarly passes into another body at death. A sober person is not bewildered by such a change.

Bhagavad-gita 2.13

We have been given life, but that life will end, giving us the ultimate chance to either reside in the spiritual kingdom or to take another birth in the material world. However, *Bhagavad-gita* 8.16 explains that one who attains the spiritual world never has to take birth again in the material world.

3. *Upasanar pranalibheda: Differences in the Method of Worship*

   People worship in many different places such as temples, mosques, churches, or even on mountains. Obviously, these places just make up some of the external differences. For people who are not grounded in their own tradition, these differences are sources of confusion. Differences that come together around a strong nucleus of love and understanding engender unity, while differences lacking this nucleus move us towards greater degrees of conflict. Unfortunately, we have seen some of the worst inhumanities under the banner of religion. People even hide behind religion while they involve themselves in all kinds of deviations.

4. *Upasya-tattvera sambhande bhava o kriyabheda: Differences in the Conceptions and Conventional Actions Concerning the Object of Worship*

   Sometimes religionists believe that there is only one process, one prophet, or one son of God, which is quite an elementary understanding. In terms of Christianity, the Bible says in John 1:12 that those who receive Jesus and believe in his name, he gives the right to become sons of God. We might compare this position of a son to a type of ambassadorship. Certain entities, who are pure servants of the Lord, represent the spiritual kingdom. To think that God sends a messenger only once and only in a particular way is a limited conception. When these prophets guide people, they give the message in a particular way. In some cases, due to their compassion, they find ways to get the same message across while using different terminology and instructions. An ambassador may come alone to a different country, but he or she has the power of attorney to represent their particular country. However, the individual must correctly represent the country if he or she wishes to remain an ambassador.

There are also different notions surrounding the form of the Lord, especially in terms of how His form can be approached by us in worship. These differences stem from different conceptions of the Lord. Some people are taught that the Lord is beyond the physical world and cannot be expressed through physical materials while others are taught that, in being unlimited, the Lord can manifest Himself in a form appropriate for limited beings like ourselves. Be it a physical icon or an abstract concept, in one sense everything is a manifestation of the Lord. With a mature understanding of the Divine, we can hold proper respect towards the various objects of worship, being able to reconcile apparent differences by seeing them in their proper perspective.

Five thousand years ago, in facing the onslaught of the present Age of Quarrel and Hypocrisy, the greatest sages of various spiritual paths congregated in the forest of Naimisaranya, Northern India. Their purpose was to perform sacrifices to help delay the degradation of the coming age. After engaging in sacrifice for a period of time, they decided to select the most qualified amongst themselves, Suta Gosvami, to explain the ultimate good for mankind. Suta Gosvami succinctly gave the reply—unmotivated and uninterrupted devotion to God. However, in his explanation he gave a definition of God appropriate for the wide variety of spiritualists in the assembly. He spoke as follows:

vadanti tat tattva-vidas
tattvam yaj jnanam advayam
brahmeti paramatmeti
bhagavan iti sabdyate

Learned transcendentalists who know the Absolute Truth call this nondual substance Brahman [spiritual energy], Paramatma [God supporting creation, and accompanying each of us], or Bhagavan [God in His own world, in His complete personality].

Srimad-Bhagavatam 1.2.11

Srila Prabhupada comments on this point in the *Teachings of Lord Kapila*:

The Absolute Truth is understood differently according to the position of the student. Some understand the Absolute Truth as impersonal Brahman, some as localized paramatma, and others as the Supreme Personality of Godhead, Krishna, or Visnu. Brahman, Paramatma and Bhagavan, the Supreme Personality of Godhead, are not different. They are simply different aspects of the complete Godhead. Looking at a mountain from a distance, we may see a hazy cloud, and if we come nearer, we may see something green. If we actually climb the mountain, we will find many houses, trees and animals. Our vision is of the same mountain, but due to our different positions we see haze, greenery or variegatedness. In the final stage, there are varieties—trees, animals, men, houses, and so on.

To truly recognize and adore how all aspects of reality are distinct emanations from the all-good Supreme Being is the essence of religion and knowledge. As the understanding of our relationship with God matures, when we encounter a different bona fide object of worship, we will be able to appreciate the divinity therein and grow from it, going deeper into our own distinct devotion to God.

5. *Bhasa-bhedanusare nama o vakyadi-bheda: Differences in God's Names and Teachings Due to Linguistic Differences*

Every great theology comes with a scripture or teaching to disseminate knowledge. It comes with *acaryas* or sons and daughters of God who are very instrumental in propagating the philosophy. The messengers who have distinct personalities come in specific types of bodies to certain parts of the world. They speak a language and may use different names to address the Lord. But in spite of these differences, we see that most theistic traditions encourage followers to call on the names of God.

In Christianity, the Bible states, "For whoever shall call on the name of the Lord shall be saved" (Romans 10: 13). In Psalms 113:2-3, "Blessed be the name of the Lord from this time forth and for evermore. From the rising of the sun to the going down of the sun, the Lord's name is great." The Koran 7:180 says, "Allah's are the fairest names. Invoke Him by them." The Koran 17:110 says, "Cry unto Allah, or cry unto the Beneficent, unto whichsoever ye cry (it is the same). His are the most beautiful names." The Book of Mormon, Alma 34:17-27 explains that we should call upon the name of God at all times, in all places, and under all circumstances. In Buddhism, the 18th Vow of the Amida Buddha emphasizes that all who sincerely call upon his name will attain his Pureland, or a paradisiacal place in which the person can continue their quest to enlightenment.

We even find in mystery schools like Eckankar an emphasis on calling on the name of God, Hu, as a means to attain greater spiritual realization. In our Vedic tradition, we address God as Krishna. We also understand that God has a masculine aspect and a feminine aspect. In *Bhagavad-gita* 10.25, Krishna says, "Of sacrifices, I am the chanting of the holy names." We find the following verse in the *Brhan-naradiya Purana* 3.8.126:

> *harer nama harer nama*
> *harer namaiva kevalam*
> *kalau nasty eva nasty eva*
> *nasty eva gatir anyatha*

In this age of Kali there is no other means, no other means, no other means for self-realization than chanting the holy name, chanting the holy name, chanting the holy name of Lord Hari.

The *Kali-Santarana Upanisad* 6 further states:

> *iti sodasakam namnam*
> *kali-kalmasa nasanam*
> *natah parataropayah*
> *sarva vedesu drsyate*

> After searching through all the Vedic
> literatures, one cannot find a method
> of religion for this age so sublime as
> the chanting of the holy names of the
> Lord.

If we deeply examine all the various religious traditions, we will see an emphasis on the power of *mantra*, and an emphasis on how sound affects individual consciousness along with the collective environment. It is often people who minimize the importance of these universalities due to a difference in form and other external factors.

Five Types of Adharma or Irreligion

1. *Vidharma* refers to irreligious concepts and actions that hinder a person's spiritual advancement. This of course causes individuals to not get the full benefit of following their respective religions.

2. *Para-dharma* refers to religious principles concocted by others that create some contamination or adulteration. These principles have entered whimsically and weakened

the potency of the process. Religion means to follow the laws given by God, but sometimes people speculate and then introduce their own philosophies and so-called religious principles.

3. *Dharmabhasa* or pretentious religion occurs when a pseudo-religious practice is adopted whimsically by people who willfully abandon their prescribed duties. According to their social and spiritual stations in life, people have certain responsibilities. Those who abandon them, adopting a pseudo-religious practice to suit their whims, only create confusion and chaos.

4. *Upadharma* or heretical religion is a faction of a bona fide religion created by people taken away by false pride. These factions appear plausible, but are actually fallacious.

5. *Chala-dharma* refers to a cheating religion in which people use a bona fide religion to meet their own ends. This is often a matter of business and politics in the name of religion, or exegeses to push one's own ideas.

Spiritual Guides: Manifest and Unmanifest

All of these different approaches to religion also affect people's understanding of spiritual teachers and guides. We must remember that we are never alone on the spiritual path. There are always personalities helping us to advance and guiding us in the right direction. Just as some teachers come in a physical form, there are many *yogis* and teachers who never enter the physical form. We can only see them if we have higher vision.

Although higher beings have at times come into this particular realm to interact, they no longer appear as frequently. The planet became more sinful after the departure of Lord Buddha and consequently many higher beings did not feel comfortable coming into environments saturated with destruction and devastation. People are now engaged in all types of sectarianism and superficialities. However, someone on this planet who has a higher level of consciousness will not have any problem seeing or interacting with such entities when they come to earth.

Very powerful rituals and *yajnas* do not just involve the people who are physically present. The purpose is to assist those who are present while simultaneously calling forth and honoring others in higher realms as well as those who may have come due to the potency of the particular ritual. In the Vaisnava community, after a ceremony is over, the Premadhvani prayers or closing prayers conclude by saying, "All glories to the assembled devotees." We are offering respects to those in attendance and hopefully to those who have come due to the potency of the ceremony. The higher beings do not necessarily manifest physically unless we have the vision to see. As we also hear in the Bible, we have a physical form as well as a spiritual form. Although we might only have the capacity to perceive material forms, we should not consider that nothing exists beyond these forms. We think this because we are using our materialistic perspective in the realms below to analyze the realms above.

None of us are defined by the costumes we wear. We have so many designations while we remain in these bodies, but we are none of these designations because the soul is completely separate from any material labels. It is eternal.

na jayate mriyate va kadacin
nayam bhutva bhavita va na bhuyah
ajo nityah sasvato 'yam purano
na hanyate hanyamane sarire

For the soul there is neither birth nor
death at any time. He has not come into
being, does not come into being, and
will not come into being. He is unborn,
eternal, ever-existing and primeval. He
is not slain when the body is slain.

Bhagavad-gita 2.20

In one sense, we are all extraterrestrials because no entities
permanently reside in this material universe. We are simply in
transit. The soul does not stay in these environments eternally;
therefore, it is just a matter of how recently we have come and
how ready we are to leave. These subjects only seem extraordinary because people try to understand the spiritual realms
through mundane references and perspectives. Being absorbed
in the normative patterns of material life, spiritual truths seem
imaginary and unreal. Nevertheless, spirituality has always
been full of adventure, excitement, and transcendental personal
relationships.

Personalism Versus Impersonalism

As we deepen our examination, we will also discover that
people have different conceptions of God, which sometimes
stem from their own experiences. Some people think of God
as being free from variegatedness. They feel that the ultimate

state of God consciousness involves a type of *nirvana*, void of relationships and heterogeneity. Other people conceive of God as an expression of universal intelligence or ultimate divine light. They are connected with systems and practices that allow them to experience a cosmic consciousness or *samadhi*. Such systems might lead to an experience of oneness with all that is, or a feeling that they are all that is. Others feel that the ultimate connection with God involves their ability to honor morality and ethics. Yet other people see God through objects in their environment such as trees, the moon, the sun, animals, and so on. Then there are those who try to connect with the Godhead in order to experience divine personality and divine variegatedness.

Material relationships are temporary whereas spiritual associations are not limited. The spiritual reality is actually creating the material objects and activities. The material realm is merely a reflection of the permanent and eternal. For instance, if you look in a mirror, you only see a reflection because of the existence of the original form in front of the mirror. Many of the mystery schools and various theologies seem to take on more of an impersonal aspect. However, if we look more scrutinizingly, we will begin to observe that everything when studied has characteristics or specific attributes.

In one sense, there is no such thing as impersonal energy because even a drop of water, a neutron, or a light wave has specific qualities, relationships, and forms. If we take a drop of water and look at it very closely, we will see how it is comprised of small parts that are variegated. The parts attract, unite, repel, and so on. It seems almost like an oxymoron. From one perspective, something might seem void of relationships, but whatever exists must be interacting and relating to other objects in the environment. Anything that exists must have some type of *dharma* or essence; otherwise, it does not exist. Therefore, the idea of impersonalism is just a conceptual consideration since it doesn't actually mean anything.

The earth itself is a living entity along with the sun, moon, and galaxy. Even our physical bodies could compare to a universe along with the dominant consciousness that we call our identity. Within a person's body are hundreds of thousands of life forms, cells, and germs, etc. Of course, physical bodies are relative according to size and duration of life. For an ant to walk across what we consider a small room might compare to miles for the insect. Size, duration, and longevity are all relative. For the little germ, our body is indefinable.

We, as living entities in association with Mother Earth, are very minute, but so many of our activities are polluting and rupturing this planet. We are rupturing the earth by nuclear tests, toxic waste, landfills, and even improper thoughts and mindsets. We are creating many disturbances on this planet. No wonder we have an increase in earthquakes, hurricanes, tornadoes, and famines. Just as our body will malfunction if we abuse it long enough, the earth also reacts to our constant abuse. Our bodies have a natural way to fight off intrusions, germs, and attacks, and Mother Earth, as an individual personality, also has a natural way to fight off sickness.

In 1998 alone, tens of thousands of people died and millions were displaced due to earth changes. We see such catastrophes all over the world. As long as we continue to abuse living organisms, we will get corresponding results. Now we find more people suffering from such ailments as heart disease and cancer, which also stem from the abuse of our physical and subtle presence. We will get various types of reactions. The unhealthy bombardments in the atmosphere are weakening our immune systems.

We need to be much more conscientious in taking care of ourselves, especially considering the hundreds of thousands of life forms connected with our bodies. When we take proper care of our bodies, we are not only giving better attention to every organ and cell, but we are also giving care to the many other forms of life inside of our bodies. For instance, our cells are alive, and in every atom, there is the presence of the Supersoul. The way we treat the physical body is also the way we treat and relate to all of the variegated life forms within the physical shell.

Dr. John Cleveland Cothran, formerly a Professor of Chemistry and the Chairman of the Science and Mathematics Department at the University of Minnesota, also supports this personal view. In his article, "The Inescapable Conclusion," he writes:

> Chemistry discloses that matter is ceasing to exist, some varieties exceedingly slowly, others exceedingly swiftly. Therefore, the existence of matter is not eternal. Consequently matter must have had a beginning. Evidence from chemistry and other sciences indicates that this beginning was not slow and gradual; on the contrary, it was sudden, and the evidence even indicates the approximate time when it occurred. Thus at some rather definite time the material world was *created* and ever since has been obeying *law*, not the dictates of chance. Now, the material realm not being able

to create itself and its governing laws, the act of creation must have been performed by some nonmaterial agent. The stupendous marvels accomplished in that act show that this agent must possess superlative intelligence, an attribute of *mind*. But to bring mind into action in the material realm as, for example, in the practice of medicine and the field of parapsychology, the exercise of *will* is required, and this can be exerted only by a *person*. Hence our logical and inescapable conclusion is not only that creation occurred but that it was brought about according to the plan and will of a Person endowed with supreme intelligence and knowledge (omniscience), and the power to bring it about and keep it running according to plan (omnipotence) always and everywhere throughout the universe (omnipresence). That is to say, we accept unhesitatingly the fact of the existence of "the supreme spiritual being, God, the creator and director of the universe."[7]

As we go deeper into orthodox religions and deeper into various mystery schools, we will constantly find more of a personal connection. Just consider how any relationship functions. If you do not know me or do not see me as a valuable person, you will treat me impersonally. Similarly, if we do not study theology deeply, we will have a general understanding of our relationship with God, but the closer we look, the more we will understand. We might see a beautiful building from afar, but, as we reflect more closely on the intricate design of the structure, we will understand that an architect designed the building as a creative expression. We can either just look at the manifestation or look to see what is really behind the creation. This type of research will always bring us back to a personal level. Not only are the minutest details personal, but the grandest phenomena are personal as well.

We can also find glimpses of higher knowledge in some of the mystery schools such as the Grail movement, Eckankar, or the Theosophy movement. Eckists, followers of Eckankar, have a book entitled *The Flute of God* by Paul Twitchell. I once inquired from one Eckankar master about this book. They say the highest experience is to hear the ultimate sound, which is that of the flute of God. I then asked for more knowledge of the flute and about the player of the flute. There was silence because the knowledge stopped at that point. However, if there is a flute or a sound, someone has put that sound into motion. A spiritual sound is not put into motion by a material being or force, but by a spiritual influence. Therefore, the knowledge and science of this spiritual personality—the Supreme Lord— is the ultimate goal of the spiritual warrior.

We find in the Vedic scriptures an emphasis on various personal expressions of the Godhead such as incarnations, plenary expansions, and so on. In different Vaisnava temples, we will see the *arca-vigraha* or the Deity who plays on a flute. We also see similarities in this conception of the Deity between religions. The Vatican accepts the conception of a self-manifest Deity. Sometimes the Madonna cries or the icons communicate with people in other ways. There are certain similarities that appear in all of the various theologies of the world as we go deeper and deeper. We touch upon very personal experiences and even miracles. We consider them miracles because we do not necessarily understand them or encounter them in our daily lives. However, those experiences that we normally call miracles or psychic phenomena mostly deal with a subtler expression of ourselves and of the personal reality. If we stop blocking them, more of the natural miracles will take place.

Personalism as the Ultimate Conclusion

Let us look closer into this conception of personalism. In Islam, the Hadith describes Muhammad's ascension called the Me'raj in which he went to the lower planets, to the medium planets, and to the higher planetary systems. The angel Gabriel, who was very instrumental in offering the world the Koran, escorted Muhammad to these different realms. However, it explains in Islamic theology that when they arrived at *sidratul muntaha*, angel Gabriel could not go any further. At this point, Muhammad went beyond heaven and met Allah face to face. The prophet had a relationship with Allah in the mood of friendship. Muhammad continues by describing how Allah put His hand between his shoulders, and gave him divine wisdom.[8] Furthermore, we also find in Islamic theology that "[s]eeing Allah is the ultimate joy of the hereafter, the most precious gift of Allah" (Jaami' al-Usool, 10/557). The greatest knowledge will lead to the greatest exchange of love.

The Bible explains how in the beginning, God created the heaven and the earth, which might lead us to ask, "Where was God before He created these places?" It indicates that He was in an eternal environment separate from both heaven and earth. Again, as we go deep into these theologies, we will find similarities between many of the different religious traditions. Unfortunately, they have sometimes been misrepresented or watered down by people pursuing economic or political considerations (*chala-dharma*) rather than unconditional love, devotion, and service to God.

The Torah mentions how the Lord spoke to Moses face to face as a man speaks to a friend (Exodus 33:11). Many people consider these descriptions to be conceptual or allegorical because they cannot understand their deeper significance. The Song of Solomon in the Bible is a loving exchange between humankind and God. However, most times when people read this book in the Bible, they just view it as poetry because they cannot understand that a living entity could have such a deep connection with God due to his or her purity. When they think of the idea of God as a personality, they can only think in terms of a material personality. Such people think personality must mean material characteristics, attributes, etc. True personality is spiritual, and all other external personalities are perverted reflections of these higher realities.

In the Torah, it also mentions that Sarah had a relationship with the Lord like a mother. It mentions that God would appear to Enoch and Abraham, and they would have wonderful ongoing exchanges. In Christianity, great mystics such as St. Teresa of Avila and St. John of the Cross did not just refer to God as a light or sound, but they had personal experiences with the spiritual kingdom and with God as a lover. The New Testament emphasizes that the pure in heart shall see God. In John 6:46, it says that not any man can know the father but he who is of God, emphasizing that there is a certain level of consciousness that will enable us to connect with the Lord.

It is unnatural to not be able to have direct communication

with one's beloved. The great 17th century saint, Tukaram, expresses this same point through poetry:

Can water quaff itself?

Can trees taste of the fruit they bear?

He who worships God must stand
distinct from Him,

So only shall he know the joyful
love of God;

For if he say that God and he are one,

That joy, that love, shall vanish
instantly away.

Pray no more for utter oneness
with God:

Where were the beauty if jewel and
setting were one?

The heat and the shade are two,

If not, where were the comfort
of shade?

Mother and child are two,

If not, where were the love?

When after being sundered, they meet,

What joy do they feel, the mother
and child!

Where were joy, if the two were one?

Pray, then, no more for utter
oneness with God.

It is unnatural to not have association with one's authority. It is impersonal. It indicates a lack in reaching that highest expression. It is natural to reciprocate with one's beloved.

The Book of Revelations in the Bible explains that there will be many plagues, difficulties, famines, and so on. However, it says that the servants of God shall wear the mark of the Lord on their forehead and shall see His face (Revelation 22:4). It does not say that they shall see the light, feel the oneness of the universe, or lose their identity; it says that they will maintain their identity and see the face of the Lord. The relationships and variegatedness in these lower realms are just perverted reflections of the perfect relationships in the higher realm. The higher states always involve specific relationships and ultimately love. How do we love a concept? We can have general feelings, but love develops through specific knowledge and exchanges. We love based on awareness. We love through service, relationships, and various interactions. Whenever we have feelings of attachment or aversion, specific attributes or experiences cause that love or distaste. And the Lord states in *Bhagavad-gita* 10.10 that He will give more knowledge to those who serve Him with love:

tesam satata-yuktanam
bhajatam priti-purvakam
dadami buddhi-yogam tam
yena mam upayanti te

To those who are constantly devoted to serving Me with love, I give the understanding by which they can come to Me.

The more we acquire bona fide and esoteric spiritual knowledge and act upon that knowledge, the more we can experience a connection with the beloved. When you love someone, you want to know what they like and how you can serve them. For instance, if you know that they like a certain type of food, you want to please them by offering that preparation. However, if you know they like soup, but you offer them a plate of rice, that does not indicate that you really care about their personal preferences. To the degree that you know their personality traits and preferences, you will create more union and togetherness. There will be much more appreciation because of the harmony and attentiveness. As we know more about our real identity, the identity of other living entities, and the real nature of the spiritual kingdom, we will be able to experience real spiritual relationships by taking away the coverings that obscure them.

The example of a high court judge can help us better understand different concepts of the Godhead. For instance, a judge interacts on many different levels according to relationship. Normally, we think of a judge as a person who has great authority and influence, even over life and death for some people. And in the courtroom, people must follow etiquette as they deal with him or her. Theists normally conceive of God in this way. They think of the Lord primarily as the supreme auto-crat who oversees the creation and dictates different orders. Of course, these are various aspects of a judge's responsibility.

The lawyer has a different relationship with the judge. Lawyers honor the judge due to his superior position, but since they are also involved in law, they do not have an excessive mood of awe and reverence towards the judge. Since both the lawyer and the judge understand the law, to some extent they can bond in friendship.

The judge has the most intimate relationship with his little grandson. When he goes home and takes off his formal robe, he plays with his grandson. Maybe the grandson jumps on his back or slaps him. In the courtroom, a person could be arrested or fined for treating the judge in such a manner; however, in a different environment with different people, there are different levels of relationships based on the quality of love and intimacy.

In the Vaisnava scriptures, the descriptions of the Lord compare to this connection of the judge with his grandson; therefore, it might come across as mythology. Some people might have a hard time envisioning the judge, who sends people to jail, chastises other lawyers, or fines people, later sitting on the floor playing with his grandson and getting slapped from time to time. Theologies that deal with this idea of a personal God might come across as strange to those who normally view God as the judge and autocrat. They might not be able to easily change this conception. The judge has a relationship with his grandson that is based on love. Formality does not exist and would actually have a way of interfering with the natural flow of love. The highest level of love is spontaneous, invigorating, exhilarating, and void of formality. The formalities stemming from awe and fear limit the relationship for those who view the judge in this way.

The Language of the Heart

Sometimes we hear mystical sayings such as, "As above, so below; as below, so above," emphasizing that some type of mysterious unfoldment goes on in the spiritual realms above, which is paralleled in the material realms below. If, however, we try to evaluate and understand truth simply from a materialistic perspective, we will only be able to evaluate phenomena according to our own limited position. If we are trying to see only through our particular glasses, we will run into problems. However, if we understand that the higher reality is coming from above, we can evaluate truths based on a more accurate perception. Then all of these variegated conceptions of religion, which might confuse an aspirant on the spiritual path, will no longer pose a threat or weaken the person's faith.

It is not that activities and relationships cease to exist in the spiritual realms; rather, in the spiritual world there are divine, eternal activities. The fact that there are activities below in the material realms means that there are activities above in the spiritual realms. The Vedic texts explain that the material world is a perverted reflection of the spiritual world. However, the activities in the material world are limited and bring on birth, old age, disease, and death. The material world below is designated to help the living entity forget God. However, the variegated activities in the spiritual world are all about remembering and serving the Lord eternally in full knowledge and bliss. The material world is like a counterfeit or a reflection—a resemblance of the genuine. A reflection or a counterfeit posits that "the real thing" exists elsewhere.

Ultimately, there is a presence of God within each and every one of us, and this presence is providing knowledge, remembrance, intelligence, as well as forgetfulness. By the blessings of the Lord within the heart, we increase our ability to deeply communicate and connect with the spiritual realms. We do not simply want to connect with the physical, metaphysical, or subtle material realms; we want to connect with the transcendental realms. We, of course, have a physical body and a subtle astral body. We have many subtle experiences associated with our subtle bodies. So many phenomena that we call extraordinary miracles or paranormal occurrences are normal activities for the subtle body. However, beyond the subtle body is the soul, which is in connection with the Kingdom of God. Communication at the highest level is the language of the heart or the relationship of the soul with God.

Access Higher Communication through Love

Everything is ultimately personal. We all want to be loved endlessly and unconditionally. We all want to be valued and appreciated. None of us want to be treated impersonally. When we are treated impersonally, we feel offended and alienated. When we love and are loved, these sentiments develop out of appreciation for specific attributes, characteristics, experiences, and relationships. To think that the Supreme Absolute Truth does not have certain attributes or characteristics would mean that He has less than the variegatedness in His creation. The Supreme Lord must have everything within creation and many more sublime and eternal qualities as well. The Lord cannot lack in any way. If the Supreme Truth is impersonal, then how can personality and variegatedness exist in this realm? The Lord must include all that exists and much more:

yad yad vibhutimat sattvam
srimad urjitam eva va
tat tad evavagaccha tvam
mama tejo-' msa-sambhavam

Know that all opulent, beautiful and
glorious creations spring from but a
spark of My splendor.

Bhagavad-gita 10.41

Higher communication really means understanding our
original and eternal identity. It means that we have genuine
communication, which can never be there when people do not
reveal what they really feel and think. Higher communication
is very difficult when we want to contact the higher realms to
acquire material commodities rather than process the spiritual
truths.

Let us remind ourselves that there is one God who has
many different names, and that same Supreme Lord, out of His
compassion, is sending different teachers according to time,
place, and circumstance. As Srila Bhaktivinoda Thakura writes
in his *Sri Manah-siksa*, Chapter 1, "The religious principles of
human beings can never be many. That religious principle that
is eternal for all human beings can never become different due
to time, place, and circumstances. In fact, an eternal religious
principle is one without a second." If all of the great teachers
from the various religious traditions suddenly appeared in one
place at the same time, we would notice how much love they
would have between each other. We must ask why, in most
cases, their followers are not able to have that same kind of love
towards one another. It indicates deviation from the original
teachings of these teachers; consequently, the followers have

less and less personal interactions. People discuss metaphysics and religion but do not experience spirituality. The great *acaryas*, prophets, or incarnations did not come to perform for us; they came to show us what we can achieve. They came to help us experience what they themselves are experiencing.

Ultimately, we want to know how to develop more love. Love eradicates lust and egocentricity, which block our ability to have these dynamic personal exchanges. Since we have the opportunity while we are still in these physical bodies to gradually work together, let us remind each other of the great adventures and pleasures available for us.

Questions and Answers

Question: Why do some of the cheating religions seem to be financially successful?

Answer: First consider how the drug industry is the top business in the world right now and defense comes in second. How are these businesses so successful? First of all, they have clients, and second, the material energy is naturally dualistic. Since we live in the material world, which we might compare to a reformatory, we will find deviation in many areas. Although there are karmic consequences for the deviations, the sinful activities do seem to get leverage. Unfortunately, when people recognize this aspect of the world, many will turn to a life void of integrity and principle-centeredness. They will just try to get some immediate stimulation without understanding the karmic responsibility and consequences. For this reason, it is important for spiritual people to bond together more since they are often in the minority. They can help remind each other of the goal as well as protect each other from much of the sinful activity in the environment. They will have a synergistic effect since like-minded people help to encourage each other to remain on the path.

Question: Why does love appear to reduce pain?

Answer: No one can hurt us more than those who we love the most, and no one can give us more joy than those who we care for the most. When something powerful is misused, it has the most devastating effect. Conversely, when used properly, it will have the most substantial benefit. When we connect with someone in a loving manner, we are making ourselves available and vulnerable because we want to receive. At the same time, relationships can be exploitive.

People need to become whole within themselves. When they then enter a relationship, they will not be so needy, expecting the other person to make them whole. Otherwise, it is just one impoverished person looking for another, expecting the other person to make a miracle happen in their lives. People usually have this conception of love: a very needy and empty person wants someone to come into their life and fulfill them. When two people with this type of mentality come together, they simply end up dropping all of their frustrations on each other. Sometimes such people have come out of dysfunctional backgrounds in which they haven't seen compassionate, loving relationships. Consequently, it becomes hard to try to create a positive relationship when they have not had any role models.

Question: Why do we have the ability to turn away from God's love?

Answer: Since we have free will, we have the choice to love the Lord or run from His love. When someone loves another person deeply, they will never act against the well being of their beloved. The relationship between a parent and a child can help us understand these dynamics a little better. A good parent always wants to give and extend love, but sometimes the child refuses to accept. Sometimes the child even runs away which means that he or she will not experience the love. However, the love is always there. When the child reconnects, he or she will once again experience the love that was always there. Similarly, we often turn away from the love coming from the Lord, or we partially turn away when we engage in sin or practice mixed devotional service. Mixed devotional service contaminates the situation without allowing the purity to come forth. For this reason, we say that higher consciousness is natural, but more people are actually working hard to maintain lower consciousness, which includes a cheating or superficial religion and which takes us away from the essence of all religions—returning to the Kingdom of God.

Hurt not others in ways that you yourself would find hurtful.

Udana-Varga: 518 (Buddhism)

Chapter 5

A Spiritual Response to Terrorism

Perspectives on Terrorism

The amount of violence pervading the planet should sound a wake-up call and provide a mirror reflecting us in the context of our own creation. It should awaken us to the degraded condition of humanity. When we stand in front of a mirror, we see our own reflection and the reflection of those around us. Everyone has to look at what we have done as members of humanity to help create this monster. We might also need to recognize what we have not done and what actions we should have taken to prevent such a creature from surfacing. There is not a single person on this planet who is not involved in some way.

The monster known as terrorism can be analyzed from many perspectives. Politically, improper foreign policies and economic deprivations can create situations that act as breeding grounds for this type of violence. Historically and sociologically, events have taken place throughout the world to create this type of threat to humanity. We can also look at it from a more philosophical, psychological, and spiritual perspective. We are not so much interested in the physicality, the historical, or the political although we should understand these influences because they do play an important role. We are more concerned with the philosophical, psychological, and especially the spiritual aspects.

Many books have been written on the subject since the September 11 terrorist attacks on America, and universities have even begun to offer courses on the psychology of terrorism. As many of these people have already said in their books and analyses, a major negative shift in world consciousness happened that day. Everything bad about humanity surfaces in terrorism. For this reason, people other than those just caught up in materialism have serious concerns, because it is an important barometer showing the current state of our collective humanity. We see people who are so violent that they are joyfully taking their own lives and the lives of others. People are being bred to think and accept such a lifestyle with great anticipation. In some places, people must face a complete lack of physical protection on a daily basis, which also shows that we never have ultimate physical protection. Abrupt events can take our lives at any moment.

Suicide bombing is one of the most intense manifestations of violence. Not only does the person violently hurt other people, but they violently assault themselves as well. Suicide bombing means that the person is ready to commit suicide in the most horrific way. To compound the situation even further, the person tries to have the most negative impact that they can possibly inflict on others. They can easily think in this way because they do not consider any of their victims innocent. However, it is just the opposite. In many cases, the victims do not have any involvement in politics or war, but because they are of a different group, religion, or race, they are considered enemies who have no right to live. An individual who turns into a terrorist might believe this philosophy to such an extent that they are ready to sacrifice themselves with the hope that they will simultaneously kill their so-called enemies. They pursue this opportunity to destroy with zeal and enthusiasm, knowing that their death is inevitable.

Think about the type of entities capable of such acts and the effects of this violence. What does this mean for humanity? People will obviously develop more fear, which in turn leads to more negative consequences. As the level of fear rises, the love quotient goes down. Love and fear do not compliment each other. For this reason, those striving to dismantle humanity strive to increase fear because it causes people to act irrationally. It causes people to sometimes look for security in unhealthy ways, which also opens more avenues for the manipulation and exploitation of such people. We can already see how many people acquiesce to the loss of civil rights as they seek shelter from leaders with ulterior motives.

Terrorism reveals the worst effects of nationalism, racism, and tribalism. It shows the worst that can come from the exploitation and depletion of resources. It develops from some of the most serious cases of poverty in which a great chasm exists between the so-called haves and have-nots. This monster is feeding on ecocide, or the abuse of the environment. It is distinctly connected with the matricide of Mother Earth. We see the earth as mother and as a living being. People who are willing to abuse their own mothers must be viewed as extremely violent and insensitive. No person can be in a healthy consciousness when they are abusing their mothers, which, according to Vedic scriptures, include the biological mother, the wife of the spiritual master, the wife of a *brahmana*, the wife of the king, the cow, the nurse, and the earth. Since those actions cause such internalization of unhealthy mindsets, that then extends itself into other areas of life.

Terrorism relates to genocide, which develops from an excessive emphasis on race, religion, or ethnicity to the point that all other groups turn into enemies who threaten our own sense of survival. Consequently, people reach a point at which they are ready to annihilate anyone who interferes with their sense gratification. The result of this mentality manifests in drastic actions such as suicide bombing.

Terrorism even has a connection with infanticide, which involves the killing of children, especially of baby girls. It is a chauvinistic mood on the part of men, which minimizes the female gender. There are many places in the world, especially in China, Africa, and India, where infanticide is very prevalent. In some cases, mothers have sonograms to determine the gender of the baby, and if the baby is female, they might have an abortion. Millions of girls meet their deaths in this way. While all of this violence continues, atheists and even some so-called theists embrace deicide, which involves the desire or attempt to kill or remove God, as if such insignificant living entities could do so. Such people wish or think that God does not exist and wish to eliminate all conceptions of theism.

As in the process of gardening or farming, we plant and then harvest. Basically, the world has planted many unhealthy seeds that have developed into the most unfortunate harvest. As spiritualists, it should present a tremendous barometer, reminding us of this difficult time in history. Of course, this Age of Kali or the Age of Quarrel and Hypocrisy has been described in all the sacred scriptures of the world such as the Vedas, the Koran, the Torah, and the Bible.

The Abuse of Mother Earth

As we monitor some of the current events unfolding on the planet, we see the importance of making a global shift in consciousness. Mother Earth is currently experiencing tremendous sickness. When a mother does not receive proper care, attention, protection, and support, the family will fall into tremendous disarray. As a matter of fact, Srila Prabhupada explains that when the mother does not receive proper protection, the population's duration of life will shorten considerably, which we can already observe.[9] He further elaborates on the nature of selfish and demonic personalities:

> The *asuras* [the most sinful class of people] want to enjoy a life of sense gratification, even at the cost of others' happiness. In order to fulfill this ambition, the *asuras*, especially atheistic kings or state executive heads, try to equip themselves with all kinds of deadly weapons to bring about a war in a peaceful society. They have no ambition other than personal aggrandizement, and thus mother earth feels overburdened by such undue increases of military strength. By increase of the *asuric* population, those who follow the principles of religion become unhappy, especially the devotees, or *devas*.
>
> *Srimad-Bhagavatam* 1.16.34, purport

These abusive mindsets and behaviors form a large part of the problems now facing the world. We constantly see child abuse, elderly abuse, spouse abuse, ecocide, matricide, genocide, homicide, suicide, and deicide. We are increasingly polluting our planet and the atmosphere. America especially plays a role since it uses an exceedingly large portion of the world's resources. *International Wildlife* reports, "[T]he world's one billion richest people—which also include Europeans and Japanese, among others—consume 80 percent of the Earth's resources."[10] At the same time, half of the people on the planet do not have proper sanitation facilities, and a quarter of the earth's population does not have access to clean drinking water.[11] *International Wildlife* further elaborates, "A sixth will never learn to read, and 30 percent who enter the global workforce will never get adequate job opportunities. The other five billion people on Earth make do with just 20 percent of the planet's resources."[12] In some cases, certain situations are imposed on us that we seemingly have little ability to change, but we can change the world as we change ourselves. Those in the developed world especially have a responsibility, due to our general *karma*, to look at ourselves and see what we can do to make a difference at a very critical time.

Living in a Culture of Aggression

We must look closer at aggression and war because it relates to our consciousness and to problems associated with modernity and institutionalization. Our generation has an interesting position in determining what the future of the planet will hold. We have the ability to blow up everyone on the planet many times over, and our global community is increasingly resorting to combative interactions. The terrorist attacks on September 11, 2001 in the United States and many others that have followed around the world distinctly reveal this violent mindset.

This mentality is also reflected by the amount of murders that occur daily on this planet. Gary LaFree describes in his book, *Losing Legitimacy: Street Crime and the Decline of Social Institutions in America*, the unbelievable amount of murder and crime occurring just in the United States alone, what to speak of other countries:

> From the end of World War II until the early 1990s, the number of crimes committed in the streets of America skyrocketed. Murder rates doubled; rape rates quadrupled; robbery and burglary rates quintupled. By the early 1990s, nearly 25,000 Americans were being murdered each year. In just two years, more Americans were murdered than were killed in the Vietnam War; in twelve years more were murdered than died during World War II.

Furthermore, if we look at how most governments spend their money, we will also find a focus on war. We can learn much about a person or group by how they spend their money. It reveals their priorities. When so much money is used to help maintain and perfect violence, we can understand that it will be hard to attain peace. In *Maximum Security*, a journal article written by Margo Okazawa-Rey and Gwyn Kirk, the authors report that worldwide expenditures on the education of an average child each year is approximately $380, while $22,000 is spent to train and equip the average soldier. In 1994 alone, the worldwide expenditures on defense totaled $700 billion. Most governments spend more on their military than on public health. For every 100,000 people in the world, there are 556 soldiers, but only 85 doctors.[13] These statistics can help us understand the extent to which the mentality of war and aggression permeates this planet. In other words, governments spend the greatest amount of money on increasing and perfecting their ability to kill.

On September 11, I was just finishing a thirty-five country world tour. The news reports that we heard in Russia differed from the reports in America. For instance, in Russia it was reported that almost one hundred nuclear suitcase bombs were missing, and it was alleged that Osama bin Laden possibly had some of them. Russia was a first world country based mainly on the military, but if you look at Russia closely, you will see that it is in some ways more like a third world country. Most of the hospitals in Russia do not have sufficient running water, medicine, or indoor toilets, and the majority of homes in Russia also do not have toilets inside. As the communist block dismantled, many military personnel and even scientists were literally starving. For this reason, the United States government has subsidized many of the scientists, but the military is not so easy to control. However, even if bin Laden did not acquire some of those weapons, there are so many other fanatical personalities in the world. He is just a small player in the grand scheme of things.

The Divine and the Demonic

Special beings have come into this world to facilitate both sides. Some entities have come to help elevate consciousness while others are empowered for destruction. Just as we have policemen, soldiers, and tax collectors, certain entities have specific responsibilities for different planets and universes. They make themselves available as we make ourselves available to receive their help. This is an incredible time period in which people can connect with empowerment on both sides.

Some of these demonic entities can act in such abominable ways because their bodies are possessed by sinister entities. Just as a rat looks for shelter and food, such demons look for a place to find shelter. At times, we hear of a serial killer who murders up to thirty or forty people and then chops them up and eats their body parts. This is no ordinary criminal. Some of these people are possessed by entities who have taken over their bodies. Certain types of possessions are comparable to the concept of time-sharing in which several entities share a single body. A very degraded or low consciousness allows such entities to enter the body and to use it for their own purposes. Conversely, if people elevate their consciousness, they can become empowered and used in a positive way. We have all heard of angels, archangels, or demigods. These are real entities who have a particular involvement in this earthly realm.

Take Responsibility

We are witnessing the symptoms of a tremendous disease, which confronts the entire planet. It should incite a wake-up call for people such as ourselves to look closer at what we can do individually. Unfortunately, when most people face these issues, they place the responsibility and blame on external factors. But everything that happens in any environment, community, planet, or universe depends on the aggregate consciousness of the living entities that occupy those environments. Therefore, each of us has major influence over whatever happens on this planet and we each have the amazing ability to make differences. We can begin with our own body, which is a universe within itself. Many life forms reside in each of our bodies, and, as we address our own consciousness, we are already affecting a universe.

A major issue confronting us relates to the consciousness of fragmentation. It puts race against race; tribe against tribe; gender against gender; political parties against each other; and it creates religious fanaticism. Basically, we must either learn to live peacefully together or die in separation. The wake-up call is sounding for all of us to choose which direction we will support. Will we facilitate the mood of aggression, anger, and retaliation? Are we looking for the problem outside of ourselves? To what degree do we honor our ability to make a difference? We first have to determine to what degree we are adding to the warlike culture. It starts with ourselves. We must introspect in order to determine what is happening with our intellect, emotions, and passions. Are the lower passions defeating our higher values and interests? If so, we are at war with ourselves and adding to the culture of war. To what degree are we honoring our higher principles? To what degree are we at peace with our bodies? To what degree do we have proper nourishment—internally and externally? To what degree are we engaged in various types of *sadhana* or spiritual practices that will enable us to engage in spiritual warfare? This planet has always been riddled with war and will always be permeated with war. However, we must determine whether the war is based on physical, metaphysical, or spiritual factors.

At this period in history, we might view ourselves as a global village because whatever happens in China, Africa, or India for instance affects other parts of the world. Never before in modern times has there been a period in which people can be so connected and close in spite of their diversity. However, too much diversity without a focus on a nucleus that can create unity can lead to chaos, pandemonium and devastation. Unless we find a stronger nucleus to unify the global village, we will only see more fragmentation. People who accept the call to spiritual warriorship can create a stronger nucleus. As we work on ourselves, we can make a difference in our environments. As we affect our own environments, we can affect cities, countries, and ultimately the world.

The Social Activist and the Selfish Spiritualist

Those inspired to initiate change should also consider how to most effectively assist in the endeavor. The social activist often wants to make a change based on political, social, or economic factors, but, due to the intensity of the problems, such endeavors are insufficient. And spiritualists are sometimes in a contemplative mood and view these concerns as unimportant or irrelevant. They focus more on internal peace, satisfaction, pleasure, and their own theologies or institutions. However, it can also indicate egocentricity at a time when people need to access more compassion and selflessness in order to make an active difference in the community and in the world.

Both extremes are dangerous. We need very profound spiritual technologies due to the intense nature of the world in which we live. If we accept the position of the activist, we will just look at the external factors and miss a chance to offset some of these difficulties. On the other hand, if we simply focus, as some spiritualists do, on our own institution, inner peace, meditation, rituals, or *sadhana*, it will also be insufficient. It does not create the kind of potency that comes out of compassionate and selfless activity. Focusing solely on our own rituals and dogma will not bring about wholesome, comprehensive, or selfless solutions. One should be chaste to bona fide teachings, but not limited. There is a need for a marriage between those who are socially or politically minded, and those who are spiritually minded. Those who choose more isolated communities still need to find ways to apply their philosophies in order to make a more meaningful difference in the world rather than focusing only on themselves and their immediate environments. The adversarial, atheistic forces want people to feel such disappointment and depression that they just move into their own scene for their own inner peace. There is a need for people to help effect a global mindshift while we still have a chance because, even at this moment, resources are being depleted all over the planet, and homicide and suicide are increasing in practically every country.

The polarities are a part of the fragmentation. We want wholeness, and we want to make our planet, institutions, families, as well as ourselves more complete. Those who just absorb themselves in their own spiritual connections and focus on nourishing themselves cannot help to sufficiently combat the negativity on the planet. On the other hand, those who remain captured by the secular paradigm will also not have the proper strength to combat the assaults and attacks. For instance, if someone has a gun, a soldier will not want to face such an enemy with a slingshot. You want to find ways to be effective so that when the attacks come physically and subtly, you will have the proper strength. You want to take care of the physical body, the subtle body, and the soul.

Final Reflections at the Time of Death

The attacks on September 11 teach us many lessons. For instance, the fourth plane, Flight 93, which crashed in the countryside of Somerset, Pennsylvania, provided insight into the minds of those on the brink of death. With modern technology, the cell phone provided several people with an opportunity to communicate before the crash. Normally, we cannot know what a person is thinking before death. However, in this case, we heard some of the conversations moments before many of those people met their deaths.

What types of thoughts and concerns did they express? Did they ask about the mortgage or their investments? Were they concerned about a business meeting? No. Many of them endeavored to connect with their loved ones in order to somehow honor their existence and the relationship. Some of them called to say, "Beloved, I love you and please tell the children that I love them. I just want you to know how much I love you." The same types of messages came one after another, and this can help us realize the real purpose of life.

We often engage in the most superfluous activities and miss the real essence. We miss taking shelter of that which can animate us the most. We all need to look closer inside of ourselves and try to eliminate that which is unhealthy or conflictive within ourselves. Then we can take a closer look at our relationships to see how we can connect with each other more profoundly and literally enter more into the mood of spiritual warfare. We realize that war is a reality and we are all subjected to it, directly or indirectly. However, we do not want to take shelter of situations that add to the problems already in motion, nor do we want to be in denial or insensitive by not doing our part.

Only Love Can Counteract the Warfare

A few months after the September 11 attacks, I visited a different country every three or four days. I was shocked to see how nervous people felt on the airplanes. If a person stood up too fast to use the restroom, people would look at him or her with fear. If someone walked towards the cockpit or reached for the overhead compartment too quickly, people would watch in fear and anxiety. As this fear becomes more dominant, it opens up more room for negative influences. As we honor our loving existence and try to radiate love, we will do our part in being able to heal the planet, and we will help change some of the karmic patterns that now exist. In our own way, we can all strategize so that we can wage peace and accelerate love.

Love is a powerful weapon that we seriously need to implement at this time. It is the only medicine that can make a tangible difference because the situation is deteriorating rapidly due to *karma*. The *karma* in many places in the world is very inauspicious because of the tremendous amount of collective sinful activities that have already taken place. These sins have already sent out a wave or current that can only be counteracted by a weapon of higher potency.

Different situations can bring out the very best in people as they now try to honor their communities and relationships more closely. They look more at their lives in order to determine their priorities. Other people remain obsessed with fear and anger since they only look at the externals. This is a strategy used to control the minds of masses of people. Such schemes are being orchestrated in very powerful ways due to some prominent manipulators in the international community. On a higher level, we might see it as a war unfolding between the pious and the impious.

Saint John of the Cross, a saint respected by both Eastern and Western practitioners, helps us understand that the essence of life is love. Life is a journey meant to enable us to become the greatest lovers of God so that we can return to the realm in which the greatest exchanges of love constantly unfold. He wrote, "Where there is no love, put love and you will find love." If we examine the Bible, the Koran, the Torah, and the Vedas, we will find how they consistently ask the same of us. It goes far beyond the normative scheme of mundaneness that we normally experience while eating, sleeping, mating, and defending. So much exists in the higher realms in the association of love.

The Weapon of Love

We have a great need to replace and offset aggressive mindsets. In these days, we should look closer to find ways to wage peace. Peace is not just the absence of war. Peace cannot exist unless there is a certain amount of inner fulfillment and satisfaction. Just as we now have so many agents endeavoring to wage war, those who have a higher consciousness need to look closer at alliances and strategies to accelerate the love and peace. We do not simply want to ignore conflicts; we must put conscious mental, intellectual, and physical energy into enhancing the primary and the spiritual.

If something is really important to us, we find a way to focus a sufficient amount of energy in that direction. If we want a new computer, car, or house, we organize so much of our life around that desire. We make all types of sacrifices in order to see that it happens. That which is most important to us receives our full attention. We should have this level of intensity as we endeavor to become more loving and empowered to make a difference on the planet. Creating love and peace should be of such significance in our consciousness that we become mindful in our eating, sleeping, mating, and defending. Every action turns into a form of meditation as we deepen the quality of the experience. In this way, it creates an armor that will protect us from the negative influences.

Questions and Answers

Question: How do we escape the feeling of isolation that might arise during these times?

Answer: First realize that the indwelling presence of God resides within each of us. We do not have to see ourselves as so distinct from the universe or from the Supreme Lord. He is very close. Some traditions refer to this presence as the Holy Ghost or as the *paramatma*. The Vedic tradition emphasizes our identity as part and parcel of God—the same in quality with God but different in quantity:

> *sarvasya caham hrdi sannivisto*
> *mattah smrtir jnanam apohanam ca*

> I am seated in everyone's heart,
> and from Me come remembrance,
> knowledge and forgetfulness.
> *Bhagavad-gita* 15.15

Our original nature is divine or godly. It is pure and full of love, which means that everything else is just a temporary covering. If we think that in order to attain self-realization, we have to become far different from our current associations, the endeavor will simply overwhelm us. However, self-realization mainly involves cleansing and removing some of the acculturation and unhealthy attachments.

We just have to become more genuine in our investigation, more intense in our prayers, and more selfless and compassionate. If we endeavor in this way, the universe will facilitate us accordingly. As people put out negative energy, it will create more negativity in the environment. However, as we focus our energy in a positive direction, we can make a positive difference in our environment and in the world.

We want to fight terror in all of its forms, but not with more terror. We want to fight the terror of incurable diseases, crime, poverty, mental illness, racism, tribalism, chauvinism, and religious fanaticism. We want to stop abusing our own bodies, our communities, and our planet. We can achieve this goal through the powerful weapon of love. The spiritual warriors are lovingly committed to helping the planet by waging comprehensive peace.

Question: The terrorist attacks in America have created a sense of mistrust against anyone who differs even slightly from the normative patterns of popular culture. How do spiritualists who might differ from mainstream culture maintain their convictions in the midst of the skepticism and mistrust that others feel towards them? For instance, some religionists even feel hesitant to wear their traditional religious clothing in public due to the increase in violent attacks against such people.

Answer: Yes, it is true that people and various customs that differ from the norms will surely be viewed with more paranoia than previously. Everyone's religion is on trial. For instance, many materialists or "humanists" think that anyone adhering to religious institutions is a party to intensifying the problems in the world. They feel that the world would be a better place if more people would just abandon these unhealthy religious attachments. Such people feel that religion and its dogmas are a constant threat because they can easily energize people to justify and engage in destructive activities. Not only are religions more on trial, but, for some people, God is also on trial. Some people wonder how an all-merciful God continues to allow such inhumanities to exist. Some feel that if people would take less shelter of religion and God, more problems could be addressed in practical and productive ways.

In one sense, these doubts and analyses are useful since they will cause the majority of the populace to scrutinize religion more closely. It will prove to be beneficial for authentic religions since it will show the benefits and potencies of those people, systems, and processes that have wholesome value. Conversely, those people, processes, and systems that are of little value or even destructive will have light shed upon them. What an important time for people, leaders, and institutions to be more authentic, and to find better ways to communicate their message so that it will be understood and accepted better.

Question: Terrorism has created such a sense of fear, especially since it can strike at any moment and take massive numbers of lives. Nor can we fully protect ourselves since we must continue living, working, eating, and so on. Therefore, how do we function, knowing that death or destruction could strike randomly at any moment, without letting the fear consume or overwhelm us?

Answer: I have given an extensive discussion on the negative effects of fear in my book, *Spiritual Warrior IV: Conquering the Enemies of the Mind.* We invite you to consult this book. There are many unhealthy consequences associated with fear, which is one of the most negative effects of the increase in terrorism. It propagates a culture of fear. However, a positive aspect of fear is that it can help us live a more responsible and focused life. Most people have a tendency to take many things for granted. To know that we can die at any moment can actually be a first-class way of thinking. Reminding ourselves that there is danger at every step can allow us to take life more seriously: *padam padam yad vipadam na tesam* (*Srimad-Bhagavatam* 10.14.58). A place where there is danger at every step is certainly not a comfortable place.

By reminding ourselves that life is temporary and full of dangers, we can try to live a life beyond eating, sleeping, mating, and defending. Even if we do these activities most expertly, we will still have them eventually taken away because, at the time of death, we must walk away from everything and everybody. Therefore, we should let the fear be a motivator in helping us attain *atma-vidya* or self-realization. In this way, the fear will not consume or overwhelm us, but will help us in better structuring our lives and increasing our desperation to attain the ultimate goal of liberation and service to the Godhead.

Question: How do we genuinely hate the sin but not the sinner? If we find ourselves in a situation in which someone is prepared to viciously attack, kill, or rape us, how do we maintain the ability to love the soul of that individual?

Answer: We should always try to protect ourselves from the constant assaults of material nature that come in three forms—*adhyatmika* (bodily or mental pains), *adhibhautika* (pains offered by other living entities), and *adhidaivika* (pains offered by supernatural disturbances). Much of our survival as humans depends on how we are able to protect ourselves from these constant attacks. Of course, the greatest attacks come from the enemies of the mind—either our own mind attacks us or someone else's mind attacks them, which causes them to act obnoxiously.

We should try to stop ourselves from being our greatest enemy, and we must also try to stop others who act as our so-called enemies by attacking, abusing, or exploiting us. By stopping our own minds from attacking us, we become more peaceful and focused on higher goals. By stopping or minimizing the attacks of material nature, we have fewer obstructions in carrying out our daily activities. By stopping the attacks from other living entities, we will help ourselves as well as them. When other living entities attack, they will incur negative *karma* and will have to suffer the reactions. If we care about them, we must protect ourselves and find ways to help them by not giving them a field of activity in which they can commit or continue to engage in their deviations. When necessary, there must be a punishment befitting the crime or offense, and, after the punishment, there is forgiveness. If a sinner does not receive a punishment, the society or community will become confused about the proper code of ethics, and it will also reinforce the deviant activity and mindset.

We should see the sinner as someone who is sick with a contagious disease or mental illness although he or she is essentially also a spirit soul:

> *acchedyo 'yam adahyo 'yam*
> *akledyo 'sosya eva ca*
> *nityah sarva-gatah sthanur*
> *acalo 'yam sanatanah*

> This individual soul is unbreakable and insoluble, and can be neither burned nor dried. He is everlasting, present everywhere, unchangeable, immovable and eternally the same.
>
> *Bhagavad-gita* 2.24

The individual is temporarily experiencing sickness, bewilderment, and madness. We must be careful about who we associate with and how we associate. We may even need to avoid a sinful person altogether in order to avoid contracting their disease or suffering from abuse due to their madness. We should not consciously put ourselves in a situation in which another person can hurt us or infect us with their deviations. We can carry as our motto, "We must do whatever will bring about the most positive human and God conscious effect."

Instead of only looking at the external sinful behavior, we can also study the situation and person closely to try to understand some of the underlying causes responsible for this dysfunctional and disturbing behavior. There are always underlying causes connected to some perverted cry for love. Still, if you cannot personally help or protect yourself, get others who can help you and the attacker. In this way, we can do the needful while separating the sin from the sinner.

Question: The American Renaissance Alliance, an organization created to address political issues from a spiritual perspective, and people such as Marianne Williamson seem to be offering some of the same ideas that you have just presented.

Answer: Very special people reside on the planet right now, and some of them have come to specifically assist with the elevation of consciousness and various other missionary activities. It is not an accident that we have people such as Deepak Chopra, Marianne Williamson, or Oprah Winfrey who affect so many people's minds in pious ways. Furthermore, it is also not an accident that we have some musicians and producers who create films of a highly sinister nature. When we watch television, it puts the mind into an alpha state which makes the individual much more receptive to suggestion. If we consider the amount of violence, promiscuous activities, and degradation that most people confront daily, we will understand why so many children have dysfunctional patterns or attention deficit disorders. Our children receive a constant diet of violence. Those raising children have a serious duty so that future generations will not have to struggle with some of the issues confronting us at this time.

Tens of thousands of people have insomnia or suffer from various types of trauma. It is a field day for therapists now. For instance, after extensive research, the World Health Organization reported on the condition of mental health around the world in their 2001 World Health Report. They estimated that 450 million people on the planet have a mental or behavioral disorder. Furthermore, depression is now a leading cause of disability around the world, and, among the ten leading causes of the global burden of disease, it ranks fourth. The World Health Organization estimates that, in the next twenty years, depression will become the second leading cause of disease.[14] People everywhere must deal with more mental challenges, especially depression. *Spiritual Warrior IV: Conquering the Enemies of the Mind*, one of our previous books in this series, presents an elaborate discussion on depression.

As we enter the twenty-first century and observe modernity, we have so much material facility, but people still feel internally bankrupt. It means that people are projecting their fear, anxiety, lust, and greed into the environment. Thoughts are energy, which means that these heavy, negative mindsets are bombarding the average person. If we do not rejuvenate or energize ourselves, this negative energy will completely bombard us. If we do not recharge ourselves with spiritual nourishment, after awhile, we will get diminishing returns. We will start experiencing new degrees of anxiety, depression, lust, and greed without understanding the source.

Imagine walking through an environment permeated with dangerous chemicals. As soon as you enter, it just bombards you. Many people have strong spiritual intentions but do not keep themselves sufficiently focused to avoid the heavy bombardments. Consequently, their consciousness will gradually change as they deny their higher principles. They will eventually be shocked to see what has happened to them. Those with a demoniac mentality first try to corrupt people in general and increase the gross sinful activities, which will add to the deviation and corruption. But they also try to influence people who have tremendously good intentions by making them so depressed that they can no longer function properly.

Question: Could you elaborate on this last point because I see myself as well as other spiritualists suffering from this problem?

Answer: It is almost scary to see the extent to which spiritualists fall under these influences. Basically, people with very good hearts and intentions feel depressed and unable to make a difference. Consequently, they play right into the current patterns. Spiritual people really need to associate with each other more so that they can help reinforce and protect each other, especially from this type of attack. It is a dangerous weapon because people have a clear understanding about what is necessary, but they simply feel too drained to act upon that knowledge. Other people falter due to basic distractions imposed by the material energy.

We all have so many basic concerns that we need to deal with such as economic or family issues, but, at the end of the day, we have to remind ourselves, "I have a job, I have a body, I have a car, I have a house, or I have bills, but I am not any of these possessions. I am not going to be a slave to such material conceptions." We can reinforce this understanding by observing people who have all of these possessions but still feel completely miserable.

Question: Could you elaborate on the media report you heard while you were in Russia about the number of missing nuclear weapons?

Answer: Unfortunately, due to the state of affairs in America and in the world right now, even when people discover such things, in many cases it does not make such a difference because the effects are already in motion. For instance, an interesting phenomenon occurs with major world powers. They basically can find out what everyone is doing, but their problem relates to misinformation; that is, the other party might purposely be giving wrong information. In other words, these nations have tricky ways to present misinformation. Knowing that they are being monitored, they distract their adversaries who now have so many ways of spying on them. Otherwise, there are not many secrets. They can find out each other's secrets, but they do not know whether it is misinformation or not. Technology is so powerful that it offers many methods to find out secrets. They know this amongst themselves. If you analyze the nature of the Russian military and see how people have given up their loyalties, you will see the degree to which some of the high-level officials were even starving. When you are starving, you will do whatever you can to save yourself. If you have some access to technology or to weaponry, you will try to find some way to make an arrangement for yourself.

However, we must know that war is an inevitable fact in these realms, either gross or subtle. The real issue is not to determine the extent of the war, but how we can use higher weapons to make a difference. What are the terrorists trying to avoid? Consider the philosophy of terrorism. The goal is to bring as much chaos, pandemonium, and destruction as possible. Therefore, they abhor unity in different religious, racial, and ethnic groups. They do not want people in different parts of the world to unite in a harmonious way. They want to bring as much fragmentation, fear, and disturbance as possible. They want to dismantle any harmonious arrangement. Unity is one of the most effective means to counteract any type of attack because unity creates togetherness, synergy, and a symbiotic effect. Therefore, the greatest way to fight terrorism involves relinquishing exploitation and fragmentation, and embracing unity with diversity. We must celebrate the diversity and find ways to appreciate and complement each other in various ways. These are the weapons of love—the weapons of the spiritual warrior who is dedicated to waging peace.

What is hateful to you, do not to your fellow men. That is the entire Law; all the rest is commentary.

The Talmud, Shabbat, 31a (Judaism)

Chapter 6

The Positive and Negative Effects of War

In the course of daily life, we often find ourselves in unpleasant environments and situations despite our best endeavors to avoid such circumstances. These strenuous situations tend to expose our true qualities. First let us consider which environments bring out the very worst in people. Among the many circumstances that might materialize in a person's life such as school, work, family gatherings, incarceration, funerals, weddings, and so on, consider a setting that elicits the most negative traits within a human. We will find that war has an unusual way of engendering the very worst in people.

Human Nature at Its Worst

Through a closer examination of the atrocities that often happen during war, we find that soldiers have the capacity to engage in some of the most vicious crimes. Death no longer has the same meaning because the fighters see death all around them and in the most wretched and horrible ways. Thus, they also react viciously for their own self-preservation. History shows that war crimes have not been limited to any particular nationality or to a specific war.

While working in Liberia as well as in Sierra Leone, several staff members told me of some of the horrors they personally experienced or witnessed during the civil wars in these countries. They explained how members of the militia kidnapped children from their villages and forced them to join the armies. In some cases, the children saw their parents die right in front of them. These children were frequently given drugs, tortured, and even killed if they refused to terrorize other villagers. During these fights, pregnant women were often killed and their babies cut out of their stomachs. Thousands of people had their limbs cut off, and men's genitals would be chopped off and forced into their own mouths while the men were still alive. Some descriptions indicate that these children could often attack more viciously than the adults.

Engaging these children in warfare devastates the future of these countries because the children are the future. After the traumas that many of these children faced at such young ages, few will be capable of raising healthy families on their own, and many will remain rebellious and violent throughout their lives. Although the governments of several of these nations have made endeavors to reintegrate these children back into society, it is a formidable task in these war torn countries. Many children cannot find their parents, and in many cases, their parents have been murdered, leaving them without a home or proper care.

Unfortunately, this phenomenon of child soldiers extends

far beyond this region. According to a November 2001 article in *Foreign Policy in Focus*: "Today more than an estimated 500,000 children have been recruited in 87 countries (including the United States). At least 300,000 children are actively participating in conflicts, and are directly involved in combat in 41 countries. Although most child soldiers are between 15 and 18 years old, others are as young as seven."[15] Girls are not exempt from the battlefield either. Often, the fighters capture young girls, force them to act as sex slaves, and order them to perform other menial services such as cooking or cleaning. These girls will also suffer the aftereffects of this trauma for the rest of their lives.

In the midst of the civil strife in this same region in 2003, rebel militias in the Northern Congo were suspected of engaging in the most vicious crimes against civilians. Investigators from the United Nations heard from victims the most horrifying stories of rape, cannibalism, executions, and torture. "They cut out the hearts and other organs of their victims and forced families to eat them," said U.N. spokeswoman Patricia Tome in Kinshasa.[16] Witnesses saw the execution of one little girl who the soldiers then cut into pieces and ate. The soldiers also looted houses and raped large numbers of women. This particular militia group which created such a devastating and fearful environment is just one of many who have been causing havoc in the region during the war.

During the period of the partition between India and Pakistan, some Muslim terrorists as well as Hindu terrorists would murder members of the other ethnic group and cut the bodies into many pieces. As if this were not bad enough, they would then load the body parts onto trains. The Muslims would send the body parts to India, and the Hindus would send the body parts on trains to Pakistan. Such actions only further deepened the hatred between the two groups.

More than half a century ago, the massive murder of the Jews during World War II reveals another tremendous display of viciousness. Survivors of the concentration camps, who lived to tell their nightmares, describe with horror the brutality they endured. To some survivors, the experience seemed almost unreal as they witnessed thousands and thousands of people including their family members sent to the gas chambers, and then their bodies ruthlessly thrown into crematoriums.

Some of the greatest horrors occurred in Auschwitz, a concentration camp in Poland, in which almost 4 million people, mostly Jews, met their deaths. Survivors have told their stories in many forms, describing the horrifying details of their experience in the camp. One survivor, Sara Nomberg, shares her account from the summer of 1944:

> Every day of that macabre last summer of Hitler's reign twenty thousand people were killed in Auschwitz. The crematoria were unable to burn all of the dead who were being gassed in Auschwitz. Large ravines were excavated next to the crematoria. The dead bodies were thrown into them, and then they were doused with benzine and set aflame. The flames leaped upwards, and the sky was turned red by the gigantic fire. At night the entire scene looked grotesque. We would go out to the front of the block and stare at the reddened sky. We were not so much mesmerized by the flames as by the sea of human blood...All summer we

groped our way around in the smoke
that belched from the chimneys of the
crematoria above and from the burning
bodies in the ravines below. That July
and August the weather was very hot
and stuffy. It was a terrible summer.
Looking back, now, it is difficult for me
to say how we were able to live through
those times, conscious of human life
oozing out of existence everywhere.
How is it that we did not all go crazy?
How is it that we were able to vegetate,
keeping our composure in this
unbearable world? The time arrived
when a scream tore itself involuntarily
out of one's throat.[17]

Imagine the mental anguish of witnessing thousands and
thousands of people, sometimes friends and relatives, walking
straight into the gas chambers, which was only the final torture
after starvation and humiliation. The prisoners were starved
and beaten without cause, forcing them to live in constant fear
of impending death.

The Nazis were not the only group of soldiers ruthlessly
murdering and torturing their prisoners during World War II.
In December 1937, the city of Nanking in China fell under the
control of the Japanese. Most war crime transcripts tell stories
similar to the one that follows:

The Japanese would take any men they
found as prisoners, neglect to give them
water or food for days, but promise

them food and work. After days of such treatment, the Japanese would bind the wrists of their victims securely with wire or rope and herd them out to some isolated area. The men, too tired or dehydrated to rebel, went out eagerly, thinking they would be fed. By the time they saw the machine guns, or the bloodied swords and bayonets wielded by waiting soldiers, or the massive graves, heaped and reeking with the bodies of the men who had preceded them, it was already too late to escape.

The Japanese would later justify their actions by saying that they had to execute POWs to save their own limited food supply and prevent revolts. But nothing can excuse what the Japanese did to hundreds of thousands of helpless Chinese civilians in Nanking. They had no weapons and were in no position to mutiny.[18]

The Japanese murdered almost 300,000 Chinese during the six-week period after they entered the city. Not only did they murder, but the number of rapes could range between eight thousand and twenty thousand.[19]

The suffering continued in other parts of the world during this same war. In the book, *Hidden Horrors: Japanese War Crimes in World War II*, by Yuki Tanaka, the author describes the vicious ways in which the Japanese soldiers tortured and killed their POWs. In one of the POW camps, witnesses reported various types of extreme torture used by the soldiers. In one case, they would force uncooked rice down a prisoner's throat and then put a hose in his mouth so that he would swallow a large amount of water. Consequently, the rice would expand, causing excruciating pain. In other cases, they would fill the prisoner's belly with water and then an officer would jump on the soldier from a high chair.

Tanaka also describes how tens of thousands of women were raped or captured as sex slaves by the Japanese. These women were starved, viciously raped, and often massacred as well. Those who survived often suffered from mental breakdowns from which they never recovered. Unfortunately, soldiers from many regions and countries take it upon themselves to exploit the region that they conquer along with its people. For instance, from the first day of U.S. occupation of Japan in 1945, reports indicate that U.S. soldiers engaged in the mass rape of Japanese women, sometimes gang raping women numerous times.[20] The soldiers who executed these acts on both sides were, in most cases, considered dedicated and loyal citizens of their respective countries.

How does a soldier kill and exploit others so viciously? Tanaka also questions, "Why do soldiers ill-treat POWs who obviously have little or no means to fight back against their captors? How do ordinary men with ordinary lives, including loved ones they care for, become capable of such brutality when they become soldiers? In ordinary life these men would be incapable of killing animals let alone other people. Everything changes, however, when certain other people become enemies."[21] The author goes on to describe how certain ideologies during the war thoroughly dehumanize the enemy. Killing becomes more possible by creating a psychological distance from the opponent. Soldiers must kill or be killed, a threat which often leads soldiers to view the enemy as inhuman and cruel. Consequently, even the women of the enemy turn into mere exploits of war rather than human beings.

Due to the environment of the war, the goal and the mission obsesses people to such an extent that they are forced to maintain this psychological distance. From these reports and witnesses, we can see that the worst can come out of people when they must function in such life threatening and dangerous environments. Many veterans feel embarrassment as they look back. Tanaka notes that some of the generals overseeing the POW camps felt some hesitation to speak of the incidents, partly due to shame. However, in the midst of the violence, most aggressors, whether American, Japanese, British, or those of other nationalities, were totally convinced of their righteousness and of the necessity of their actions. They felt angry and took revenge. They saw their friends die and realized that they could also die at any moment. Consequently, they just saw the other person as inhuman and felt that the other race, country, or group must be destroyed. Thus, when they did kill them, they would kill in the most vicious ways.

The Vietnam War also has many dark stories that veterans have shared over the years. One of the more famous atrocities occurred at My Lai on March 16, 1968. On that night, almost four hundred villagers, including women, children, and babies, were gathered together for a massive execution. The order to fire came from superiors, and although some of the soldiers had moral objections to fulfilling this order, circumstances led them to comply. One can imagine that most of the soldiers at the time of the massacre did not feel too much guilt in executing the order, but surely in peacetime, many realized how inhumane they had become.

From history and scripture, we see that vicious acts of

violence do not limit themselves to our modern age. Even the *Mahabharata*, the great epic of India, describes a tremendous war. After the pious Pandavas won the war at the Battle of Kuruksetra, Asvatthama, a warrior on the opposing army, snuck into the Pandavas' camp at night and beheaded the five sons of his enemy, Arjuna. In that same night, he killed countless other warriors in the most gruesome and cowardly way. Rather than facing them in battle as an honorable *ksatriya* or warrior, he killed them at night while some of them still lay in their beds:

> Asvatthama slew all of the surviving warriors...Horses and elephants, terror-stricken, ran about wildly. Confused warriors came out of their quarters and looked around in the darkness to see what was happening. Seeing Asvatthama whirling his bloodied sword, many of them mounted horses and sped toward the camp's gates. Others ran on foot, trying to escape. As the men left the camp, Kripa and Kritavarma met them and killed them. Having no weapons, with disheveled hair and garments and crying in fear, they were cruelly butchered even as they fled crying for mercy.[22]

Despite knowing the principles of religion as stated in the ancient Vedic scriptures, Asvatthama did not hesitate to break these codes in order to seek his revenge. However, in previous ages, wars were fought according to certain principles and guidelines. According to the Vedic scriptures, an enemy who does not resist should never be killed. As stated in the *Srimad-Bhagavatam* 1.7.36:

> *mattam pramattam unmattam*
> *suptam balam striyam jadam*
> *prapannam viratham bhitam*
> *na ripum hanti dharma-vit*

> A person who knows the principles of religion does not kill an enemy who is careless, intoxicated, insane, asleep, afraid or devoid of his chariot. Nor does he kill a boy, a woman, a foolish creature or a surrendered soul.

Human Nature at Its Best

Not all people respond in negative and vicious ways under pressure. Some individuals have a great level of love, compassion, and devotion, which will manifest the most when put to the test. Therefore, consider which environments bring out the best in people? Actually, when we examine human nature, we will see that some of the same situations that bring out the worst in people will also bring out the very best in other people. War is one of the situations that can also bring out the very best because difficult situations will expose the true nature of people. The most amazing qualities can shine forth if they already exist within the person in a dormant condition. The more that a situation challenges an individual, the more it will expose what the person really has in their consciousness.

Florence Nightingale, a famous nurse in the 19th century, felt a unique calling to dedicate her life to the care of the sick. Born of a wealthy family in 1820, she went against her family's wishes by pursuing her study of nursing and dedicating her life to increasing the standards in hospital care. In 1854, during the Crimean War, she arrived with 38 nurses at a hospital in Turkey. The conditions in the hospital were torturous for the wounded as they lacked cleanliness, sufficient supplies, and qualified nurses. After arriving, she worked selflessly, day and night, to mitigate the suffering of the soldiers. A newspaper report at that time wrote, "She is a ministering angel in these hospitals; and, as her slender form glides quietly along each corridor, every poor fellow's face softens with gratitude at the sight of her. When all the medical officers have retired for the night, and silence and darkness have settled down upon those miles of prostrate sick, she may be observed alone, with a little lamp in her hand, making her solitary rounds."[23] She became known as the "Lady of the Lamp" because she would walk around at night with a lamp, checking on the patients to ease their suffering. The phrase itself was coined by the sick soldiers who looked forward to her nightly visits as she lit the corridor with a lamp.

Harriet Tubman exemplifies rare courage and compassion in the face of great danger. Born into slavery, she escaped in 1849 and became one of the most successful assistants of the Underground Railroad. Through her efforts, she led more than 300 slaves to freedom, which was not an easy task. At the time, the officials placed a reward of $40,000 dollars on her head and would probably have burned her alive if caught. However, this threat of death did not stop her from returning five times to bring around 300 slaves northward into Canada. She became known as the "Moses of her people" for delivering numerous slaves to freedom.

The stories of her rescues reveal a deep faith in God and also a concern about her fellow slaves who remained in bondage. She did not just rescue herself and rejoice over her own freedom but felt compelled to help those still suffering the torture of slavery. Even though she knew that she would be immediately tortured and killed if caught, this did not diminish her compassion and eagerness to help others out of their sufferings. During the Civil War, she assisted as a nurse and as a spy and scout for the Second South Carolina Volunteers. She never tired of helping others and in her later years she established a home for the elderly in Auburn, New York in which she helped the disabled and sick.[24]

Father Maximilian Kolbe, a Catholic priest, provides an extraordinary example of heroism during war. He lived his life in service to God and died that way as well. Survivors of the death camps remember him not only for his death but for his behavior in life as well. He had deep faith in God and would not waver under any circumstance, in spite of torture, hunger, pain, and so on:

> On 17 February 1941 he was arrested
> and sent to the infamous Pawiak prison
> in Warsaw. Here he was singled out for
> special ill-treatment. A witness tells us
> that in March of that year an S. S. guard,
> seeing this man in his habit girdled with
> a rosary, asked if he believed in Christ.
> When the priest calmly replied 'I do',
> the guard struck him. The S. S. man
> repeated his question several times and
> receiving always the same answer went
> on beating him mercilessly.

In Auschwitz, where hunger and
hatred reigned and faith evaporated,
this man opened his heart to others and
spoke of God's infinite love. He seemed
never to think of himself. When food
was brought in and everyone struggled
to get his place in the queue so as to
be sure of a share, Fr Maximilian
stood aside, so that frequently there
was none left for him. At other times
he shared his meager ration of soup or
bread with others. He was once asked
whether such self-abnegation made
sense in a place where every man was
engaged in a struggle for survival, and
he answered: "Every man has an aim in
life. For most men it is to return home
to their wives and families, or to their
mothers. For my part, I give my life for
the good of all men."[25]

He meant this last statement very literally as his death
revealed. In 1941, he was deported to the death camp, Auschwitz.
In the end of July, a prisoner escaped which meant that the S.S.
men would choose ten random prisoners to execute. Among the
ten, a younger man with both wife and children was selected.
Father Maximilian stepped out of line and offered to take the
place of Francis Gajowniczek, explaining that he wished to die
for the man since the man was younger and had a family. The
S.S. man did not care who died as long as he had ten men. He
then led the ten away to meet their slow deaths in a starvation
bunker. An eyewitness, one of the janitor's assistants, recalls
those last days:

In the cell of the poor wretches there were daily loud prayers, the rosary and singing, in which prisoners from neighbouring cells also joined. When no S. S. men were in the Block, I went to the Bunker to talk to the men and comfort them. Fervent prayers and songs to the Holy Mother resounded in all the corridors of the Bunker. I had the impression I was in a church. Fr Kolbe was leading and the prisoners responded in unison. They were often so deep in prayer that they did not even hear that inspecting S. S. men had descended to the Bunker; and the voices fell silent only at the loud yelling of their visitors...Fr Kolbe bore up bravely, he did not beg and did not complain but raised the spirits of the others.... Since they had grown very weak, prayers were now only whispered. At every inspection, when almost all the others were now lying on the floor, Fr Kolbe was seen kneeling or standing in the centre as he looked cheerfully in the face of the S. S. men. Two weeks passed in this way. Meanwhile one after another they died, until only Fr Kolbe was left. This the authorities felt was too long; the cell was needed for new victims. So one day they brought in the head of the

> sick-quarters, a German, a common criminal named Bock, who gave Fr Kolbe an injection of carbolic acid in the vein of his left arm. Fr Kolbe, with a prayer on his lips, himself gave his arm to the executioner. Unable to watch this I left under the pretext of work to be done. Immediately after the S. S. men with the executioner had left I returned to the cell, where I found Fr Kolbe leaning in a sitting position against the back wall with his eyes open and his head drooping sideways. His face was calm and radiant.[26]

Pope John Paul II later canonized Father Maximilian Kolbe a Catholic saint in 1982. Advanced spiritualists of all traditions exhibit these same unique qualities of selflessness, humility, and devotion. They uplift the environment wherever they go. They dedicate their lives in the service of God and humanity due to their higher knowledge and love. The more devastating the situation, the more the divine qualities of the saints manifest.

Other heroes emerged during that time period as well. A young Catholic girl known as Stefania Podgorska was 16 years old when the Jews were segregated in Poland. She heard of the hunger, disease, and death occurring in the ghettos and made secret visits to the ghetto with food, clothing, and medicine even though she risked her life each time she crossed the barbed wire. One night, Max, Stefania's friend, made an escape, but after knocking on the doors of many people who refused to take him in, Stefania agreed to hide him:

After she agreed to help Max, she and her sister built a false wall and ceiling in the attic of their small apartment with wood from abandoned apartments. Designed to hold seven people, the space eventually served as a hideaway for 13 Jews. For two and a half years, the 13 kept watch out of spy holes, spoke in whispers and survived on bread and onions. When one of the Jewish women became ill with typhus, Fusia secretly obtained lifesaving medicine for her.

Such behavior was a rarity in the years of persecution throughout Poland and other European nations under Nazi control. Rescuers like Fusia were few, numbering only several thousand. Most citizens complied with the Nazi edicts and did not assist the Jews; to be caught meant arrest and possibly death. What made people like Fusia risk their lives for the sake of Jews? What qualities and characteristics did they have that others lacked?[27]

Obviously, their compassion was much stronger and they were more selfless. In many cases, they also had a deeper faith in God.

Some of my own staff members risked their lives in Liberia and Sierra Leone during the war. Several were even assassinated while trying to facilitate the needs of millions of suffering people. In former Yugoslavia, several Hare Krishna devotees risked their lives on a regular basis while giving out free food and water to people in need.

Spiritual Warfare

These points can help us realize how war transforms the consciousness of people, nations, and continents. It has an unusual way of honing into different emotions—positive as well as negative. While war dehumanizes some people, it empowers others to go the extra mile and to act far beyond their normal capabilities.

The idea behind my series of books entitled *Spiritual Warrior* is to tune into this concept and use it in a positive way. Since war creates an environment that can bring out the very best in people, we want to help people see their lives as a daily mission. Adversarial situations and dangerous environments arise in daily life, but we want to constantly access love in spite of the challenges. Instead of conventional or traditional warfare, we are engaged in spiritual warfare.

The character, weapons, and battlefield of the spiritual warrior are all wholesome and extraordinary. The word "war" usually carries negative connotations, but realizing that war indicates an emergency will encourage us to develop strategy and clarity about our deeper goals. We must maintain our focus and determination. All of these qualities can be very powerful and positive as we depart from conventional settings.

The Weapons, the Battlefield, and the Goal of the Spiritual Warrior

A spiritual warrior is unconventional to say the least. We do not fight with conventional weapons, we do not fight on conventional battlegrounds, and we do not fight for conventional objectives. Unconventional warfare in a spiritual setting uses weapons of love, compassion, and fearlessness in order to do the right action in the right way. Devotion, pridelessness, and selflessness lay the foundations for our weapons. Consequently, we have this tremendous armor and arsenal of very progressive and powerful connections.

Secondly, the spiritual warrior's battlefield is the battlefield of consciousness, or the realm of human consciousness where we wage war against the ignorance and lust that now pervades human society like an occupying army. Conversely, conventional wars take place in a country, city, or village and, in any of these settings, the material situation focuses on sovereignty or egocentricity. One nation, group, or religion in one part of the world is trying to dominate others and capitalize for themselves at the demise of other groups. Many of the wars in human history have had some religious overtones, but a closer look generally reveals that the combatants were actually more interested in some political or territorial gains. People can use religion for all types of personal motives. At times, our consciousness comes under attack, which helps us realize that the intruding armies of lust, greed, selfishness, avarice, and other negative qualities can overpower our consciousness.

Finally, we want to consider the actual objective of the spiritual warrior—how to bring about the greatest good for the greatest number of people. We want to help people free themselves from slavery to their senses and from the orthodoxy and fads constantly imposed upon them which forces them to act as blind followers. The objective is to gain freedom from the illusions imposed by the material body, material world, and the material planets so that we can return to the spiritual realm where we will find ultimate association, peace, and freedom. Our objective is a civilization in which people live in harmony with each other and with God, awakened and in tune with the effulgent spiritual environment available to us. Such spiritual warriors have gone deep into their bona fide religions and will be absorbed in experiencing the most universal, confidential, and loving essence of these teachings. Toward these ends, we endeavor to develop our self to ensure an understanding with the people we meet. We want to give them the tools they need to discover and experience the truth for themselves.

Conventional Warfare Versus Spiritual Warfare

The warrior conception is powerful because the thought of war indicates danger. We realize that some alliances are healthy and friendly, and some associations and environments are unhealthy. We must constantly try to distinguish between the two because, in war, we must deal with issues of survival. When conventional soldiers fight on the battlefield, they have strategies to protect themselves, particular areas of expertise, and specific targets. The soldiers realize that they must do what is required while at the same time endeavoring to return home. Similarly, spiritual warriors see themselves on a mission. Whether we are lawyers, engineers, doctors, teachers, priests, or housewives, we must realize that we have a mission. As we carry out our mission, we must acknowledge that dangers inherently exist because war means danger. At the same time, there are opportunities for victory and for high achievement.

Conventional warfare focuses on saving oneself or one's own group. In each case, it involves an obsession or passion. The soldiers who committed the violence previously described were normal fathers, uncles, cousins, brothers, and boyfriends who became obsessed soldiers. The subsequent violence they did to people was vicious and the violence imposed upon them was also vicious. Just as these conventional soldiers became so obsessed to the point of acting far beyond their normal mindset in horrendous ways, the spiritual warriors should become so obsessed with divinity that they become empowered to act far beyond their normal capacity in a healthy, positive, and progressive way. The spiritual warrior in this frame of mind does not take a moment for granted and looks at each situation in an opportunistic way for the benefit of the society and in the service of God.

The conventional warrior's goal in each situation is to cause as much destruction as possible and then to somehow get back to the camp and ultimately back home. These soldiers are just eating, sleeping, and drinking war. A conventional warrior's whole mindset is entirely captured. The classical warriors or *ksatriyas* think, dream, strategize, and play war. They analyze everything including economics and politics in the paradigm of war. The more a challenge confronts them, the more it stimulates them to do the necessary.

In the Middle East, the number of suicide bombers is growing every day. In many cases, the so-called martyrs are just children in the Islamic communities who see it as glorious to one day kill themselves along with other people in the process. They believe that they will go to paradise and bless their families. Just as someone can become obsessed with the idea of hurting others and failing to see them as human, the spiritual warrior has to possess love and devotion to an even greater extent.

The Battlefield of Consciousness

We must realize that we cannot avoid war since it is an inevitable part of material existence. As long as people have existed on this planet, wars have been fought and they will continue to rage. The root of all of this violence is consciousness. It takes a certain consciousness to abuse women without the capacity to see them as someone's sister, mother, or wife. It takes a certain type of consciousness to kill. In most cases, soldiers are young men. The average age of the soldiers in Vietnam was approximately twenty-three years old. They were kids who were sent to war while the admirals and generals strategized far away from the front line. They sent these boys out by the hundreds of thousands. Some of the children fighting as soldiers in Liberia, Rwanda, and Sierra Leone were only nine to ten years old. The leaders of these wars capitalize on the pioneering mood and unrealistic conception of life and death carried by youth.

The greatest battlefield is the battlefield of consciousness. Beneath the consciousness of war is the consciousness that leads to war—the negative mental culture of lust, greed, envy, indecency, and domination. As this negative mental culture prevails, war is inevitable; in one sense, the next war has already begun. As it now pervades human civilization, we find ourselves surrounded by a battlefield of consciousness and an atmosphere of war. Assaults encroach upon us through every facet of our culture and through our own minds, threatening our potential as humans and as spiritual beings. This is not surprising considering that the material world is suited for this strife, being a place to accommodate our separation from God. As long as we have a material body and are a part of the material world, the battlefield of consciousness is something we must face.

We cannot remain neutral on a battlefield. Attacks are underway, and if we do not find some way to save ourselves, the atmosphere of war will destroy us. We are all on these battlefields and we all play a role. We either allow the devastation to go on until we become products of the fallout, or we elevate our consciousness. Not only do we elevate our own consciousness, but we also want to help elevate our communities, corporations, and environments by acting as warriors for righteousness and by having the armor of love, devotion, compassion, and selflessness.

Waging a War of Peace and Love

We do want people to eat, sleep, and dream about war, but a war of peace and love. During any interactions, we must see ourselves as on a mission. "To pursue the transcendental path is more or less to declare war on the illusory energy. Consequently, whenever a person tries to escape the clutches of the illusory energy, she tries to defeat the practitioner by various allurements" (*Bhagavad-gita* 6.37, purport). As we make plans, we want our plans to involve strategies to raise consciousness. In any situation or environment, we realize that we have to find a way to do the necessary without becoming wounded or killed. We must realize that the day-to-day attacks we experience come from lust, greed, and envy. We must understand these enemies and combat them without becoming captured or wounded by them. When we have this sort of consciousness, we can begin to counteract much of the conventional warfare around us.

Many devotional and pious people look at others and wonder why they act so warlike. Such people have not yet realized that the only way to counteract the war is to have higher consciousness and engage in waging love and peace. Love and peace do not simply manifest by conceptualization; they manifest by using strategies to counteract the negative strategy. It does not just happen by thinking about acting kindly or lovingly. Love is a relationship and involves active exchanges. Love is a verb. It is not just a matter of thinking lovingly; it is a matter of acting and relating with love. It involves expressions of loving associations. We create a loving environment based on the aggregate amount of loving activities.

Planetary Warfare

Many events indicate that it is a very critical time on the planet. Some of the recent conflicts could even accelerate into a massive third world war. We see the extent to which people with this conventional warlike mentality are shaking up the planet. Some of the violence that is happening in the Middle East is due to years and years of aggression, abuse, sadness, and depression. By studying the law of *karma*, we find that in periods of conflict, those involved often remain similarly oriented in their succeeding lifetimes. Many of the people who are now in Middle Eastern countries have repeatedly taken birth there after several lifetimes under oppression and limitations. Therefore, some entities who have come into the environment are now empowered for destruction. They have been in situations in which they have lost hope for the future due to such oppression that it creates grounds for fanaticism. After so many lifetimes, such tension will not simply go away overnight.

When war happens in different places on the planet, it has much to do with the collective consciousness of the people and with the current and previous activities in that environment:

> In the West, slaughterhouses are maintained without restriction, and therefore every fifth or tenth year there is a big war in which countless people are slaughtered even more cruelly than the animals. Sometimes during war, soldiers keep their enemies in concentration camps and kill them in very cruel ways. These are reactions brought about by unrestricted animal-killing in the slaughterhouse and by hunters in the forest. Proud, demoniac persons do not know the laws of nature, or the laws of God. Consequently, they unrestrictedly kill poor animals, not caring for them at all.
>
> *Srimad-Bhagavatam* 4.26.5, purport

Due to the intensity of the warlike energy today, war cannot be checked simply by remaining passive. We have to be activists carrying the weapons of love and devotion. We need to think and strategize as we sleep, work, shop, and interact. We must find ways to act as entities of divinity and love. We must be entities who allow divinity to work through us and around us. If a sufficient number of people can accomplish this achievement, we will change the course of what is about to happen on this planet.

The general *karma* on this planet is a mess right now. It doesn't take a mystic or a scholar to come to this conclusion. Just look at all of the negative actions that are producing corresponding reactions. Look at the tremendous amount of abuse that is and has been going on such as spouse abuse, child abuse, elderly abuse, resource depletion, racism, tribalism, religious fanaticism, and so on.

The Necessity of Spiritual Warriorship

If the lifestyle you want is always escaping your grasp, maybe it is because you haven't yet mastered the art of spiritual warriorship. In these days and times, the art of spiritual warriorship is essential to those who want to experience personal fulfillment, loving relationships, and overall well-being in a world riddled with negative influences that degrade our consciousness. Spiritual warriorship is no longer a recreational sport or a luxury. It is actually a strategy for survival, especially for those who want to avoid toxic thought patterns and their devastating after effects.

A great number of spiritually evolved souls and seekers recognize the need to resist a common pitfall that plagues so many members of society. Unbridled lust is, of course, foremost among the elements that have a harmful effect upon our success and happiness. Keep in mind that many of the causes of negative obsessions stem from lust. Purifying methodologies like those found in this book and in our previous books in the *Spiritual Warrior* series are critically important. These approaches can profoundly alter the fatal attractions and habitual patterns of self-deceit from which so many people are now suffering. If conventional warriors would learn to have more appreciation, value, and love for those they desire to fight or annihilate, their combative mood would disappear.

The Prevalence of Conventional Warfare

Wars are often held to bring about so-called peace and eradicate conflict, but they usually have the opposite effect by producing more conflict. As the wars rage, people are uncertain of the outcomes and of what entities will be a part of those outcomes. As we wage a war based on love and devotion, we have a chance to be a part of the Golden Age that will ultimately come about in full after all of this chaos escalates and permeates throughout the planet. Many of the hostile events occurring now stem from abuse and improper thinking, which have led to inauspiciousness.

In 2003, SARS, a type of deadly flu, as well as AIDS and mad cow disease sickened and killed many people. This also indicates that wars are unfolding in our own bodies. Some germs and viruses have entered which create a disease. Due to some foreign matter, imbalances are taking place. The determining factor depends on which bacteria is stronger—the good or the bad germs. As people build up their resistance and take proper medication, the good bacteria and organs get strengthened and their bodies are in better shape.

Just as our bodies, organs, and cells are undergoing different types of conflict, our planet is similarly undergoing such conflict. The orthodox culture of a combative nature that pits people against each other in a vicious and precarious way is destroying millions of lives. People act beyond their own limits as they become possessed and obsessed with the warlike mentality. The conflicts in Afghanistan and Iraq did not bring peace to the international community, and many situations continue to manifest in unhealthy ways. Whether a man batters his wife, a group of people engage in ethnic cleansing, or countries fight over territory, such aggression is symptomatic of the same kind of disease that coerces people to fight over material sovereignty. This disease creates scarcities and warlike mentalities in which one sees others as inhuman and thus harms them in the most vicious ways.

Therefore, we want to become so intoxicated with love and affection that we accept accountability for the consequences before we speak, eat, or enter different places. We are on a mission to see how we can play our role and do our part in creating an environment of love and peace.

The Path of the Spiritual Warrior Is Not Easy

Through these books, we are trying to address material, metaphysical, and spiritual concerns to help with the discipline of spiritual warriorship. We want to solve material problems with spiritual solutions. We want to go beyond the point of just having peace solely for ourselves. We want to go beyond our own meditation, chanting, praying, *yoga*, and nutrition. We also want to go beyond just thinking about change, becoming active in the role we can play in making the world a better place. Naturally, we must work on our own universe first. We must work on our own body and consciousness. In this way, we will all make a contribution that can influence the bigger universe.

The path of the spiritual warrior is not an easy path. It demands courage, determination, discipline, intense compassion, and unconditional love. It requires an understanding that this world is not the final chapter. We are on a mission. Spiritual warriors undergo adversity and challenge; however, in a positive and equipoise state of mind, they see the challenges as purifying and understand how the obstacles force them to achieve higher, accelerate faster, and try harder. Even gold, the most valuable and costly of metals is brought into its glory by fire. The diamond, the most precious of gems, is formed by intense pressure and heat. Spiritual warriorship is similar; thus a spiritual warrior should thrive on intensity. The more our desire to help and make a change flourishes, the more we will want to be a part of the struggle.

Spiritual warriors are not alone. They carry the Supreme Lord in their hearts. *Acaryas*, *devas*, and angels guard and guide them, and the residents of the spiritual world cheer them as heroes and heroines on their journey back home to the transcendental realm. Just as in conventional warfare people receive supplies, resources, encouragement, and honors, spiritual warriors are backed up by angelic hosts. Do you want to join the ranks of this transcendental army? If so, you must take a stand. You must make a choice.

As the negative forces struggle to maintain their foothold in our lives, only two sides will emerge—the spiritually enlightened and the materially oppressed. Beloved, we do not have the luxury of time. Your current thoughts and actions are already placing you in one camp or another. The earth is merging into a millennium of spiritual enlightenment and purity. The residents will become conspicuous by their loving natures and peaceful minds. The *devas* and angels will again visit the planet and tranquility will permeate throughout the atmosphere. We invite you to take your place among the inhabitants of the Golden Age. Pick up your weapons of austerity, mercy, compassion, and love and join the ranks of the spiritual warriors as we forge a new beginning under the banner of the Supreme Lord.

Questions and Answers

Question: With all of the wars surrounding us and rumors of war in all of the scriptures, what is the key to maintaining one's focus as a spiritual warrior, especially if we must function around people of different mindsets?

Answer: Consider the conventional warrior. What are some of the keys that keep the warrior in the mindset of war? Most importantly, the person has accepted that identity. He or she is a soldier fighting for the United States of America, for instance, with a certain area of expertise. The individual has accepted that identity, and others also think of him in this way. First, we must develop more of an identity in which we really believe that we can make a difference. We can have a role in consciousness raising by monitoring what we say, what we do, and how we think.

Secondly, warriors are always planning. By connecting with their external plans and goals, they are bringing their mind and body into a certain state. If we don't plan, *maya* or Satan will plan for us. If we don't use our energy for strategizing and trying to have certain short-term and long-term goals, then the fallout will disturb us. First, focus on our identity, then plan and strategize. We do it anyway, indirectly. We make some plans to clean, to shop, or to get a degree. We make some plans about what will happen when we meet that princess or that prince charming we have dreamt about. We make all of these plans, which is natural, but we should plan our whole life based more on a spiritual paradigm.

Question: We may want to do something to advance ourselves and humanity, but, at the end of the day, we never feel that we have accomplished enough. How do we deal with these feelings, and how do we open our creativity so that we can make effective plans?

Answer: First, this mentality is actually healthy. Both the conventional and the unconventional warrior never feel satisfied. Even after a victory, they are ready for the next victory. After a good fight, they are ready for another fight. They realize that, although they won this scrimmage, the enemy will return and attack in another way. This lack of satisfaction is a sign of a good warrior, and it is good for him or her to maintain this type of mentality. If a warrior begins to feel satisfied and takes a victory for granted, he or she increases the chances of more attacks. For a soldier, the worst mistake is to let down his or her guard or think that the war has ended while it actually still rages. While we are constantly trying to see how to improve, we also want to access quality through the practice of mindfulness. We have to go deeper into all of our activities. Furthermore, as we want to help more, the Lord will also help us more.

Question: Wars have always gone on, but the current warfare seems more stressful because we cannot quite pinpoint the enemy. Is it our own people, the government, or the governments of other nations? Could you address this point?

Answer: You have touched on an important theme. In very intense wars, it becomes hard to recognize the adversaries. We are dealing with a very unusual combat environment. When people who are really into war have certain targets and goals, they can make all kinds of sacrifices, including even their own people. That is war. Consciously as well as unconsciously, we see that people also die under "friendly" fire.

However, in a war situation, some people give their lives

through suicide missions in order to accelerate the cause and help increase the accessibility of the goal. War involves casualties, traitors, and espionage. Sometimes people begin on one side but then shift to the side that they later want to support. When some people feel that their side will not win, they will switch sides. In other cases, some soldiers are just cowards. They are only bold when they have sufficient resources and equipment to hide behind. Therefore, we must be very alert to see the ways of the enemy, both gross and covert, so that we do not become wounded or a casualty.

Question: In a situation that involves intense warfare and fighting, often times we may find ourselves expressing our fears. In terms of courage and the empowerment of the spiritual warrior, can you offer some practical things that we can do to begin to experience some of those transformations?

Answer: In my book, *Spiritual Warrior III*, I describe twelve qualities of a spiritual warrior: sense control and mastery of the mind; humility; fearlessness; truthfulness; compassion and pridelessness; material exhaustion and disinterest in material reward; no idle time; patience and selflessness; firm faith; perseverance; curiosity and enthusiasm to learn and grow; and surrender to divine will. I also offer four principles of community building which are very practical and distinct techniques that people can use to make a transformation:

> 1. Treat everyone you encounter as if the success of your spiritual life depends on the quality of your interactions with them.

2. Reflect on the person you love the most and aspire to treat everyone with that same quality of love.

3. Anytime a conflict arises in a relationship, view it as your own fault first.

4. Realize that the people in your present environment might very well be the people with whom you will live out your life and who will be with you at the time of death.

One should definitely not get caught up in the mindset of fear. When fear overwhelms you, it will lead you to act in irrational ways. If you are in a fearful state, you become vulnerable and can become a casualty. We do not want to become fearful, but, at the same time, we do not want to deny the complexities of the times. Once again, one can refer to my book, *Spiritual Warrior IV*, for a more elaborate discussion on fear.

Question: How do we overcome a fearful attitude?

Answer: That comes with replacement. How do we overcome addictions and bad habits? We can read and hear endlessly about the negative effects, but it is not so easy to give them up unless we can replace an unhealthy habit with a positive engagement. It is not easy just to try to stop unhealthy activities, but, as we redirect our focus and attention, we can become absorbed or even attached to a positive alternative.

Question: Although it is difficult to look at war in a positive light, it can provide a foundation for growth by tearing down the old and creating an opportunity to build the new. Similarly, by beginning with ourselves and undergoing a thorough self-examination, we can begin to see the world in a different light. After the terrorist attacks on September 11th, there seems to be an increased national interest in spirituality. For those of us on the spiritual path, this is a wonderful opportunity to help others connect with genuine spiritual truths.

Answer: Very good points. It is a wonderful time to try to help people who are anxious, wounded, confused, and in need. For this reason, we began this chapter by considering which settings bring both the worst and best out of people. These are times when people can come to the call of service far beyond their rational scheme of activities. However, for some people, it brings out the worst because negative patterns are more dominant in their consciousness and the current situations open up avenues for their paranoia.

Question: Sometimes we focus on our mission to such an extent that we lose sight of anything but the mission. As you stated, there are many negative forces in the environment today that could take advantage of us and cause us to think that we are fighting for the good when we are really fighting for the bad. How do we remain attentive and true to the mission so that we can accomplish our goals instead of falling prey to some of these other negative influences?

Answer: For this reason, we emphasize the qualities of a spiritual warrior. One of these qualities is humility. If we lack the ability to honor feedback, then in spite of our good intentions, we might become an integral part of the problem. Instead of helping to raise consciousness, we might remain stuck in negative patterns and consider them to be the only ways to function. By thinking of ourselves as special or "chosen," we resort to fanaticism and fundamentalism. In many cases, we have some good intentions, but we also have a misguided consciousness. We must take constant inventory and receive feedback with humility.

In this way, we always remain aware of the battlefield of consciousness, which can be overtaken by the intruding armies of pride, lust, and enviousness. When we see these mindsets as invading enemies, we will act more carefully to not imbibe them within ourselves while simultaneously trying to do good work. We might have an awareness of what is improper and know how to make a difference, but instead of making a healthy change, we just add to the problems. For this reason, I addressed some of the metaphysical aspects of the karmic influences in the Middle Eastern areas. Many of those people have repeatedly come back into that environment after several births and they come with a good deal of anger, depression, and frustration. Many have experienced poverty and violence lifetime after lifetime. These mindsets create existentialism, fanaticism, and desperation to try to find a way out. Such people will become motivated and enthused by the conception of paradise. By being locked into such negative karmic patterns, many of these people become compelled to continue in a digressive and destructive course.

Question: You have given us so much insight into acting as spiritual warriors so that we can continue to function on the planet during these transition times, but how would you advise us to prepare for a transition in another way if the Lord decides that He wants us to leave our material body?

Answer: For instance, an intense conventional warrior is ready to die and realizes that, in war, some people will die. They function with the idea of doing as much as possible before that might happen because they accept the situation as a reality. The spiritual and unconventional warriors fully understand that we are dealing with a battlefield and casualties are an inevitable fact.

We must either practice our spiritual path or weaken to the point that we do not maintain our principles, vows, and determination. All the fallout surrounding us will simply overwhelm us. We must recognize the reality of the situation and the possibility of death. However, by constantly trying to keep the goal in mind, we will not be as likely to fall prey to such even when it challenges and tempts us. When we have intensity about our goals, we will have the ability to continue moving forward. Even if and when a true spiritual warrior meets death, he or she dies with nobility and dignity because the spiritual warrior leaves behind a great legacy. He or she is always promoted to higher realms in the next life since they do so much good in the world and since they do not inflict unnecessary violence, pain, or death on others.

That nature alone is good which
refrains from doing another whatsoever
is not good for itself.

Dadisten-I-dinik, 94,5
(Zoroastrianism)

Chapter 7

Vegetarianism as an Aid to the Elimination of Violence

A Wake-Up Call

We remind ourselves that the greatest inhumanity takes place in an environment of war. Conversely, some of the greatest acts of heroism and sacrifice also happen during war. What does war mean? Although some people do manifest their most heroic moments, we mainly see war as a time in which we see the worst of humankind. We may wonder if we, as humans, are violent by nature? And if so, is there any way to really overcome this tendency? As long as we remain in the material world in these material bodies, we will face war. However, this does not justify cruelty or minimize its horrific impact on civilization. Even though we live in a warlike environment saturated with conflict, we have a duty as spiritualists to not play into it. We want to create environments that can minimize conflict and violence in order to show people alternative ways to live.

The Correlation between Diet and Violence

We want to consider how diet and food influence violence. It is impossible to have a healthy sense of peace and well being when our actions oppose that goal. We obviously cannot have peace if we are eating violently and consuming violent foods. Nor can we have it if we consume violent drinks or drugs, listen to violent music, hear violent sounds, read violent books, have violent relationships, absorb ourselves in violent television, and support or elect violent leaders. Therefore, we return to our initial statement—we really cannot embrace peace within ourselves, in our relationships, in our communities, or within the world if our actions revolve around violence.

The body is a machine, which is directly influenced by the fuel we put into it. It is a serious contradiction when we take to a life of polite cannibalism by eating dead bodies, but then try to project an artificial life of civility or piety. Imagine the irony of people who are killing so many animals then wondering why there is so much death around them. People who are killing are wondering why so many other people are killing each other. People who are killing are wondering why the world is being permeated with killers. Killers bring forth more killers. There is a need to look deeper at the negative aspects of human consciousness and to look closer at how it can be stopped. For this reason, we want to examine the more subtle causes of the problems facing the world since people are only addressing them in superficial ways while the crisis continues to amplify. If your house is on fire and you try to put the fire out with a small bucket of water, it is mere sentiment. If the fire is raging and the wind is blowing, the fire will increase in spite of the few drops of water in the bucket.

False Religionists

As we have previously mentioned, religion can function as a major nucleus, bringing people together; however, in many cases, it functions as the complete opposite by creating fanaticism and causing people to murder others viciously in the name of God. Some of the worst abuses and inhumanities take place under the name of religion. It is even worse when the people who are supposed to be religious leaders and maintainers of civilization spend their time creating capitalization and exploitation. We expect this behavior from a criminal, but not from those representing the highest truth. However, this is what is happening with the destructive influences presently. Some of the biggest destructive influences have entered into religious institutions in order to purposely gather people and use them to commit horrible acts against humankind. Even worse, when the people act in this way, they will see themselves as righteous and religious.

In order to get more in-depth knowledge of this subject matter, we can go to the *Srimad-Bhagavatam*, one of the oldest scriptures in the world. It gives us extensive information on all aspects of life including history, politics, science, geography, religion, and so on. It also reminds us of the many truths that we need to embrace on a deeper level in order to see the effects of improper activities in the world. We will also understand how positive and powerful activities can make a serious difference. People who have some knowledge, but not complete knowledge, are actually adding to the acceleration of violence. The problems in the world never stem from just the evildoers. They increase when pious people minimize evil, do not sufficiently offset the evil, or when they do not raise their consciousness to a level that can check present as well as future deviations. It is as if the Supreme Personality of Godhead is sending a message, telling us to look at the way we are living, thinking, and interacting. Look at the type of world that it is creating—a world permeating with fear in which many people honor violence and want to commit suicide while killing others.

As transcendentalists, we should be able to offer more knowledge of how we have created our current state of affairs and how we can eradicate such an unhealthy, violent culture. The *Srimad-Bhagavatam* 11.5.14 gives some very astounding verses in regard to false religionists involved in a lifestyle of eating flesh:

> *ye tv anevam-vido 'santah*
> *stabdhah sad-abhimaninah*
> *pasun druhyanti visrabdhah*
> *pretya khadanti te ca tan*

> Those sinful persons who are ignorant of actual religious principles, yet consider themselves to be completely pious, without compunction commit violence against innocent animals who are fully trusting in them. In their next lives, such sinful persons will be eaten by the same creatures they have killed in this world.

In the purport, Hridayananda dasa Gosvami writes:

> In the Western countries such as America, many people proudly proclaim themselves to be most pious religionists

and sometimes even prophets or representatives of God. Boasting of their religiosity, such foolish people experience no fear or doubt in cruelly slaughtering innumerable animals in slaughterhouses or on hunting trips for their whimsical sense gratification. In the state of Mississippi there are sometimes pig-killing festivals, in which entire families enjoy watching a pig cruelly butchered before their eyes. Similarly, a former president of the United States from Texas did not consider any social occasion complete without the slaughtering of a cow. Such persons mistakenly consider themselves to be perfectly observing the laws of God and due to such arrogant foolishness lose all touch with reality. When a man is raising an animal for slaughter, he feeds the animal nicely and encourages it to grow fat. Thus the animal gradually accepts its would-be killer as its protector and master. When the master finally approaches the helpless animal with a sharp knife or gun, the animal thinks, "Oh, my master is joking with me." Only at the last minute does the animal understand that the so-called master is death personified. It is clearly stated in Vedic literature that cruel

masters who kill innocent animals will
undoubtedly be killed in the next life
by a similar process...In other words,
one who kills an animal or who eats
meat undoubtedly acquires a debt to
the living entity who has contributed
his body for the satisfaction of the
meat-eater. The meat-eater must pay
his debt by contributing his own body
to be consumed in the next life. Such
payment of one's debt by offering one's
own body to be eaten is confirmed in
the Vedic literature.

In other words, some people openly intend to sin and
engage in violence and murder. However, it is even graver
and more serious for people to think that their actions will
make a positive difference when in fact their actions may add
to the violence and war through their insensitivity toward the
animals. The above text and purport in the *Srimad-Bhagavatam*
basically describes people who think of themselves as religious
and pious but who only add to the problem by their thought-
less actions. Those involved in such crimes will have to pay in
the next life, even to the point that similar animals may attack
and abuse them. However, some people may not be ready to
embrace such an extreme understanding, but the great sages
have tremendous insight about *karma* and the consequences of
acting improperly. They detail the type of reciprocation that
awaits us.

In the next verse, *Srimad-Bhagavatam* 11.5.15, we see the
false pride and envy maintained by the living entity. This false
pride itself creates unhealthy lifestyles and mindsets that lead
to war as well as terrorism:

dvisantah para-kayesu
svatmanam harim isvaram
mrtake sanubandhe 'smin
baddha-snehah patanty adhah

The conditioned souls become completely bound in affection to their own corpselike material bodies and their relatives and paraphernalia. In such a proud and foolish condition, the conditioned souls envy other living entities as well as the Supreme Personality of Godhead, Hari, who resides in the heart of all beings. Thus enviously offending others, the conditioned souls gradually fall down into hell.

The purport further elaborates:

Materialistic persons express their envy of animals by cruelly killing them. Similarly, the conditioned souls become envious even of other human beings and of the Lord Himself, who dwells within everyone's body. They express their envy of God by preaching atheistic science or pseudophilosophy in which they ridicule the fact that everyone is an eternal servant of God. Envious persons express their bitter feelings toward other human beings by creating wars, terrorism, cruel

> governments and cheating business
> enterprises. The sinful bodies of such
> envious persons are just like corpses.
> *Srimad-Bhagavatam* 11.5.15

This verse addresses the envy that people have towards God and other people. Enviousness is one of the root causes of sinful activities. It is a lack of compassion that manifests as the abuse of other races, genders, political parties, religions, species of life, etc., and it ultimately leads to wars.

The Unnatural Effects of a Carnivorous Diet

Consider for a moment the characteristics of wild animals. What are some of their habits? They are fearful and create fear in other animals and sometimes in humans as well. They are constantly on a vicious and aggressive search for food. Wild animals, especially when hungry, instinctively hunt and kill. Nature does not make any mistakes. Wild animals in general have claws and canine teeth, which enable them to catch their food and eat it immediately. They do not cook their meals. For a wild animal, their ability to attack and kill is essential for their survival.

The bodies of carnivorous animals versus herbivorous animals are naturally different. For instance, those who have a natural tendency to eat meat have shorter digestive tracts to enable them to eat and digest the meat raw. Their claws and teeth allow them to hunt and catch their prey. We will not find any of these characteristics in the human body. Our bodies do not have such sharp canine teeth or claws. Many animals have a natural proclivity for violence and murder, and cannot survive unless they hunt for their food.

Animals such as cows and chickens are not wild, but they are raised in very cruel and violent environments, and are full of antibiotics and fear. When we eat their flesh, we imbibe much of the mentality of what we eat, especially the violence and fear from their life and death experience. How can we become peaceful when we are filling ourselves with violence? It creates within us a perverted tendency to kill. We see this manifesting in wars, conflicts, and riots.

There have been many scientific experiments showing how the foodstuffs we put in our bodies affect the cells, brain, and mind. Just as many women are suffering from breast cancer, many men are having prostate problems, and some doctors and scientists have been trying to treat prostrate problems in men with estrogen or female hormones. However, the side effects of the medication can create additional problems such as heart attacks and strokes that kill the person faster than the prostrate cancer. Artificial hormones can cause the heart and brain to malfunction, leading to death.[28]

What does this have to do with meat eating? Let us look at a book called *Molecules of Emotion* by Candace Pert, a neuroscientist whose extensive research has shown that the brain does not reside in the head alone. Rather, cells throughout the body receive and transmit information, which means that consciousness is not just limited to the activities of the brain. Actually, our cells are alive. We are like massive batteries or energy force fields, which indicate that the whole human physiology is like an amazing amalgamation of vibrations of electromagnetic vibes. And when one electric system is connected with another electric system, they exchange energies and influence each other. When we eat an animal, we are ingesting its cells. We are ingesting an entity with a certain electromagnetic field and consequently incorporating that into our system, which affects our body, mind, and consciousness.

We can find many examples of people who have received a heart transplant that start adopting some of the idiosyncratic tendencies, emotions, and even appetite of the person whose heart they received.[29] This happens because a person's consciousness extends into the organs. For this same reason, some people who practice black magic, juju, or other sinister activities sometimes kill a human and eat their flesh with the idea of gaining certain powers based on that particular body.

Imagine all over the world people taking to a carnivorous diet. As people ingest so much of the mentality of animals that prey on other animals for food and the mentality of animals raised in an environment of violence and fear, the same mentality also becomes ingrained in their own cells, which then creates more of the animalistic activities on the part of humanity. Furthermore, Juliet Gellatley, in her book *The Silent Ark*, explains how some of the animals in slaughterhouses show symptoms of madness due to their perpetual isolation and incarceration.[30] Therefore, this madness surely is having a negative effect on those who eat these animals.

An Interconnection between All Things

Some scientists, especially physicists, tell us that we live in a holistic universe, meaning that the study of one piece or part contains the essence of the whole. Quantum physics also looks more at an almost spiritual conception of interconnectedness in which we are all influenced by a certain cosmic consciousness or energy. One thing is always affecting another. People are beginning to understand through modern technology that one event in the world affects another, but many still do not understand the actual profundity of this truth.

Alternative medicine, which is gaining more recognition, deals with the influence of subtle energies. From the Chinese perspective, physical sickness develops when the energies in the body are in disarray, which they treat with acupuncture, and by introducing herbs whose energies bring balance to the body. Most physical sicknesses also have a subtle counterpart. If you adjust the subtle energies, you can fix the symptom manifesting through the physical body. Of course, it is even better to prevent diseases from the beginning by developing a proper balance of the energy.

The Chinese call this subtle energy *ch'i* and the Japanese call it *ki*. In Sufism, it is called *baraka* and some of the Native American traditions such as the Lakota Sioux tribe call it *waken*. In some of the Pygmy tribes in the Congo, it is called *megbe*. In mystical Judaism or in the Kabbalistic tradition, it is called *yesod*. In the Indian and Tibetan traditions, it is called *prana*.[31] All of these traditions have some understanding of the subtle energies and their impact. Even the whole realm of parapsychology should at least help us appreciate the existence of certain phenomena that we cannot fully understand by orthodox perceptions. There are now conferences taking place especially in the West on health and spirituality and even on health and prayer. Some studies have shown how prayer has a tremendous impact on healing and recovery, sometimes even leading to spontaneous remission. Again, this has to do with how one entity projects onto another through something beyond the mere physical exchanges. An emerging field known as energy psychology also deals in this area. Some of the experiments have shown that just by altering energy, people with chronic diseases have been able to rid themselves of those diseases in a short time.

It cannot be denied that we are giving and receiving

energy regularly. We are constantly involved in exchanges of energy. Every object has a certain level of energy, vibrancy, or consciousness emanating from itself. Therefore, as people associate and move around in their environment, they are constantly receiving and projecting energy and moving into different force fields. Considering all of these points, imagine what is happening as people are imbibing and ingesting more violent energy during their activities of eating, sleeping, mating, and defending. It should surprise us that our species is still surviving.

Martin Luther King Jr. mentioned some very interesting points on this topic. He said, "Injustice anywhere is a threat to justice everywhere." Injustice to someone has the effect of injustice on everyone. Basically, where there is evil and sin in one environment, it adds to the sin on the entire planet. From a more positive perspective, as each person acts lovingly and frees themselves from racism, tribalism, exploitation, ecocide, matricide, homicide, infanticide, deicide, and so on, less of these activities will take place on the planet. Everyone can make a difference. As each person decides to accept vegetarianism and minimize killing or murdering on all levels, it influences the entire world. As one person or even one community becomes healed, the whole world becomes healed.

The *Srimad-Bhagavatam* tells the pastime of Dhruva Maharaja, the son of a king who went into meditation. By harnessing the *prana* or the life air within his own body, he influenced the *prana* within the whole universe. Srila Prabhupada further elaborates on the influence of Dhruva Maharaja in the *Srimad-Bhagavatam* 4.8.80:

When hundreds of persons are sitting
in an airplane, although they remain
individual units, they each share in
the total force of the airplane, which
runs at thousands of miles per hour;
similarly, when unit energy is identified
with the service of the total energy, the
unit energy becomes as powerful as
the total energy...Dhruva Maharaja,
because of his spiritual advancement,
became almost the total heaviness, and
thus he pressed down the whole earth.
Moreover, by such spiritual power his
unit body became the total body of the
universe. Thus when he closed the holes
of his unit body to firmly concentrate
his mind on the Supreme Personality of
Godhead, all the units of the universe—
namely all the living entities, including
the big demigods—felt the pressure of
suffocation, as if their breathing were
being choked. Therefore they all took
shelter of the Supreme Personality of
Godhead because they were perplexed
as to what had happened.

Due to his intense meditation, Dhruva Maharaja affected
the entire planet. This again reminds us of the interconnec-
tion between all things. As Dhruva Maharaja became more
powerful within himself, he influenced the planet and even the
universe.

The Detrimental Effects of Slaughterhouses

Juliet Gellatley shows in *The Silent Ark* how livestock production is at the heart of most environmental catastrophes and even health crises. Raising animals to sell on markets and then slaughtering them adds to many problems such as acid rain, global warming, desertification, and deforestation to name a few. All of these effects are directly connected to the excessive breeding and slaughtering of livestock.[32] It takes sixteen pounds of grains and soybeans to produce one pound of beef, which means that twenty vegetarians can feed on the land that it takes to feed one meat-eater.[33] With almost half the world dealing with malnutrition, millions of these people would be able to sufficiently eat if more people followed a vegetarian diet. For this reason, some of those who often appear to have good intentions and act as religious leaders are also involved in propagating poverty on the planet by their consumption of meat. By changing their diet, they will minimize poverty and minimize the violent mentality.

If Americans alone reduced their meat consumption by just ten percent, 60 million people in the world could be fed enough to avoid starvation.[34] It takes about 4,200 gallons of water a day to feed a meat-eater in contrast to 1,200 gallons for a vegetarian according to the amount needed to feed an animal versus the amount needed to water crops.[35] Keep in mind that one of the greatest threats to human existence is a lack of water. Some statisticians predict that in the near future, countries will go to war over water just as some countries are now going to war over oil. Again, taking to a vegetarian diet can minimize the problems confronting the whole world in terms of scarcity of water. Finally, on an individual basis, those who take to a vegetarian diet are fifty percent less likely to die of heart disease and cancer, which are two of the greatest killers today.[36] Just by changing their diet, people will have a much greater chance of avoiding these major killers.

Many studies also reveal the cruelty animals must endure in the slaughterhouses, which Gellatley thoroughly exposes in her book. Just that knowledge alone should be sufficient to stop meat consumption. Furthermore, slaughterhouses also carry a karmic effect for all those involved in its maintenance. The ancient and authoritative *Manu-samhita* gives detailed information of such effects:

> According to Manu, the great author of civic codes and religious principles, even the killer of an animal is to be considered a murderer because animal food is never meant for the civilized man, whose prime duty is to prepare himself for going back to Godhead. He says that in the act of killing an animal, there is a regular conspiracy by the party of sinners, and all of them are liable to be punished as murderers exactly like a party of conspirators who kill a human being combinedly. He who gives permission, he who kills the animal, he who sells the slaughtered animal, he who cooks the animal, he who administers distribution of the foodstuff, and at last he who eats such cooked animal food are all murderers, and all of them are liable to be punished by the laws of nature. No one can create

a living being despite all advancement of material science, and therefore no one has the right to kill a living being by one's independent whims...The material world is itself a place always full of anxieties, and by encouraging animal slaughter the whole atmosphere becomes polluted more and more by war, pestilence, famine and many other unwanted calamities.

Srimad-Bhagavatam 1.7.37, purport

As explained in the *Manu-samhita*, six different activities can implicate a person in the same sin. For instance, if someone robs a bank, he might have assistants who help him. One person might help plan the crime; another person might stand at the door as a lookout; another person might drive the get-away car; and another person might take the stolen money. The police would consider each of these people guilty of some aspect of the crime. Similarly, Manu explains that six people share the *karma* involved in the killing of an animal. This shows meat-eating's serious effect on the collective *karma* of human civilization.

Acts Meant to Destroy the World

The *Srimad-Bhagavatam* describes Kali-yuga as a time in which people lack mercy, and a time of increased passion and ignorance. The killing of animals will also lead to the killing of people in war. In other words, there is an unfortunate and direct connection between the merciless slaughtering of animals and the merciless slaughtering of humans. The *Srimad-Bhaga-vatam* 4.26.5 explains:

> *asurim vrttim asritya*
> *ghoratma niranugrahah*
> *nyahanan nisitair banair*
> *vanesu vana-gocaran*

> At that time King Puranjana was very much influenced by demoniac propensities. Because of this, his heart became very hard and merciless, and with sharp arrows he killed many innocent animals in the forest, taking no consideration.

Srila Prabhupada discusses this lack of mercy in our present age known as Kali-yuga. Actually, we are more likely to find people who lack mercy rather than people who are kind, compassionate, and considerate. And even when someone seems kind and compassionate, if we study their ulterior motives, we might find that it is not genuine or consistent. The great sages understand this mood to predominate in Kali-yuga:

> When a man becomes too proud of his material position, he tries to enjoy his senses in an unrestricted way, being influenced by the modes of passion and ignorance. He is thus described as asuric, or demoniac. When people are demoniac in spirit, they are not merciful toward the poor animals. Consequently,

they maintain various animal slaughterhouses. This is technically called *suna*, or *himsa*, which means the killing of living beings. In Kali-yuga, due to the increase of the modes of passion and ignorance, almost all men are asuric, or demoniac; therefore they are very much fond of eating flesh, and for this end they maintain various kinds of animal slaughterhouses.

In this age of Kali the propensity for mercy is almost nil. Consequently there is always fighting and wars between men and nations. Men do not understand that because they unrestrictedly kill so many animals, they also must be slaughtered like animals in big wars. This is very much evident in the Western countries. In the West, slaughterhouses are maintained without restriction, and therefore every fifth or tenth year there is a big war in which countless people are slaughtered even more cruelly than the animals. Sometimes during war, soldiers keep their enemies in concentration camps and kill them in very cruel ways. These are reactions brought about by unrestricted animal-killing in the slaughterhouse and by hunters in the forest. Proud, demoniac persons do not know the laws of nature, or the laws of

God. Consequently, they unrestrictedly
kill poor animals, not caring for them
at all.

The *Bhagavad-gita* 16.9 explains how such activities will
not only create war, but will eventually create nuclear war:

etam drstim avastabhya
nastatmano 'lpa-buddhayah
prabhavanty ugra-karmanah
ksayaya jagato 'hitah

Following such conclusions, the
demoniac, who are lost to themselves
and who have no intelligence, engage
in unbeneficial, horrible works meant
to destroy the world.

The purport goes on to explain:

The demoniac are engaged in activities
that will lead the world to destruction.
The Lord states here that they are less
intelligent. The materialists, who have
no concept of God, think that they are
advancing. But according to *Bhagavad-
gita*, they are unintelligent and devoid
of all sense. They try to enjoy this
material world to the utmost limit and
therefore always engage in inventing
something for sense gratification. Such
materialistic inventions are considered

to be advancement of human civilization, but the result is that people grow more and more violent and more and more cruel, cruel to animals and cruel to other human beings. They have no idea how to behave toward one another. Animal killing is very prominent amongst demoniac people. Such people are considered the enemies of the world because ultimately they will invent or create something which will bring destruction to all. Indirectly, this verse anticipates the invention of nuclear weapons, of which the whole world is today very proud. At any moment war may take place, and these atomic weapons may create havoc. Such things are created solely for the destruction of the world, and this is indicated here. Due to godlessness, such weapons are invented in human society; they are not meant for the peace and prosperity of the world.

How Do We Really Become Vegetarian?

We would like to discuss a few last points about the consumption of vegetables for those who do consider themselves vegetarian. Some recent studies estimate that 50% of food is now being genetically manipulated which includes vegetables. Some of the genetic manipulation involves the use of animal by-products. This means that even most people who consider themselves to be vegetarian still consume meat in some form since vegetables have been manipulated with animal parts. For those trying to live a lifestyle free of the consumption of dead bodies, they will gradually have to become more conscientious about how they acquire their food. If we do not come to a point in which we can grow our own food or supervise it, we will become more and more ignorant about what is on our own table. As more vegetarians also begin to understand the dangers of what they eat, they will also want more of a guarantee in regards to the source of their food.

It is powerful to have a clear understanding of what we eat because it is not just about being vegetarian, but it is also about the way we produce, cook, and then prayerfully accept the food. As we hear how everything has energy and constantly projects energy, we see the significance of cooking in a consciousness of love and devotion because we understand its importance on our physical, psychological, and spiritual sense of well-being. How wonderful if we can plant, harvest, and then cook the foodstuff as an offering for God at a time when people are ingesting more violence in this culture of manipulation and exploitation.

The greatest terrorist that we have to fear is the terrorist in our own hearts, minds, and behaviors. This is a call for our institutions and leaders around the world to act as examples of what we expect to see in the world. It is a call to those already engaged in a life of vegetarianism to follow it more carefully. It is also a reminder that it is not just a dietary preference, but it is a matter of really trying to allow oneself to be a powerful agent of love at a time when violence has escalated to such a point that people are ready to take their own lives in order to hurt others.

Questions and Answers

Question: Is it not true that humankind is inherently evil; therefore, there will always be excessive killing of other humans as well as other species?

Answer: First we should realize that the violent tendency is an acculturation. It is not that humankind is inherently evil. The philosophies that propagate such beliefs are dangerous because they cause those who could otherwise be agents of change to not sufficiently address problems. After all, if humankind were inherently evil, we would not be able stop or arrest inhumanities to humankind. However, as we have said, in our original identity, we are *sac-cid-ananda* or full of eternity, knowledge, and bliss. We are naturally loving and compassionate. As we adjust and adapt to environments focused on unhealthy survival methods, we begin to accept that kind of lifestyle. For instance, if a person who is a very conscientious and ethical citizen takes a job with a corporation that has a culture of deviation, that same person in their attempt to function as a good worker will end up taking the mentality of the wicked environment in order to survive. Similarly, in their attempts to survive, people have become so acculturated to the environment that they end up acting harshly toward each other. They might consider exploitation and manipulation necessary for their own survival.

Recently I was counseling a prominent diplomat from Croatia who was confronted with this problem and was consequently thinking of resigning from his work in international affairs due to such corruption. With his wisdom and maturity, my advice was that he should remain in order to focus on being an agent of positive change. In this way, he could help to inspire others who would benefit tremendously from his dealings. He would be able to help protect many others who could become engulfed by the deviant, unethical environments.

Instead of thinking that we have to create a new human or change all of these negative tendencies, we really just have to revitalize the higher qualities within ourselves and others. We need to wake up from our illusion and eliminate the acculturation. And each person makes a difference. We are in a holistic universe. As each person makes a change within him or herself, it then affects the whole world. We cannot make that change if we do not realize the actual gravity of the problem in the first place. This discussion should help us revisit the gravity of our situation.

Question: Since many of the vegetables are genetically manipulated, what effect does that have on the consciousness of vegetarians who are trying to follow a healthy and ethical diet?

Answer: Just in terms of the physical body, we are all being bombarded to various degrees with toxic substances in the environment such as chemicals in soap, perfume, cologne, and even in furniture and building materials. For this reason, we see a drastic rise in cancer and other diseases that were not so prominent even fifty years ago. It means that some of these things are creating increasingly bad effects on our minds, bodies, and environments. Our conscious and physical immune systems are constantly attacked due to exposure to these chemical and meat products.

We can also consider this practice of eating flesh in terms of our judicial system. If someone commits a premeditated murder, it is not evaluated in the same way as someone who accidentally kills someone in self-defense. At the same time, a life has been taken in both cases. Similarly, in material existence, we cannot avoid killing. Just by drinking water, breathing, and walking, we are killing all types of species of life. However, we do have a duty to minimize the killing and live more naturally. We cannot exist if we do not eat, drink, or move in our environment, but we can live in a healthier physical, psychological, and spiritual way by eliminating flesh from our diet as much as possible.

Those activities that are most natural for maintaining body and soul together may also incur some sin or some death, but it is not the same. Some people can even correctly argue that vegetables are alive. It forces us to see how one material body is food for another material body, but some diets are more natural in the food chain. When we act according to the laws of nature, we will get auspicious results. If we act unnaturally, we will get more of what we already see—violence, pestilence, wars, sadness, and suffering.

Question: The *Manu-samhita* lists the six people who must accept the *karma* for killing an animal. A person who gives permission is the first individual on that list. Many countries use a democratic process of election, which means that those who vote for a person who supports slaughterhouses might also be implicated in that sin. Could you give advice in regard to this dilemma since both candidates usually support the eating of flesh?

Answer: For this reason, there are groups of people who are working hard to try to educate the masses. There is a massive movement comprised of people who understand the precarious situation on this earth right now due to ecological contamination. Such people are looking at political candidates and trying to make them aware. They are ready to support candidates who are working to make the earth a safer place. As people understand more about the consequences of their actions, many will also make changes. There are millions of vegetarians in America and in many places throughout the world. However, in most places they do not understand how the *karma* of the meat industry also plays into the culture of violence. As they understand this better, then we will begin to see people campaigning and trying to hold some of their leaders accountable in these areas.

It is quite an awesome task; however, we can start with consciousness. We start with our perception of ourselves in relation to other species, to other people, and ultimately to God. When we change our worldview and our philosophical understanding of things, many issues automatically align according to our shift in consciousness. We have already read several passages from the ancient scriptures explaining the karmic consequences of mistreating animals. The *Manu-samhita* also explains that a leader is accountable for one-sixth of the impious deeds of the people and one-fourth of the pious deeds, which can help us understand why so many of our heads of state suffer so much. They are responsible for a certain percentage of the pious activities of the citizens as well as their sins. Taking responsibility for so many people is a serious issue.

Question: We are in the last age known as Kali-yuga. In this age, it is very difficult for the inhabitants to conquer over their lower desires and passions. How does one get the strength to give up so many bad habits?

Answer: It is very difficult for many people to stop smoking. Some people even consider the addiction to cigarettes more difficult to break than the addiction to drugs or alcohol. But although all of these addictions are so overwhelming, they are activities that people have accepted and internalized to a strong extent. Just as they have accepted that addiction at some point, they now have a need to recondition and detach themselves. It starts of course with education and then replacement. Education is very necessary so that people can understand why they should replace with something different. Then from replacement, there can be a transformation. But education alone is not enough. There must be ongoing good association and other reinforcements.

For instance, why do we have hundreds of millions of people smoking although they know that smoking is hazardous to their health? It is written on all the cigarette packages and on all the advertisements, but, at the same time, hundreds of millions of people just can't wait to put a cigarette in their mouth. This is how unfortunate it is—millions of people have accepted such an unhealthy habit and have become slaves to their addictions even though they have information that it is unhealthy.

Freedom, peacefulness, and love are all connected. Conversely, control, incarceration, and addictions force people to act in unhealthy ways by controlling their lives. We can see how they are opposites. However, when someone is exposed to healthy alternatives, they can put their energy in a healthy direction. We call this *param drstva nivartate* or replacing the lower taste with the higher taste. It is not so easy to just stop an activity because we cannot become vacuums, devoid of activity. If we can access healthy replacement, we can transform that same energy. However, healthy replacements happen with knowledge, ongoing good association, and with successful role models.

Question: I have heard that some impious people also are vegetarians and take to various austerities. Sometimes such people can really confuse others.

Answer: There are some people who are engaged in sorcery and witchcraft who also imitate a pious lifestyle. They may engage in austerity and even have a vegetarian diet. However, it is quite rare because most people engaged in such activities kill animals. Generally, when people take to austerities for unhealthy reasons, they cancel out the ultimate benefit of the austerity because they are using such principles and even religiosity just to create *chala-dharma* or cheating religion. They pretend to engage in religiosity to ultimately go against religion. Some people study religion and ethics to understand how to help themselves and the world. Other people study these same principles in order to find more ways to control and abuse people. There are those who make money in order to enjoy life on a higher level and include others in their good fortune. Others simply make money in order to have more power and control. In each case, it is a matter of the consciousness of the person using the resources. The consciousness will determine whether the result is healthy or unhealthy.

People may even go to the extreme of undergoing austerities to get power in order to do evil and malicious acts. This is unfortunate, but it is a sign that austerities bring power. Someone might fast or perform a ritual just to do an evil and harmful act. That kind of person will actually suffer more than one who commits sin out of pure ignorance. The *Sri Isopanisad* explains that people and leaders who know what is proper but use their leadership for deviation are like killers of the soul, and they will suffer even more than just a normal sense gratifier.

Question: You have helped us understand the importance of vegetarianism and the advantages and disadvantages of this diet. You also described the consequential results waiting for those who kill animals. Can you clarify this even more?

Answer: According to the Vedic tradition, when someone leaves the body, they have to go to the court of Yamaraja, who is expert in evaluating each person's situation and what kind of body and environment they will have to accept in the next lifetime. Just as we have national laws established by the government, there are also universal laws. It is not difficult for those who are astute in overseeing the judgment of souls to arrange certain experiences based on their past. In this case, a person involved in animal slaughter accumulates a certain kind of *karma*. It may even lead to a point in which they have to receive some difficulties and abuse by some of the entities that they have slaughtered.

It should remind us that nothing goes unnoticed—we are accountable for all of our actions. But *karma* is not just negative; we can benefit from our healthy actions. Positive or negative *karma* does not just disappear when we finish that action. We will later receive or experience some consequence based on the initial action. It just shows how the universe is so intense and systematic. It reinforces the fact that everything affects something else, and every person influences another in some way. We are in a holistic existence.

Question: You explained that those who eat violent animals will also pick up that same mentality. In many parts of the world, people eat mostly cows, pigs, and chickens who do not kill for their food. Is the violent effect less for those who eat less violent animals?

Answer: In one sense, eating a peaceful animal such as a cow will have an even worse effect than eating a violent animal. Killing a robber is a crime, but killing an innocent citizen is even worse. So, people who eat flesh should especially not eat the cow due to spiritual principles, and physically they should avoid animals that eat abominable food. A pig will eat stool, worms, or any other edible item it comes across. That is the nature of a pig. And a boar will kill in order to acquire such abominable food. Some religious traditions forbid its followers to eat pork for this reason. They realize that the flesh of a pig can lead to all types of unhealthy worms and diseases within the body because of what the pig eats. Again, eating affects eating. Just watch a pig and you will see that it eats stool. It will go right into the slop and eat the most abominable stuff. Similarly, a vulture will eat dead bodies. Therefore, when you eat such animals, not only do you eat them, you eat what they have eaten. The cells and hormones of one animal connect with the consciousness of the animal from previous meals. This chain of connections might make you hesitate before ingesting certain types of food because you will be accepting whatever the previous entity has ingested. Everything is interconnected. Why should we make our bodies into graveyards?

From time to time when I visit some of our own farm communities where we grow our own food, I can immediately experience the wonderful difference when I digest food that has been grown organically and prepared devotionally. Most people do not have any options since they can only buy what is available in the store. And fast foods also add to so many problems, including aggressiveness and even attention deficit disorder in children. Not only are the children eating flesh, but they are also eating food prepared quickly without devotion and, in some cases, with anger. How happy do you think the people are who work for so many hours at minimum wage, almost like slaves? Where is their consciousness? Whatever fills their minds goes into the food. This is what is happening within modern day society. People are being surrounded and bombarded by violence on every level. What is the result? Obviously more and more violence.

Question: Having eaten meat throughout my childhood and adult life until I gained more knowledge, and having worked in a research lab where we used to kill animals for our studies, is there any way I can clear my consciousness now? And will any of those animals be waiting for me at the time of my death?

Answer: The cruelty towards animals in laboratories and in scientific experimentations is a serious issue drawing tremendous attention and campaigns. Millions of animals meet their deaths in that way. I faced a similar situation when I attended Princeton University. In the psychology lab we had to do experiments, and, even previously at another school, we had to dissect frogs, cats, and rats. However, I just had to let the chairman know that I could not do those experiments. I explained that I was interested in the degree, but it is against my religion. I wanted to have an alternative to the hands on work in the laboratory, and they honored my request.

Yes, we have all done many things in the past in this life and in previous lives that might embarrass us. If we could do it over again, we would probably do it differently. The Lord doesn't hold us fully accountable. Gaining knowledge and making a change by engaging in transcendental activities changes our entire *karma*. Endless reactions from past *karma* would be waiting around the corner for us, but, due to the power of devotion, our *karma* has been altered.

From a biological perspective, the influence of those cells on the body is cancelled out after a number of years. If a person has only been a vegetarian for one or two years, they carry a heavier influence, but, as the years pass, the influence will decrease more and more. This shows how the body is a machine. Consider those children raised in a spiritual community who have never been exposed to such things. Their bodies will be more geared toward lives of higher consciousness in which they can make a difference in this world through their thoughts and actions. They will add to the love rather than adopting cells and energy that cause people to increase their violence towards each other.

How wonderful it will be for world peace when we have generations of people whose lives and eating habits are an act of collective love and consciousness raising rather than a massive expression of violence to themselves, to the environment, and to others. This is an integral part of the mission and vision of the spiritual warriors. Are you ready, beloved, to join us in yet another global mission of waging peace? You might like to put the book down for several hours or a day to reflect on the implications and ramifications of what you have finished reading in this chapter. Reflect on the information we have just shared in relationship to yourself, to your family, to your country, and to the world.

Do not do to others what angers you if done to you by others.

Socrates

Chapter 8

Stop Letting So-called
Differences Create War

Working Together Towards Peace

Interestingly, most people want peace. They want to live in peaceful environments, have peaceful relationships, and enjoy peaceful exchanges with their friends and family so that they can then feel secure about themselves and their environment. We see advocates for peace all over the world, but in many cases, their actions take them in a different direction due to their violent thoughts, violent music, violent movies, violent books, violent diets, violent relationships, and their support of violent leadership. We may then wonder how we can ever have peace when the majority of people's lives revolve around violence. It is practically impossible because we reap what we sow: Whatever we do, we will get more of the same in the future. In this context, we want to discuss points in relation to unity with diversity because peace is even harder to embrace without a sense of community. We want to look at what inherently creates separation between people and also at what all people have in common that can help bring about real unity.

First consider what leads to war and what separates people from each other. What stimulates people to want to violently fight each other and to accept a life of aggression? A few of the many catalysts might include money, religion, race, ethnicity, and politics. Just these words can have such an impact that they can make community or break it. They have the ability to create a sense of unity, or they can dismantle institutions, nations, families, and marriages. Now, consider what leads to peace and the ability to co-exist harmoniously. Many of us might immediately think of qualities such as truth, righteousness, tolerance, justice, compassion, love, acceptance, and respect for others. We see that it is a list of beauty. These traits allow people to express a higher aspect of their humanity whereas divisions caused by the former list causes us to feel unvalued, disrespected, and insecure. They weaken our ability to receive and give love.

When a person is experiencing incoherence, fear, and insecurity, those emotions spill over onto those closest to the person. It is the people closest to us who suffer the most when we feel incomplete or dysfunctional due to our unmet needs. Conversely, when we feel loved, protected, and appreciated, those closest to us will also be the receivers of such positive feelings. We will bring whatever we have into each interaction and share with those closest to us. We all owe each other, especially those we love, the best of ourselves by working and improving on ourselves. In this way, they can receive a greater sense of love, affection, appreciation, and protection from us.

As interconnected human entities, we all influence each other on a daily basis. We exchange energy and consciousness at practically every moment. By looking at those things that produce war versus those things that produce peace, we see that most of our activities are geared toward war. As we begin to take inventory of our actions, we can find ways to direct them towards the goals that we want. As more individuals attain those goals, they can share a greater sense of well-being with others, especially those closest to them.

Causes of Fragmentation

Religion

When we see all of these different religions, we might wonder if God made some mistake. Why did He create so many religious doctrines, teachers, and principles that often seem to be at odds with each other? Is it that religion itself produces war? If this is true, then where there is atheism, we should see less war and conflict. However, we do not see more peace in atheistic environments. It is not just a matter of atheism or theism; it is a matter of consciousness.

Right now, religious fanaticism is engendering one of the greatest threats on the planet. Such fanaticism is increasing in all communities because of fear and insecurity. When people are insecure about their own religious alignment or identity, they feel that everyone must do exactly as they do. They need to see more people following their own path so that they can feel better about what is weak within their own consciousness. Often, they overcompensate for this weakness.

Ernest Hemingway, for example, had fanatical Catholic parents who detested his lifestyle. After some time, his mother refused to see him. Once she mailed him a cake on his birthday along with the gun that his father had used to kill himself. Another year, she wrote him a letter, explaining how she as a mother had given so much to her children. Now, just as a bank expects payback, she expected them to steadily deposit paybacks as well to keep the account in good standing. She made a list of things he must do, emphasizing that he must be determined to accept Jesus as his savior and to perform his duties to Jesus.

Religion is very powerful, and when something powerful is misused, the assault can be devastating. At the same time, when it is properly used and cherished, it can give the greatest solace because religion is about love of humanity and trying to honor the law and blessings of the Supreme Lord. When religion is dealt with superficially, it produces fragmentation. Unfortunately, people fail to see the great unity between the essential aspects of all religions. In actuality, there is one religion—service to and love of God. There may be diversity between the many different names of God and scriptures which glorify God, but, ultimately, it is based on humanity's relationship with God. All major religions emphasize that we should love God with all our heart, love our neighbor as ourselves, and understand the world to be our temporary home, for we have a higher existence than what we are presently experiencing. These are universals that reveal the unity of all people.

Race

Race has also been such an element of fragmentation. But what exactly is race? Several decades ago, some scientists claimed that only three or four major races existed. However, some studies now reveal thirty to forty possible categories. And besides race, there are hundreds and hundreds of ethnic groups. Is race really a distinct category? Can we unequivocally define race based on hair texture? No, sometimes people from the same region have more diversity in their hair texture than someone from a different background. Is race distinctly based on the color of the eyes? No, sometimes people of the same so-called race have eye differentiation. Is race defined by skin color? No, people from the same region often have a variety of skin tones. And sometimes their skin color is more similar to a person of another region than to the majority of those from their own region. Is race based on height? No. Is race based on weight? No, not at all. If a person needs a blood transfusion or organ transplant, the organ or the blood type that he or she needs is not associated with race. Someone in the same race might have a different type of blood, and people in different races might have the same blood type. Then how exactly can we define race? If it is not based on the texture of hair, color of eyes, color of skin, height, weight, intelligence, blood type, or organs, how can we define race? Race is not an absolute category.

If someone has a baby in America but then moves to Germany, the baby will adopt many characteristics based on the country, the associations, the climate, and especially the diet. The child will speak German with a perfect accent because he or she has grown up in that environment. What we call race also has to do with migration, socialization, environment, and hereditary influences. So much has to do with our present and past associations. To make such a big issue of race is another form of violence, which separates people from being whole and from being able to give and receive love. Love is based on consciousness. It is not limited to geography, ethnicity, politics, or religion. If anything, these categories cause obfuscation. They interfere because people get distracted by the physicality. They miss the chance to connect with consciousness. This planet needs more people who are accelerating and accepting higher consciousness. Regardless of gender, race, or religion, people need to go deeper. As we go deeper within, we will be able to have greater influence outside our particular group.

Needs

Psychology and anthropology explain that we are all pursuing five basic needs. According to their consciousness, people focus on different gradations of these needs. At the lowest level of consciousness, people are focused on physical needs. At the second level of consciousness, people are pursuing needs for protection. At the third level, people are pursuing needs for affiliation; at the fourth level people are pursuing needs for self-esteem; and lastly they are pursuing needs for transcendence and self-actualization.

Basically, we see so much war and violence because people are failing to accept higher aspects of themselves and are mainly pursuing just physical needs. When people get so captured by their physical needs, they will focus more on the superficial differences. They will think primarily of themselves and of their own particular desires and pleasures, consequently missing the chance to honor someone else's existence as well as their own higher existence. They miss the chance to be more wholesome in their politics, education, relationships, and in their religion since they only approach these things in a myopic way. They will have difficulty nourishing their soul or connecting with the Godhead due to their limitations. Since they approach life with limitations, they will get more and more of the same in return.

Mind and Senses

As we look at unhealthy community, we realize that we can never really achieve external peace if we do not have internal peace. Actually, the external situation is a manifestation of the internal reality. In most cases, people are at war with themselves because they are at war with their minds and senses. When the senses begin to dominate and make demands of a person who does not have a strong devotional mind or intelligence, he or she will simply become their slave. A person under the control of the senses cannot genuinely love because love is based on selflessness and attentiveness to the needs of others. When the senses enslave us, we will involve ourselves in our relationships mainly as a way to see what we can get out of them rather than what we can give and share. Many relationships are falling apart for this very reason: People have come together to rob their partners rather than to give, and they are missing the opportunity to make deeper loving connections. In some cases, they have never experienced love coming towards them; therefore, it is hard to give love because they do not know what love is. It is hard when we handle our relationships like a business. We end up focusing on what we can get rather than on what we can share. People are suffering all over the planet due to this opportunistic mentality.

Appreciating Diversity

Imagine going to hear an orchestra, only to find everyone playing the same exact instrument. Would you want to stay and hear the same note played on the same instrument for several hours? How boring it would be to visit an art gallery only to find the same picture on every wall. It would feel unnatural because it is unnatural. Every person is unique. For example, everyone has different fingerprints. We will not find two faces on this planet that are exactly alike. The electronic recording of speech is different for each person, and brain patterns are different in each person. Siblings may come from the same parents, but there are still differences. Even Siamese twins have many differences.

If your friends like a certain type of food, would you then give them a meal that they dislike? No, you would want to honor them by appreciating and respecting their desires and differences. You can create unity based on the differences that you all bring into the relationship. But, at the same time, we want unity because it is also through genuine and healthy unity that people feel more secure.

Considering how differences are an undeniable reality, let us look at some of the positive aspects of diversity. For instance, diversity is needed to produce the highest creativity and productivity because they develop out of variegatedness. It is only from diversity that we can get synergy and symbioses. When there is only conflict and adversity, 1 + 1 equals less than 1. Due to the adversity and conflict, people are having much of their humanity taken away. All parties suffer and lose something. Through compromise, 1 + 1 can equal 2. However, synergy is when 1 + 1 equals at least 2 or more. We can only have greater achievements and accomplishments when people with differences come together and allow those differences to compliment each other.

A symbiosis is the benefit of people bringing their differences together in order to produce greater results than each individual could produce on their own. It is through diversity that people can share and bring about more creativity, productivity, synergy, and symbiosis when it is aligned with unity. However, it is still true that too much diversity will lead to anarchy because everyone will then do whatever he or she wants without respecting or sufficiently complimenting their neighbors or colleagues.

Artificial Conformity

Excessive unity, which can stem from fundamentalism, can also have drawbacks. If everyone dressed, talked, and walked in the same way, the world would be a pretty dreary place. Excessive unity is artificial because it doesn't allow people to express their individuality. It stifles creativity and opens people to abuse and fundamentalism from their leaders. It doesn't permit people to be themselves and to be valued based on who they are.

Several years ago on a flight from Ghana to Nigeria, one of the stewardesses who had seen me on a recent television program came up to me and said, "I heard you speak on television and you are quite an intelligent person, but you are so lost." I just smiled at her and said, "Well, maybe you can help me." She replied, "God is Jehovah, and only 144,000 people will attain heaven. You have to know the truth." She went on and on. Then I asked her, "What is your truth, and what are the principles that you live by?" She mentioned certain principles and I asked, "Is it possible for me to still get Jehovah's mercy if I live by those very same principles, but don't attend your specific building of worship and don't call God by this specific name?" She said that it would not qualify a person because the individual must be recognized under Jehovah's order. Then I asked, "What about a person who is part of your society and who is recognized, but who doesn't follow the principles. And what about someone else who is in another society but follows all of the principles of your religion? What is the position of a person who is not recognized specifically as a Jehovah's Witness, but who actually follows the essence of all of your principles very strictly? Is there any hope for them?" She said no. However, I asked these questions to help her reflect on her viewpoints. Basically, from her perspective, a cheating person in her society who doesn't follow any of the principles is closer to salvation than a person in another organization who serves God faithfully and who follows all of the principles rigidly.

In one sense, I also considered her to be a very nice and intelligent person, but unfortunately she was very caught up in dogma. After I presented the points and saw that she would not hear, I thanked her. She told me that she would send a book to my temple to read. However, since she had already closed her mind, she was not at a level where she could understand. Therefore, instead of putting her into a situation in which she might make offenses or get overloaded, I just said a few basic points to plant some seeds in her mind.

Sometimes if the egos are too strong, a person will not be able to hear because the discussion will simply turn into ego versus ego. I certainly did not want to come to the level of attacking someone for their participation in another group. At the same time, I could not allow her to speak so strongly without at least offering another perspective on her arguments. I also had to consider that God arranged the opportunity for me to serve Him by trying to glorify Him. A person does not have to be argumentative; it is a matter of appreciating and communicating to others the supreme position of the Lord. We should always see every situation as a chance to glorify the Lord, and the Lord will take notice.

When there is actual love rather than sentimentalism, we will say what is necessary in a way that does not disturb the ego. It still might cause a disturbance, but out of love, we address the issue as a service. On the other hand, when there is sentimentalism, we may be afraid to speak truth because we have to make friends, and we have to be concerned about our image and other superficial considerations. We want to be warriors, engaged in spiritual warfare. We have to be ready to live the truth even if we have to live it in the minority. Ultimately, if we take that philosophy to its fullest extent, and speak and live the truth, then we can depend on the mercy of God and not be overly attached. That is real faith in God. We want to become spiritual warriors armed with compassion, which means that we want to abandon arrogance. At the same time, we do not want to be wimps or cowards, afraid of trying to grow by addressing troublesome issues. If we see a way to grow from a situation or to help someone else grow from an exchange, we want to honor that.

In some situations, we should be careful how we address people. In other words, there are some people who will not be able to maintain a sense of alignment if they step too far outside of what they are comfortable with. For instance, although we say that sectarianism is bad, some religionists will not be ethical at all if they don't think that they have the only truth. Even though it is an immature stage, at their level of evolution they almost need to think that their theology or branch of a religion is the only way to attain salvation. That belief will help them remain free from grossly sinful activities. Although that type of mindset should not be accepted as the all in all, sometimes people need to function in this way at their state of evolution. Nevertheless, Srila Bhaktivinoda writes in this regard, "If even to develop one's own firm faith, one accepts that the teachings of the *acaryas* of his own country are better than the teachings of *acaryas* from other countries, one should not preach such a quarrelsome and controversial doctrine. No auspiciousness results from this" (*Sri Caitanya-siksamrta* 1/1).

Fundamentalism is actually a very heavy avenue of attack on people because it is a tremendous means for mind control. It gets people to exert their full energy in ways that can be very destructive. As there is an increase in the study of cults, terrorism, and mind control, hopefully people will also increase their understanding of how to be a spiritual person while at the same time relevant. Otherwise, the whole pursuit of God consciousness remains merely theoretical. Spiritualists must be compassionate, maintain their own principles, and also share their principles. Unfortunately, as this emphasis on terrorism and cults increases, there will also be more of an emphasis on fundamentalism. As people's insecurity increases, they begin grabbing in a sectarian way. We will see more branches of Islam attacking other branches of Islam, more branches of Christianity attacking other sects, and more cults such as hate groups who simply want to destroy others. When people with this mindset have personal problems, they want to find someone to scapegoat. They blame the Asians, the Jews, the Muslims, the Christians, and so on. This creates a greater sense of scatteredness, and the real problems do not get addressed.

When fundamentalists hear something that differs from how they have been indoctrinated, they strike out immediately. For instance, fundamentalist Christians vehemently claim that people have to accept the blood of Christ or they will be damned and lost at the time of judgment. They come up with these kinds of propositions without realizing that such a philosophy is insensitive because it denies so many other people who are seriously involved in spiritual pursuits on other paths. Such people might even be more serious in their dedication to their own path than those who criticize or condemn them. This kind of dogma and fundamentalism is one of the ways in which negative entities have tried to destabilize religious institutions. Some of these people are actually saboteurs of religion who have entered into spiritual communities with the idea of dismantling them.

Michael Baigent and Richard Leigh, who authored *The Dead Sea Scrolls Deception*, provide valuable insight on this topic of sectarianism and fanaticism:

> The Dead Sea Scrolls offer a new perspective on the three great religions born in the Middle East. The more one examines those religions, the more one will discern not how much they differ, but how much they overlap and have in common—how much they derive from essentially the same source—and the extent to which most of the quarrels between them, when not precipitated by simple misunderstanding, have stemmed less from spiritual values than from politics, from greed, from selfishness and the presumptuous arrogance of interpretation. Judaism, Christianity and Islam are all, at present, beset by a resurgent fundamentalism. One would like to believe—though this may be too much to hope for—that greater understanding of their common roots might help curb the prejudice, the bigotry, the intolerance and fanaticism to which fundamentalism is chronically prone.[37]

Actually, sectarianism not only attacks other religions, but it attacks one's own system as well. The Koran 6:108 states, "Revile not those unto whom they pray beside Allah lest they wrongfully revile Allah through ignorance. Thus unto every nation have We made their deed seem fair." This means that believers in the Koran may relate to the Lord as Allah, but they should not abuse those who call on a different name of God. People who think that they can access divinity only through their particular name of God are literally sabotaging the spiritual paradigm and are even dishonest about their own theology. The point of religion and spirituality is to develop love of God—a point which Srila Prabhupada emphasizes in a speech given on August 18, 1974 in Vrndavana, India:

> If we actually want peace, *samprasidati*, then we must learn how to surrender to the Supreme Lord. It doesn't matter through which process. Either by Hindu religion or Muslim religion or Christian religion, it doesn't matter. We want to see that everyone is becoming a perfect lover of God. This is our definition of God. It may be, due to circumstantial changes in the country, the Muslim religion may be little different from Hindu religion so far the ritualistic ceremonies are concerned, but actually we want to see whether you have advanced in the matter of loving God. Not that 'Superficially I am very advanced in religion, but I do not know how to love.' This is the test. *Sarve sukhino bhavantu.* This is the test. A devotee wants to see that everyone is happy. It doesn't matter

whether he is a Hindu or a Muslim or a
Christian. It doesn't matter. We want to
see that everyone is happy.

If everyone happily follows their prescribed bona fide
theology, they will get fantastic results and experience deeper
and deeper levels of consciousness.

Unity with Diversity

Problems arise with both excessive individuality and with
the denial of individuality. Too much unity means forced
conformity or repression, and too much diversity means
anarchy and chaos. Such situations are breeding grounds for
war. We previously listed a few categories that will produce
either war or peace. Unhealthy diversity in which people are
not honoring each other's existence and not appreciating what
is universal to all of us will produce conflict and will even
dismantle civilizations and communities. On the other hand,
forced conformity will also lead to a similar result. It will just
take longer because people will agree to conform under pressure in fear of retribution. However, their creativity and individuality will be repressed, and, at some point, they will begin
to want to experience what is natural to their particular human
experience. They will want to be appreciated and valued based
on their own individual needs and desires.

Nonsectarianism does not mean that people must abandon
their identity—identity is inherent in each of us and is a natural
part of existence. Every organization has a certain atmosphere,
but, at the same time, it is dangerous when an organization or
group of people are so dogmatic that they cannot appreciate

truth when it comes in a different form. When we are not sharper in our spiritual investigation and spiritual attunement, our faith weakens and our potency also weakens. If a person does not have a strong belief system, it will lead to incoherence, which will cause a lack of focus or absorption in any area, secular or spiritual. When a person focuses, whether they are a lawyer, architect, or spiritualist, they will have more potency to move through situations. It will help a person to be more wholesome and productive. When a person does not penetrate the surface of their belief system and maintains superficial conceptions, then naturally they will feel insecure when faced with differing conceptions. Naturally that person will strike out and defend themselves against anything that differs from their own conceptions.

For some people, if they do not have distinct things that they can have war over, they will find a difference that will lead to in-groups and out-groups, in order to create fertile ground for disputes. We can look all over the world and find people trying very hard to create differences. Sometimes the differences are very overt such as a rare language or religion, but, in other cases, the differences are minimal. The people might have gone to the same school, look alike, talk the same language, have the same religion, and have the same eating habits, but because one group lives in the North and one group lives in the South, they allow this difference to be a catalyst for creating war. Howard Bloom, in his book *The Global Brain*, gives an insightful perspective on this impetus to separate:

> One of the most powerful diversity generators in today's humans and animals is a force Freud called "the narcissism of minor difference." For

simplicity's sake, we'll refer to it
as "creative bickering." Individuals
extremely similar to one another find
some petty distinction, then raise
unholy hell about it. To paraphrase
[sociologist] Emile Durkheim, a
community of saints will classify a
bit of lint on the heavenly robes as
intolerable, and will viciously hound
those who aren't lint-free. Eventually
the supposedly unkempt may seek out
others with a sloppy bent, and wall
themselves off as a separate sect sworn
to a messy destiny. A primitive form of
this impulse far precedes us hominids.
The closer insects are to each other
in physical form and habits, the more
likely they are to be enemies.[38]

As we honor the diversity while simultaneously connecting
with a genuine nucleus that accesses unity, the diversity will
compliment each person and produce synergy. The diversity
will allow each person to experience individualized love and
will increase their ability to give more of themselves in a loving
way. Otherwise, we will see more people shut down emotion-
ally and psychologically. Actually, the greatest unity resides
in being cognizant of who we really are. As spiritual entities
undergoing material experiences, we have a physical body
which we might compare to a garment or a costume. Although
we are using these bodies at this particular time, we are all
much more than just these temporary machines. The ancient
teachings and great scriptures of the world teach us that we

are much more than just the physical presence. Greater experiences are accessible for us as we begin to connect more with our real identity. We are just travelers temporarily occupying this particular vehicle or body.

Each vehicle has a specific orientation, which we cannot deny. We take proper care of the body so that it can function well, but we simultaneously acknowledge its limited and temporary nature. People are making their bodies and institutions the all-in-all. They are living as if nothing exists beyond this limited realm; consequently, they are overly involved in excessive attachment to a temporary machine.

Of course, we do need to take care of the body, and we need to recognize our differences. We cannot have unity without recognizing diversity; therefore, we do not say that all people are the same, nor should they be. If we try to put everyone into the same category, we then minimize individuality. Nevertheless, we realize that all people have similar needs and desires. All people are similar in that they are ultimately spiritual entities. We can appreciate and honor each other's existence by honoring the differences. As we appreciate the differences, then we connect together through our similarities.

We will continuously find reasons to have war if we do not have peace within ourselves. As we develop more peace within ourselves, we can find ways to extend our peace and tranquility to others. This is what we need. We need to have a greater sense of well-being and peace within ourselves. Then the slight differences between individuals will not create a distraction, and people will not produce unhealthy conformity, nor will they branch out into unhealthy diversity or anarchy. Rather, people will be able to honor diversity, realizing that it is ultimately spiritual. However, as we maintain this consciousness of separation, we will spend lifetime after lifetime undergoing so many experiences in different types of bodies. We can perpetually engage in the drama of separation and fragmentation.

Questions and Answers

Question: Are you still working directly with the United Nations in your efforts to try to help create more of a just and peaceful world?

Answer: Not as much as in previous years. Some years back, I did some work in New York, but mostly in Geneva and Switzerland. I had opportunities at least two or three times every year for extended periods of time to interact with many diplomats. However, I am a celibate monk, so even though I am active in many different communities in the world and on different boards, my life is really one of contemplation. So, at one point, I decided that exposure to this tremendous bureaucracy was putting too much strain on my life. Sometimes after I had returned from four or five months of traveling, I would find that one of the people with whom I had associated had died from hypertension or stress because of the very intense politics and finances. Many times people's hands are tied, which also happens to the presidents of different nations. They sometimes can only make small improvements in many areas because they are surrounded by bureaucracies. Many of the diplomats I counseled were bound up in this way; stagnated by bureaucracies. Each year, I still meet with diplomats, prime ministers, presidents of countries, celebrities, etc., but I also reach out more now to the masses of people through my television shows and books, which have been translated into thirteen languages.

Question: What is your perspective on the current situation between the United States and Iraq?

Answer: We are all a part of it and we have all been listening to the news, wondering what the cowboy is up to next and what consequences U.S. foreign policy will create down the road. It is about influence, money, and business. It is about stationing strong military influence in that part of the world. It is about oil. It is about power and dominance. It had little to do with weapons of destruction although it appeared to be the main concern. This issue distracted people, but that is basic politics. Politics, however, does not have to be exploitive and manipulative, but when people of lower consciousness are in positions of power, they find ways to exploit whatever position they have.

Right now there are also people of lower consciousness who act as religious leaders. They are hiding behind religion while they have other agendas. They enter into religious communities and take on roles of leadership just to create fragmentation in order to move towards their own self-invested goals. It is not that religion itself is a distraction or an evil imposition on humanity, but evil or exploitive people can enter commerce, education, politics, and also religion.

You should not be intimidated. This is your world; you are making the decisions right now with every choice that you make in your own life. You students are determining what the future will be because every leader of any organization was also a student or child at some point. Based on some of their aspirations and socializations, they made certain choices and now think in a certain way as a result of those experiences. Hopefully some of the things that you hear in these kinds of discussions will help you as you go out into the world of work, as you take positions in different places, as you become parents, or as you become leaders. Hopefully it will help you to lead with integrity, and to function based on valuing others. It will hopefully help you structure your life in such a way that you will be chaste to your own path while appreciating others who might think and act a little differently.

Live in a way that your life is your message. In this way, your lives can encourage people to be more authentic with themselves, and to examine just who and what they really are. Let us accelerate our own productive activities in order to guarantee a better world for our children and for the young adults.

Question: In terms of finding or maintaining inner peace, both diet and meditation are important. Do you also recommend any forms of *yoga*?

Answer: Yes, diet is important as well as our environment. All of these play a part. We notice that we feel very drained in some environments while other environments leave us feeling peaceful. Some music might make us feel agitated and even sad. Everything produces different types of vibrations, which stimulate our consciousness accordingly. We should look closer for quality so that we can associate in environments and with people that will stimulate our minds positively. What we see, where we go, and what we hear all send messages to the consciousness.

Chanting, meditating, and praying in good association are very important. If we take a bath, we clean the physical body, but engaging in prayer, meditation, and chanting cleanses the internal faculties. Reading is very important since it can help us uncover some of our creativity, and increase our understanding of our actual identity. Our reading habits can also degrade our consciousness, so we should focus on reading material that enhances self-actualization and transcendence. What we are really saying is that every aspect of our existence has some influence on us. We should be more selective about what influences we accept. Most important is the type of association that we have. Whatever we do, we learn a lot from the people in our environments. We bring what we have into an environment while others also bring what they have.

All of these aspects are extremely important. We do not want to just act mechanically because we will then subject ourselves to the influences in our immediate environment. Sometimes the immediate stimulation and environment is not what we want to embrace. A thoughtful person is constantly working on themselves by strengthening and recharging themselves. Even when they go into environments that are hostile and degrading, it will not bother them too deeply because they come into that environment with love and strength. When they leave, they recharge themselves by reading, diet, music, prayers, and chanting. This allows them to once again fortify themselves against more attacks in the future. Otherwise, even people with higher consciousness will start to get diminishing returns. They might have good intentions, but, as they go out and interact, the negative energy will just drain them. As they get drained, they will get weaker and weaker. As they get weaker, they lose their own individuality along with their higher values and principles.

Most people just blindly follow whatever fads and normative patterns are currently predominating. Since their basic needs for survival distract them, the average person has little time to think. Sometimes people are purposely put into that type of situation due to the influence of globalization and centralization. Many people are now losing the luxury of deep thought. Commercialization and the media are force-feeding people who plug themselves in on a daily basis. When they do have some time for leisure, they are so tired that they just sleep.

People who do not develop higher consciousness will end up like robots who follow the norms. This is unhealthy conformity since people are not able to express their individuality. When they do, they get harassed. Some places have this herd mentality to such an extent that people trying to lead ethical and spiritual lives will stand out. Others will make them feel uncomfortable. People who are not strong will not be able to act upon their individuality. They will just merge into the group because it is a comfortable space for them. They will move without thinking because everyone else is moving the same way. Unfortunately, people are becoming easier and easier to control. There is an attempt to get all people to think similarly. When this happens, a few small adjustments can get a mass of people to follow one alignment. Sinister forces want this to happen because it then becomes easier to dominate and control the masses. Again, this is the danger of unhealthy conformity.

Question: I want to focus on spirituality and consciousness in my life, but the people around me who I really care about do not have the same interests. It seems that if they don't see it for themselves, I can do nothing to affect them. I see them come home from work with no time to think and, as you said, they just fall asleep. It is the same pattern day after day. So, I don't know how to get through to my family members and especially my mother in ways that would most benefit them.

Answer: For most people, it is very hard to break out of that monotony. Some are even afraid of change because the monotony has become their identity. Some people are afraid

to slow down and think because when they do become intro-
spective, they have to think too much. When they really start
thinking about their lives, they become depressed. So, even
when they have a chance for a little silence, they will turn on
the radio or television to distract them. Unfortunately, many
people operate in this way.

Nevertheless, as you develop a greater sense of love and
peace within yourself, that will spill over onto your family
members. Your mother has her own free will just as you have
yours; therefore, the best that you can do is to try to share
what you are experiencing with her, realizing that she loves
and cares about you just as you love and care about her. She
is also a product of heredity and socialization just as you are a
product of your heredity. Her socialization has been different,
but you can bring something different back into the house. Just
go on trying to grow in your own life without being conde-
scending towards her, but, from time to time, try to reach her
in a wonderful way by letting her know how much you care
for her, and how much you want to see her take better care of
herself also.

We all know so many people who live a very mechanical
life. As they get older and older, they start looking back sadly
because they realize that they have done things just to acquire
commodities that are no longer as important to them. They have
lived their lives according to what other people wanted them
to do. Or they have acted in ways that prevented them from
ever realizing who they are. Years might pass like this until
one day death takes them away. Everything that they acquired
and valued as important will then vanish because everything
material leaves us almost as fast as we get it. This is why we
must look closer at our lives, our families, and our positions
as spiritual warriors who are dynamic in waging peace rather
than war.

No one of you is a believer until he desires for his brother that which he desires for himself.

Sunnah (Islam)

Chapter 9

A Few Extraordinary People Can Save Civilization

It Only Takes a Few People to Change the World

What is our essential purpose and duty on this particular planet and in these bodies? We see so many varieties of bodies on this earth such as insects, birds, fish, mammals, and humans to name a few. Even within each species of life, there is so much variety and difference. However, the human form is unique. Although all bodies, both animal and human, are absorbed in eating, sleeping, mating, and defending, the human form offers a rare opportunity not found in other species. In the human form, we have a higher level of cognizance and the ability to gain knowledge. We have the chance to ask, "Who am I and why am I here? What am I supposed to do while I am here? If this is not my permanent home, where is my home and how can I return?" Anyone who is away from home is not fully

245

connected to their essence or associated with their highest level of pleasure. We want to look deeper into these questions and especially research the location of our real home.

Spiritual life involves growth and discovery. It is a culture, not just a philosophy, which involves the way we eat, sleep, mate, and defend. It involves our entire existence. Therefore, I particularly want to discuss topics that can enable us to find out our true purpose on this planet. Not only do we want to create a revolution in our own lives, but we also want to affect the entire world. It does not require many people to make wonderful changes. As a matter of fact, Margaret Mead, a top anthropologist, said, "Never believe that a few caring people can't change the world. For, indeed, that's all who ever have." Revolutions happen through the efforts of a few people. Those who follow the Lord in this material world may only comprise a small number, but they are backed up by the greatest connection—God. As spiritual warriors, we can make a difference at this crucial time in world history.

Indications of the Demise of a Civilization

There are ten basic indicators of the fall of a community or civilization as given by J. Bradley Keena in his essay, *Ten Sign's of a Culture's End*.[39] History continues to repeat itself, so we can reflect on these points to understand the current predicament of our own civilization. It is often very important to have the ability to recognize the negative so that we can move it far away from ourselves and weed it out of our community. We will see that all these items are relevant to our community today and in the world in which we live. The following ten factors show signs of the decline of a culture:

1. *A society that no longer worships or acknowledges God.* In the recent past, children could pray in school. Now, if a teacher brings prayer or scripture into the schools, students or parents might confront the principal or even sue the school. These laws minimize the fact that we are part of a theistic world. It sees knowledge and education as separate from spirituality. We have top universities all over the world and few seminaries or departments that seriously study religion. The seminaries are often situated away from the city. Many people assume knowledge is sectarian and can be cultivated outside of a spiritual connection. They believe that we only need material education in order to function better in this hostile world. They ultimately view people as animals anyhow; therefore, they send some of the animals who want to learn more about a romantic, idealistic conception of God to a separate department to investigate.

2. *Decline of the family.* The family is a microcosm of the community. When the family unit is in disarray, it will lead to an unhealthy civilization and fragment people's understanding and appreciation of healthy family life. In America, some sources estimate that it takes $300,000 to raise one child, which does not include university. You add the cost for a good university education and it will come easily to $400,000. These high expenses make it more appealing for many to not have children, and when they do, to abort, abandon, or put them up for adoption. In many families today with children, both parents work, and the children sit all day in front of the one-eyed monster—the television. All the nonsense that pours into their minds fragments the family even more.

Approximately sixty percent of marriages in America currently end in divorce, and the percentage is higher in other parts of the world including some of the CIS countries. This indicates how many people feel that they should not be held accountable to their vows. We now have no-fault divorce, which makes it easy for partners to lack accountability. In some of the so-called developed countries such as Sweden and Denmark, marriage is considered to be archaic. It is not so easy to find a church in most of these places although the theaters, casinos, and bars are quite accessible. These are people's present day shrines. The most gorgeous buildings in many Western cities are banks and insurance companies. Their leaders have expertly created a culture of greed and materialism. People no longer feel any necessity to come together and honor each other's existence because they are more caught up in the "take" society.

3. *Society's low view of life.* We hear more and more about abortions, assisted suicide, and partial birth abortions, which are legal in many places. Within a few weeks and months of pregnancy, doctors can detect a heartbeat, brain waves, and even the gender. However, this does not stop people from discarding the unborn baby, considering it to be merely blood and tissue. The quality of life means less and less. People are ready to discard the elderly by simply shoving them away in homes for the aged. Besides ruthlessly destroying life or devaluing the elderly, scientists are even manipulating life through cloning and altering the genes in the body.

4. *The prevalence of base and immoral entertainment.* We, as modern day people, are enjoying ourselves to death. According to *U.S. News and World Report*, there were 40,000 sex-oriented websites on the Internet in 2000, and the number is growing every day.[40] It is one of the biggest growth industries. Much of the current popular music is very degrading toward women, family, and authority, and many of the movies are saturated with violence and death. Instead of actors playing the roles of doctors or nurses, some shows even go into the hospitals to video real people undergoing trauma, because people do not just want to be entertained by actors any more; they want to see the gruesome blood, anger, and fear.

In ancient Rome, gladiators would literally fight to the death, an event highly enjoyed by the spectators. The people engaged in such heavy, gross sense gratification that they were enjoying themselves to death. In some cases, the wealthy would eat and then vomit in royal spittoons so that they could eat more. Similarly, immoral entertainment is currently increasing in popularity on the television, in music, and in the theaters.

5. *Increase of violent crime among young people.* We see gangs developing everywhere and could compare certain parts of cities to battle zones. People in the medical field know the amount of trauma developing because people are getting so wounded physically and mentally. On the West Coast of the United States, a so-called sport known as extreme fighting is becoming more popular. People literally bang each other on the head with garbage cans, bats, sticks, and so on. It involves real blood, and enthusiasts watch to see who will get knocked out first, fall into a

coma, or even die. This is gradually spreading throughout America.

6. *Declining middle class.* Basically the middle class is becoming more and more poverty stricken. We see in our society the upper class and then the poor or people who are one paycheck away from poverty. When civilization has less people in the middle class, it means that the cheating has become so intense that the majority of people are just struggling. Even though they are supposedly working according to the standards, they are struggling and suffering. Most people are simply working hard for someone else to make money.

7. *Insolvent government.* The bankruptcy of governments, not just of individuals or businesses, indicates a serious crisis. This type of crisis engendered the French Revolution. Many great falls of civilizations happen when the government cannot carry out its promises. People begin to see that the government does not have secure arrangements for their well-being.

8. *A government that lives off of society's moral decay.* Imagine the effect on our children who constantly see how the world is a big lie. Leaders give all kinds of promises but rarely keep them. It is time for people to walk their talk and to find ways to bring more inclusion into an environment already full of confusion. Governments encourage and support all kinds of illicit activities like organized gambling, prostitution, and slaughterhouses. Politicians talk about the welfare of the people while instituting policies that encourage degradation.

9. *The ruling class loses its will—counterfeit leadership.*
Real leaders make great people and do great things for
the people. It does not matter whether it is religious,
cultural, educational, or political, we are finding more and
more counterfeit leaders who speak one way and then act
differently. Counterfeit leaders are interested in their own
achievements and have tremendous ulterior motives.

We constantly hear now that a person's private life
should be separate from his or her public life and that
we should not try to mix them. What does this mean? If
a man batters his wife in private, how can we accept him
as respectable in public? If a person minimizes life by
cheating and abusing their children and family, how is
the leader going to take care of dependents who fill all
the cities of the nation? The leader is the same person
in private and public. Your private life is the real you;
your public life indicates your ability to perform well.
Counterfeit leadership is leadership devoid of principle-
centeredness, a service attitude, and character. This type
of counterfeit leadership indicates the fall of civilization.
My books, *Leadership for an Age of Higher Consciousness: Volume I* and *Volume II*, go into great detail about
what constitutes authentic leadership.

10. *The failure of the people to see what is happening.* In the
midst of these societal problems, people continue to think
that somehow they are being protected, their welfare is a
major priority, and that all is well. As people's civic rights
are being taken away, people continue smiling, thinking
everything is alright. Propaganda and lies begin to control
people more and more. Centralization and monopolies
take away freedoms, but instead of the masses being
alarmed, they welcome such "progress" with happiness.

Preachers of Materialism and Consumerism

Some of the teachers on this planet have helped to create these situations, and their teachings have infiltrated the consciousness of the people. By increasing our awareness of their influence, we can find ways to release ourselves from their shackles. We have teachers and philosophers such as Francis Bacon who had a major impact on this planet through his ideas, which promoted the separation of nature from God. He opened up an avenue which views science as supreme. Rather than working with nature and understanding the real proprietor of nature, he promoted the concept of humankind conquering over nature. People somehow think that their lower nature is more profound than the universal nature belonging to the Lord. The eternal soul is the same in quality with God but different in quantity. We must understand that our physical bodies are just external garments and separate from the soul:

dehino 'smin yatha dehe
kaumaram yauvanam jara
tatha dehantara-praptir
dhiras tatra na muhyati

As the embodied soul continuously passes, in this body, from boyhood to youth to old age, the soul similarly passes into another body at death. A sober person is not bewildered by such a change.

Bhagavad-gita 2.13

The Bible also explains in 1 Corinthians that we have a

terrestrial body and a celestial body—the terrestrial body is separated from God. It is not flesh and blood that returns to the Kingdom of God. Then what aspect of us returns to the Lord? It is the celestial body, the eternal soul. We are much greater than just our beautiful clothes, cars, and houses. We are more beautiful than we can possibly imagine; therefore, let that internal beauty come out. These great teachers of oppression and illusion want to prevent people from accessing their greatness. We want to understand what they have brought onto this planet in order to recondition ourselves and reach the internal greatness dormant within each of us. If we read about philosophers such as Francis Bacon, we need to read more scrutinizingly so that we can bring a real sense of unity into our spiritual lives.

Another propagator, Adam Smith, taught that society develops properly by laying a foundation of greed, prompting people to buy what they do not need. He did a good job because people now run to malls every day, spending endless hours acquiring so-called necessities. Unfortunately, some parents do not spend nearly as much time with their own children. He has accomplished the tremendous task of causing us to think that, in order to attain happiness, we really need many material commodities. Technology reinforces this mindset of greed because everyone wants to keep up with the other person. However, we know of someone much greater than Adam Smith. Just as spiritual warriors are eager to reveal the deviation and energize people to move forward in their spiritual lives, there are other personalities who will do anything to sabotage religion and devotion to God. Just as the spiritual warriors are eager to wage peace, those of gross lower consciousness are fixed at waging war.

Charles Darwin, another well-known teacher of the 19th century, said, "The evolution of the human race will not be accomplished in the ten thousand years of tame animals, but in the million years of wild animals, because man is and will always be a wild animal." Animals must constantly struggle to see who is the strongest and greatest in combat. He said that sophisticated animals are only territorially conscious and try to exploit for their own aggrandizement. Therefore, the most successful are those who accept their animalistic tendencies and put all of their energy into acting accordingly. Since he had this type of animal mentality, he projected it onto everyone else. He was empowered for destruction. These people have made a huge assault on human spiritual growth.

Millions of people have honored the ideas of Karl Marx. He also saw people as animals but considered the distribution of commodities to the masses as most important. He wanted to get rid of the classes in order to make this mass distribution possible. If people work like donkeys and animals, they will resort to antitheism. He considered religion to be the opium of the people. He felt that one day his vision would be successful—no classes and no spiritualists. Consequently, society would lack a brain. When the masses come together, it creates a crude crowd mentality, which makes people act in unhealthy ways. His idea of successful human development meant that everyone would analyze the world through dialectic materialism. Basically, it is all about ridding society of classes in terms of the spiritual pursuit and putting the idea of God farther and farther in the background. The more society gets rid of the God conception and the spiritualists, the more it tries to kill the idea of the Godhead. When society tries to kill religion, it means that it is giving life to the deviant culture, and life and encouragement to the tyrants. He propagated this through books and other types of coalitions to try and bring people away from their connection with the Lord.

Machiavelli, although more gross, also felt that humans are animals, and that selfishness is good. He taught that one should beg, borrow, or steal but "get yours." He encouraged people to manipulate and exploit others for their own benefit. At universities and business schools all over the world, many people read this philosophy and accept it as very significant. Sigmund Freud went on to say that everyone basically wants to have an affair with their mother or father, and he did not sufficiently appreciate self-actualization. Imagine the type of people writing books and influencing the world. My alma mater cost almost $40,000 a year just to scrutinize this kind of garbage.

We Cannot Cheat God

Interestingly, many Americans profess to be religious and seemingly adhere to a specific religious tradition while still acting ridiculously and thinking that they can get away with their sinful behaviors. Let us approach this topic in an unusual way by teaching from one of the materialists' bibles—*Newsweek*. When the materialists begin to preach to us and come to the same conclusions as the spiritualists, we cannot help but recognize the pervasiveness of spirituality and the obvious realities.

Newsweek reported that almost twenty percent of Americans believe the end of the world will come in their lifetime. In other words, 36 million people consider that civilization will end in the coming decades.[41] Forty percent believe it will end in the Battle of Armageddon between Jesus and the Anti-Christ. Twenty percent of those people believe that the Anti-Christ is now on the planet. Almost seventy percent believe they will go to heaven, and three percent believe they will go to hell.[42] No wonder so many of the people who profess to be religious do not operate on spiritual culture for many do not see a need to go deeper because they feel they are already properly situated.

As we said earlier, more people are reading religious self-help books in several countries. It is just that people need to take the lessons and messages more serious, and those who accept a religious lifestyle should be more authentic. There are sincere people who recognize the seriousness of our current time period. Whether they follow Islam, Christianity, Buddhism, Hinduism, or Judaism, they see events unfolding according to prophecies in their own scriptures. On the other hand, those who oppose theism are very forcefully expanding the culture of sense gratification and degradation. Only about three percent of those people believe that they will be held accountable. It is amazing that people acknowledge the seriousness of the times but still continue to act sinfully. Many of the seventy percent of the people think in this way. Obviously, some of the seventy percent are genuine and accurate in their evaluation, but more than likely, most are of a lower standard.

We understand that God cannot be cheated so easily. He monitors all of our actions and He does not have favorites. He is not concerned with what part of the world we live in, how old we are, or what gender we have; rather, He is concerned with what we do and who we are. Nevertheless, although seventy percent of the people acknowledge the existence and greatness of the Supreme Lord, those who deviate and lack account-ability reveal their perception of themselves even more. This raises a serious issue. The more we know, the more we are held accountable to act according to that knowledge. We have heard the maxim, "When much is given, much is expected." When we have knowledge and do not act properly, we will suffer even graver consequences. At this time in the world, we have so much knowledge available and so many opportunities to use that knowledge in a healthy way, but, in most cases, we are using it to deny our accountability to God's law. Instead, we foolishly try to run away from His jurisdiction, thinking that we can run faster than God Himself.

The materialistic prophets encourage us to think that we can in fact outrun the Lord. Along with the teachers, preachers, and servants of the Lord who work very hard, there are servants of Satan, *maya*, and sin who also work very hard at promoting degradation. Many of them take fewer vacations than the spiritualists. And what do you think they do when some of us take vacations or act hypocritically? When a spiritualist speaks one way but acts another, and has knowledge but fails to act upon it, the servants of *maya* or illusion will act more aggressively in trying to drag him or her to their side. Knowledge will naturally lead to certain alignments. However, we must decide in which direction we wish to travel. Do we want to align ourselves with the servants of the Lord, or with the servants of oppression, degradation, and incarceration? Do we want to wage war or wage peace? The recruitment of members constantly persists on all sides.

Hypocrisy sabotages the mission of the servants of the Lord. When those who work for Him then try to cheat Him without fulfilling their own promises, it sends a message to the world that God is unkind and does not fulfill His promises. It causes many people to accept cheating as proper and to consciously or unconsciously accept that God is not truly reciprocating on merit. We do not understand the conception of God held by many of these seventy percent of people. We do not understand their conception of God who they try to cheat through deviation, sense gratification, lust, and greed. As Michael Ellner, a certified hypnotherapist, reports, "Everything is backwards;

everything is upside down. Doctors destroy health, lawyers destroy justice, universities destroy knowledge, governments destroy freedom, the major media destroy information, and religions destroy spirituality."

Releasing the Ordinary, Embracing the Extraordinary

We want to eliminate the ordinary because the ordinary blinds us to the deprivation around us. Most people think that life should revolve around eating, sleeping, mating, and defending, but, in the final analysis, one cannot even enjoy these activities to their fullest. The body itself is a bad bargain. It gets old and sick to the point that simple activities such as respiration and defecation become painful and laborious. We want to look beyond the limits of the body to discover something greater than just the physicality. Even as we look at some of our civil rights advocates and social reformers, we will see by their own examples that they were not about to accept the ordinary. And of course the spiritualists were definitely not ready to accept the ordinary. Let us pause to reflect on some of these agents of change who were not willing to accept mediocrity.

Mahatma Gandhi first developed his creed of passive resistance against injustice while living in South Africa and witnessing the maltreatment of the immigrant Indians. Later, after returning to India, he led the movement for independence while never wavering from his unshakeable belief in nonviolent protests and religious tolerance. When fighting broke out during the struggle, he would even endure rigorous fasts for weeks until the fighting ceased. His unordinary determination and endurance led to change. Sojourner Truth was not going to accept the ordinary. She was a woman and a slave in America, but she said she felt a divine hand protecting and guiding her so that she could rescue people again and again. She did not accept the ordinary. Booker T. Washington valued the simplicity in God's wonderful creation. He understood that if we used God's gifts in the right way, we would be able to amplify them so much more. Even though he was a simple man, he was not ready to play into the ordinary.

Martin Luther King Jr. had tremendous dreams. People who dream are intuitive and have ideas, aspirations, and vision. Martin Luther King kept focusing on his dream and left the world focusing on his goal. Extraordinary people live extraordinarily. When they have to leave, they maintain their vision but are ready to go beyond this present material scheme. They are concerned about community and about other people. Mother Teresa of Calcutta lived a life of sacrifice and service to those in need. After serving for almost twenty years as a nun and a teacher at St. Mary's School for girls in Calcutta, she felt a divine calling, leading her to dedicate her life to serving the poorest of the poor. Her service and love affected the hearts of millions and strengthened the faith of many disheartened people. Her love surpassed the barriers of sectarianism and reached people of all faiths.

Malcolm X initially tried to focus on ethnicity and religion in a sectarian way, but, as he increased his vision, he went beyond the ordinary to realize that it is a matter of conscious-ness. Elijah Muhammad and Louis Farrakhan went beyond the ordinary by talking about higher beings and the mother-ship. President Sadat of Egypt had a vision of Muhammad appearing to him, telling him to make peace in the Middle East. Even though he faced a challenging situation, he was ready to make the sacrifice. In some cases, people lost their lives because others wanted to remain ordinary.

If we look closer into the different religious orders, we will also see extraordinary personalities. George Fox was the founder of the Quakers, one of the organizations against slavery and the repression of women. People thought he was mad and even considered him schizophrenic because he could communicate in the higher realms. He was not ordinary. If he had been ordinary, he would have supported slavery and the exploitation of women because most ordinary people adhered to those conceptions. He wanted to reject the ordinary and embrace the extraordinary. Many people saw Charles Smith, the founder of the Mormons, as completely crazy. However, he formed an ideal Christian organization because of his extraordinary internal connections.

Baha'u'llah, the founder of the Baha'i faith who lived from 1817 to 1892, was not an ordinary man. If he had been ordinary, he would not have given up his family, wealth, and power to teach the word of God for forty years. Although exiled from his native land, imprisoned, and tortured, he continued to maintain his conviction in his purpose. His objections to slavery of any kind, to religious prejudices, and to politicized religion disturbed many of the leaders of his time. He ultimately believed that religion should be the cause of love, uniting all varieties of people around the globe.

God does not have any favorites. He does not care what religion you call yourself nor is He limited to just one name of an organization. He does not care whether you pray in a synagogue, mosque, cathedral, shrine, or temple. However, He does take notice of your consciousness and what is in your mind. He reciprocates according to the consciousness of the devotee, and deviants who do not have genuine devotion and love cannot bribe the Lord. A cheater is a cheater. He or she might seem to follow Buddhism, Vaisnavism, Christianity, Islam, or Judaism, but it is actually hypocrisy. A cheater is a cheater regardless of which tradition he or she follows. We must be able to identify those who are counterfeits. We must be able to reclaim our relationships so that people will feel refreshed when they leave our temples, churches, synagogues, mosques, cathedrals, and other places of worship. They should want to come back because they will realize that spiritualists offer great solace.

These few personalities mentioned were not in any way ordinary because they went beyond the orthodox and traditional patterns of materialistic society. They knew that one person could make a significant difference and they were ready to do their part. They realized that the Lord far surpasses the ordinary. They understood that if they endeavor to serve and help others, the Lord would help facilitate them. They also knew that He does not have to wait around to be noticed or bribed in order to reciprocate. He does not have to wait until we call ourselves a particular religion, but He is waiting to see if we are ready to receive His love. If we are bound by commodities and sense gratification, we will be too filled with mundane pleasures to have the space to receive His love. When we empty ourselves of all these superfluous desires and aspirations, then the Lord will pour His love and fill us up.

What do we do when we see the demise of a culture? We want to see what we can do individually by relinquishing selfishness, intoxication, and self-illusion. In order to be selfless, we have to understand the difference between pleasure and happiness. Pleasure is often material, and it gives some initial stimulation which later turns into frustration when it is gone or no longer satisfies us. Enduring happiness brings long association within community, and it creates appreciation. We want to move away from those things that just feel good; we should be good. We have to get away from receiving honor; we should be honorable. When we look at ourselves as human beings, we have to watch our thoughts because our thoughts lead to words. We watch our words; they lead to actions. We have to watch our actions because actions become our habits. We should watch our habits because they become our culture. We want a culture of divinity, not a culture of sectarianism, fanaticism, incarceration, and war. We want a culture of liberation that is about love and service to God and all creation.

As we look at our problems, we realize that every challenge can be turned into something positive. God did not make a mistake by giving us certain problems, because they can in fact facilitate our growth if we use them for our growth. Our problems can remind us about the goal, but they should not define us. If we allow them to define us, then we will end up thinking of ourselves as failures. We may make a mistake, but we are not a mistake. We should pick ourselves up, realizing that we made a mistake, and learn from the experience so that we can be in touch with our true identity. We realize that we have a job, but we are not the job. We might be lawyers, ministers, teachers, carpenters, and so on, but we are not that profession in our original nature. We might have a sickness, but we are not defined by that sickness. The soul never tires, grows old, or suffers from hunger and diseases. The soul is always bathing in loving exchanges in the spiritual realm. While we are in this temporary situation, we should realize that we might fall and trip at different times, but we are not defined by that mistake. Every day is another opportunity to come back into focus and reclaim our full essence.

The Dynamic Experience of Religion

When the natural order of a civilization falls into such an intense state of disarray, it begins to influence people to live a life void of righteousness. Many of the patterns are beginning to develop in this way. No wonder more and more people are turning away from spirituality when they have trouble understanding what it really is. In some groups, they hear, "Do as I say and not as I do." We want to go more into the interior. From time immemorial, people have realized that God is the greatest and that real greatness is in serving the Lord. They realize that, with God, all types of miracles can happen even beyond what we can plan.

There are people who have gone so deep into their religion that their lives have become their message. All of the six *gosvamis* of Vrndavana, India were perfect examples of selfless, unalloyed servants of God. They lived their message. At times, they were even in association with Krishna in the spiritual world while still in the physical world in seemingly material bodies. They would have pastimes in both worlds simultaneously. In the Bible, Jesus said, "Truly, truly, I say to you, He who believes in me shall do the works which I do; and even greater than these things he shall do, because I am going to my Father" (John 14:12). He emphasized that we should all ultimately act as he did. He did not say, "My Father who is in Heaven." He said, "Our Father," emphasizing that the same Father loves us all to the same degree.

Sometimes a person can reside in a physical body but have full awareness of their spiritual identity. They are in contact with the spiritual realm as easily as our computer or telephone can reach a person in another place on earth. It is just a matter of focusing our consciousness because the connection is accessible. These entities literally come into this world in disguise. They might appear to be normal human entities who eat, sleep, and experience pain, but they are far from ordinary. God loves us so much that He sends special souls to help bring us back into the spiritual culture. Sometimes He even empowers special souls while in the physical body and helps them have contact with the spiritual realm.

Padre Pio, a great saint and monk who lived in Italy, confined himself to a monastery for many years and never came out. Before he committed himself to the monastic order at the age of nineteen, he prayed to the crucifix and an empowerment of light and love came out of the icon and penetrated throughout his body, giving him the stigmata or the marks of Jesus' wounds. These marks constantly bled, but he never suffered from weakness due to loss of blood. The blood was sweet and smelled like roses. He also had the ability to bilocate just like St. Francis of Assisi. The Vedic tradition describes *yogis* who had this ability to appear in many places at the same time. Such abilities are known as siddhic powers in which a person who sometimes comes closer to God begins to imbibe and take on some of the qualities of the Lord. Such individuals are less stagnated by the gross physical body and begin to access more of their celestial essence.

An incident involving Padre Pio is documented in the United States Air Force Records during World War II. The Nazis planned to bomb a city in Italy at which point the people called upon this saint, knowing that he had tremendous powers. As the pilots prepared to drop their bombs, they claimed to see in the air a monk who had the stigmata waving his hands at them. As some of them dropped their bombs, they dropped them off course into vacant fields. Padre Pio was known to minister to the people in the communities while he simultaneously confined himself to the monastery. He could be in more than one place at the same time. He was even known to have had a discourse with the Pope although he never left the monastery.

Saint Francis of Assisi, another extraordinary saint born in 1181 in France, felt that he had a personal relationship with God, as did St. John of the Cross and St. Bernard. In the Bible, it says that Sarah had a relationship with the Lord just like a mother and daughter. Abraham related to the Lord as a friend. The Koran describes Mohammed's relationship with the Lord as a friendship. In Catholicism, especially in the monastic order, nuns enter into a bridal mysticism and accept Jesus as their husband. Saint Teresa of Avila had a similar type of connection with the Lord. The Vaisnava theology explains in detail the science of *rasa-tattva*, the different relationships that the living entities eternally can have with the Lord. These relationships include *santa-rasa* (adoration of the Lord), *dasya-rasa* (servitude), *sakhya-rasa* (friendship), *vatsalya-rasa* (parental love), and *madhurya-rasa* (conjugal love).

Was Abraham or Moses ordinary? Abraham was ready to slay his own son. It was not that God wanted him to slay his son; He wanted to show the glories of a person who put nothing before Him. It does not matter whether it is our job, our security, our spouse, or our house, we should put nothing before our relationship with God. When we have that mentality, He will bring us all kinds of security. Moses could barely speak as he had a serious speech defect, but the Lord gave him powerful work. In spite of the adversarial material situation, he carried out the Lord's will. He was not ready for an ordinary achievement; rather, he embraced the extraordinary.

It is documented that at times when Saint Teresa would pray in the cathedral, she would levitate. When she would go into deep prayer, the other nuns had to hold her down, knowing that she would rise. She was addressing the Supreme Person who is not limited to the three-dimensional, geographical environment or to the gross incarceration of the physical. In the time of Noah, civilization was crumbling all around them, but God would never leave His agents unprotected. Some people would not even listen to Noah since they had become very much controlled by the routine. When a person tries to rise above the material patterns, other people might even try to pull them back or ridicule them. The more the Lord sees that we want to serve, the more He will make opportunities available to us. If we are captured by the ordinary, we cannot make ourselves sufficiently available to serve.

These great teachers and *acaryas*, who have appeared in all the different religious traditions of the world, were trying to find more ways to give and share their love; consequently, the Lord reciprocated to such a high level. Religion is not only a matter of reading scripture, undergoing rituals, or hearing about great personalities in their particular line based on their theology, but the essence involves having the experiences and becoming an instrument in the service of God. The great teachers and *acaryas* give us this knowledge. We are not limited to the physical, which means that we have to look closer at our interior to find the cause of our bondage to the physical. What is it that we have to remove or take away so that we can actually be able to experience our divinity?

The Highest Purpose of Community

As we have seen throughout these discussions, many dysfunctional patterns are surfacing within the individual, the family, the institution, the community, and the planet. However, we want to move towards our actual purpose in this lifetime, which will remind us of our real identity. This understanding can help us make profound changes because our ultimate identity is far greater than just the material commodities that we use. As we look closer at our existence, we see ourselves as part of a community. We can understand our essence more clearly as we research it in relation to other entities. Actually, we cannot really understand ourselves outside of *sambandha* or relationship because relationship is an integral aspect of our eternal identity.

In South Africa, they have a conception known as *unbuntu*, which means that we understand ourselves as we give value to others. It means that we understand and appreciate life when we add to life in a healthy way. Not only is relationship essential to understanding our true identity, but the quality of relationship is of utmost importance. Ultimately, we have relationship based on God; therefore, when we honor our real identity, we will develop into more wholesome individuals and communities that will naturally create a healthy culture.

Ideally, we should work together and relate to each other based on our real identity as eternal servants of the one God. To the degree that we remind each other of our true selves, to that same degree we will honor authentic community. Conversely, to the degree that we take each other away from our constitutional position, to that degree we will only prolong our amnesia and schizophrenia. Most people currently view themselves as temporary entities whose purpose is to increase their quality of eating, sleeping, mating, and defending. However, God did not make a mistake. He would have made a mistake if He gave us these bodies simply to gratify our senses because our bodies cannot even perform in these areas very effectively as in other species. The bear can sleep many more hours than any of us.

The pigeon can have sex dozens of times more than we can. The giraffe, hippopotamus, and elephant can eat more than a whole group of human beings. If we were meant to enjoy through these bodies, then God would have made a mistake since He did not give us the most effective machine to do so. However, we know that the Supreme Lord does not make any mistakes. We are the ones who make mistakes when we minimize the Lord's guidance. We constantly fail to respond to what God makes available. We turn our ears and bodies away from the Lord.

Communities form in different ways. There are communities by accident, communities, by force, and communities by design. Only community by design is an authentic community. Accidental communities can compare to a group of people on a subway train who find ways to tolerate each other during the trip. They tolerate each other while they execute their duties, and if possible, even try to avoid the other people as much as possible. Although they happen to be with those particular people in the train, they all have totally different goals and aspirations. Of course, that is not an authentic community. Every family is not a family, every home is not a home, and every church or temple is not necessarily a place that glorifies the Lord.

Some communities develop when external circumstances beyond their control force people together. Although these people might end up in the same institution, country, or environment, they do not necessarily form a genuine community. Rather, the lack of community that created the problem in the first place often perpetuates to create more of the same. When a community develops by design, it means that people are more aware of why they have come together. They are aware of their goals and are able to honor the other community members as they move toward their particular goals.

An authentic community is like a living entity. It only comes together and stays together with the help of constant planning. For instance, a relationship between two people can begin fairly easily, but it requires work to maintain so that it develops rather than stagnates. When we have an authentic community, we can celebrate diversity because a real community does not involve forced conformity. However, we must have more unity than diversity so that the community can constantly enthuse people about their common visions and goals. Community is meant to find ways to come together, but it should also encourage people to go inward and rejuvenate themselves. In this way, when they do come together, they can access more of their God consciousness. People in genuine community do not dishonor others in the community. When someone is not whole, they are more prone to inject that type of mentality into others and into the atmosphere. There is a need for people to individually develop more wholeness so that they can add to the community. A strong community should give us a chance to share while also allowing us to go deep inside.

Community is significant these days because it is through community that we can experience a sense of security and can understand our duties. It is through community that we can honor *samskaras* or rites of passages because these transitions in our lives are to remind us of what to do, when to do it, and how to do it. Such rites of passages are gradually losing their importance in our culture, and, in the process, we miss our real purpose and forget how to keep motivated on a daily basis. Consequently, we lose our focus on spirituality, and replace community with commodity. This brings the society closer to waging war rather than waging peace.

Expressions of Gratitude

There is a need for a global mind shift and a need for us all to have some involvement in this process. We can assist by reflecting on the greatness of God and the greatness of those who have accepted Him in their lives. We discussed some examples of people from a few orthodox traditions who have shown that God is alive and that He works in ways far beyond the normal patterns of this material world. It depends on how much we want Him to use our lives in His service. We allow the Lord to use our lives by putting nothing before Him. We accept that He is watching, rewarding, and protecting.

We want to come to a point in which we can look at our lives and say, "Thank you God." When we are sick, we can thank God for giving us time to be more reflective, and when we have good health, we can use our time better. We can thank God when we do not have sufficient financial endowment. We understand that if we had more, we would only use it improperly. We thank God for keeping us in a situation in which we can remain more closely under His protection.

When we have an abundance of wealth and opulence, we can thank God for enabling us to use our wealth in His service. When we have fame, we can thank God because He knows that unless we receive that type of motivation, we might just fall into depression. We can thank the Lord when we fall into a state of infamy and people harshly criticize us because He knows that we have such a large false ego. We thank Him for putting us in a situation that will help us develop humility. In this way, we will not think of ourselves as the proprietors or the doers. He is helping us recognize our position as the servant of the servant. When we are lonely, we can thank the Lord for letting us go deeper because He is always there waiting for us. When we have so many people to associate with, we can thank the Lord for allowing us to see Him manifest through so many of the people in our environment. We can thank the Lord because, instead of making a permanent residence in this material world, we are already arranging for our eternal existence, which is not based on the duality of any environment.

We want to come to a level of consciousness in which we can say, "Lord, You may disappear or You may embrace me. You may deny me or seem to abandon me when I need You the most, but I know that You are there. Thank you God because when I do ultimately connect with You, I know that it will be that much more wonderful." Furthermore, we must know that no situation in our lives is outside of the Lord's jurisdiction and ability to resolve, nor is there any trickery or exploitation that the Lord cannot counteract. We can realize that our husband, wife, children, and teachers may disappoint us, but the Lord will never ultimately disappoint us.

As we keep this focus, we will not fall apart in spite of the falling civilization around us. In fact, we will make a difference in the acceleration of God consciousness. Then our life will speak our message because we will live it, and it will work through us even while we remain in the physical body. We can perform miracles when we are not depending on ourselves because God is the master of all mystics. He performs the miracles. We can accomplish fantastic feats if we simply move out of the way and let God work through us.

Questions and Answers

Question: How should we prepare our young children when educational institutions are materialistic and corrupt?

Answer: It is healthy to know some of the ways that the force of opposition thinks in order to protect ourselves. For instance, my book *Spiritual Warrior I* emphasizes two important points—acting properly and knowing what to avoid. A warrior cannot simply act properly without knowing what to avoid. The prophets and *acaryas* have given us so many instructions to help us distinguish between proper and improper behavior. They have also taught us by their own example. If we can shelter our children by giving them proper guidance, they will learn from those corrupt environments rather than allow the atmosphere to abuse or exploit them.

Question: Can you explain bi-location in more depth?

Answer: We can better understand bi-location through such concepts as mind over matter. Mind can directly influence matter, a fact that even doctors recognize today through the study of psychosomatic diseases. Some people have the ability to heal the sick since sicknesses affect matter as well as consciousness. This helps us realize that aspects of our existence go far beyond what we normally can touch, smell, taste and feel. Some people have the ability to travel to other planets. Our eyes can hardly perceive the intricacies of this universe, nor can our limited minds understand the vastness of the Lord's creation.

Sometimes certain entities come into our environment from the spiritual realm but keep some of the characteristics associated with that abode. For instance, a person might enter a prison to visit an inmate, but the visitor does not become a prisoner simply because he or she entered the environment. Entities such as angels, archangels, Apsaras, Gandharvas, and so on are not fully confined to the same laws because they are more evolved. They are a part of a higher spiritual reality, which allows them to have many places to manifest.

Question: In terms of the ten indicators of a falling civilization, can you give us specific ways to really handle these challenges and changes in society?

Answer: For this reason, we emphasize the importance of re-spiritualizing our culture. We currently live in a culture of lust, but we want to create a culture of love. The culture of lust covers every aspect of our lives. In a culture, we have relationships and an identity. We eat, sleep, mate, and defend, but instead of eating, sleeping, and living in unhealthy ways, we want to find more uplifting ways to execute these activities. For instance, we want to be more careful about what type of food we put into our bodies. The body is a machine that works according to the type of fuel we put in it. In terms of mating, we already see so much abortion and divorce. When people come together for so-called union, they fail to honor each other's essence. Instead, they connect in order to get some pleasure for themselves rather than sharing and putting God in the center.

People come together and just try to rob each other. What we normally call romance is robbery. A man thinks, "She is a wonderful woman who has just what I need." A woman sees the man and thinks, "He can make me feel complete." She looks at what she doesn't have and then balances that against what she can get from him. Basically, she wants to rob him. Then they come together and rob each other. One day they will wonder what happened to their assets and simply get angry. At the end of the day, they are both miserable. Instead of trying to rob the other person, two people can develop a healthy relationship by giving and sharing as much as possible.

The present day patterns of incarceration bring a civilization down. People begin to think that they need convenience rather than love—just marry someone who will take care of you. However, if a person puts God in the center, he or she will look for a partner who will assist in their spiritual evolution. You want to find a partner who will help you advance spiritually. If that type of relationship does not manifest, you have to realize that you do not have the right connection.

When we make our prayers, we want to stop asking for material commodities since they have caused our current predicament in the first place. We want to pray, "Dear Lord, You know what I need and surely know what I want, but please let me have what I really need. Thy will be done." It involves an individual, institutional, and global mindshift. We invoke the most powerful prayers when we simply try to connect with the Supreme Lord. We emphasize calling on the names of God to make that powerful connection. We don't want to pray for cars, houses, friends, or more money; we want to get out of the same old paradigm.

When we do have money, we do not want to involve ourselves in gambling. Estimates suggest that 5.5 million people have a pathological gambling problem and 15 million people are at risk.[43] We are quite an addicted group of people in America, and we need to make changes. We do not want to gamble because we want to see all of our possessions as the property of God and use them in ways that make Him happy. We do not take intoxication because we want to be intoxicated by love and devotion. We want to experience ecstasy—not the drug—we want real ecstasy that cannot come by trying to cheat God or by having some altered state artificially. We want to become free of illicit affairs, and this means no adultery. When we come together, it is a festival as a service to the Lord. We cannot serve the Lord when we lack accountability or come together based on greed and lust. We want to make a shift in our individual lives in order to take us higher. It is a revolution! This is all part of the science of waging peace, not war.

Question: Do you feel that we are entering an era in which a spiritual revolution will take place, leading to more positive changes?

Answer: These changes are occurring on the planet right now, and we currently see a demarcation—pious versus impious. We will see people becoming more viciously sinful without any regret or compunction. At the same time, we see people trying to understand God and align themselves with some type of discipline. This kind of fragmentation is really a part of the unfolding process in this world. As these separations take place, people will go to one side or the other. This fragmentation is due to the impending dispensation we might refer to as the Golden Age. It means that in the near future, wonderful things will happen, but, before these changes can take place, we have to get rid of some obstructions.

We are witnessing the deposition of negative patterns along with those empowered for destruction. When you try to overthrow a very powerful tyrant, you start seeing the worst of that tyrant come out. For this reason, we will see some of the heaviest changes on this planet now. Many of these sinful agencies are being exposed which means that their time is coming to an end. An insubordinate child gets angrier when you tell them to stop and might even kick over the table before leaving. They cause havoc because they realize they have to go. We have to brace ourselves as we enter this higher period so that we do not get caught in the negative current of devastation.

Question: You discussed various teachers and, as you call them, spiritual warriors, who could bi-locate and heal others. As a leader and spiritual warrior, do you not also possess those same gifts? If so, do you have the opportunity to apply those techniques of healing or ability to deliver your message when you are not physically present?

Answer: Not only do those few saints have those abilities, but every one of us also has them. The soul itself is full of unusual expressions and activities, but our physical body may interfere. When people try to dedicate themselves more to the mission of the Lord, the Lord will give them spiritual technologies and weapons according to their mission and level. Any highly evolved spiritual messenger will be used in very dynamic ways because the person is interfering less and less. If we do not see miracles, it means that we are just working according to our own finances, intelligence, and resources. However, when things happen beyond our normal capacity, it is a sign that some higher strength is beginning to engulf us and affect others. Spiritual life should always be progressive. We realize that we are always students, and, as we are hungry to know more, the Lord will constantly feed us.

For many years, I worked in Europe, and later lived in Africa for about fifteen years. By the Lord's arrangement, I now have the chance to spend more time in America. There is a special reason why we take birth in a certain place and why we receive a specific type of body. A person can take birth in many different bodies and in many different parts of the world, but these arrangements are made so that each soul can learn the necessary lessons or even teach them to others. I am happy for this opportunity to come to America more often, and, in the next few years, I hope to have a greater impact on the spiritual communities in America as well. I want to reach people who are trying to go deeper into their religious traditions. In other words, the great *acaryas* and saints let us know that we come from the same connection. It is not just a matter of reflecting on their performance; it is a matter of gaining our own sense of divinity through humility, compassion, and love. We encourage all of our beloved readers to take inventory during all of your activities and look at the internal work that you need to do.

Please take the time now to look at three areas in your life in which you see blocks or stagnations to your spiritual growth. Be honest with yourself because you know the areas that you need to address. Maybe you have several bad habits, lack honesty in your relationships, or need to work on your role as a parent, leader, spouse, etc. Give yourself a time frame to work on those weaknesses and, as a part of your daily meditation, try to see how you are freeing yourself from those particular problems. Take whatever help you need from your peer association and from mentors. Give yourself one month for each issue and, in three months, make a vow that you will eliminate such inappropriate behaviors from your life. If you seek out good association, you will get sufficient help to make the necessary transformations.

We want to go deeper and remove that which is preventing us from experiencing God's love. In this way, we will find our lives to be more exciting and exhilarating. We will have more protection because we will draw to us divine protection. We will have a greater understanding of our purpose here, and when we leave this body, we will not have to return to another body. With this type of spiritual greed, desperation, and destitution, the Lord who resides in the heart will notice. We want to focus in a very devotional way, realizing that the Lord is receiving our prayers, and has already made arrangements for reclaiming us. It is important that as we observe civilization falling into great decadence, we do our part to make a significant difference. As spiritual warriors, we want to do our part in helping to arrest the violence, sectarianism, fanaticism, and the fall of civilization. As we improve ourselves, we bring improvements to the world.

Closing Reflections

Sometimes people wonder how we, as Vaisnavas, can follow the *Bhagavad-gita*, a book compiled in the midst of a great war in what seems to be an atmosphere of violence. Why do we not just hear from God when He speaks from the heavenly kingdoms or in a very palatial environment? Why do we not just adhere to those saintly people who speak realizations and revelations in a forest or while meditating in a cave? Why do we embrace a scripture in which Arjuna, a great devotee of the Lord, seems duty bound to engage in what we might consider violence? First of all, it shows that there is a misconception about violence. It also shows that spiritual life is not based on the opposite standards of the material world. It is not based on anyone's mind, intelligence, or intuition; rather, it comes from God who gives us the understanding of actual ethics, morality, and violence.

From the Vaisnava scriptures, we see that violence involves

anything that interferes with our ultimate healthy position and anything that takes away from our glorious status as pure servants of the Lord. Violence is much more than a physical assault. Violence is anything that we do to ourselves or to others that causes us to think that God's love is not available for us. Violence is whatever causes us to get distracted by the mundane material energy and fail to act godly. Basically, people are violent towards themselves and others on a daily basis because they are constantly acting in unhealthy ways. It is suicidal to the living entity and homicidal to the family, institution, community, and environment.

Even as devotees and spiritualists, we need to look at our lives and see how much violence we constantly involve ourselves in. If we look at this week, how many times did we say or do things in this violent frame of mind? And how many times did we experience violence from someone else? Violence also involves those discussions and interactions that simply help another person feel comfortable with sinful and degrading activities. We act violently towards ourselves when we go about our duties without remembering the Lord in the background. We are violent when we go through our daily activities thinking of ourselves as the ultimate controller. Violence even involves the times in which we excessively think of ourselves as a victim—playing God by putting ourselves in the center of attention as the victim.

People who always position themselves as the victim will never grow. They always think that other people are hurting them in some way. Although it could be a reality, if they anticipate and look for it, they will just create that around them to an even greater extent. They will begin to chant the same *mantra* in their minds, "Somebody didn't treat me right, someone didn't look at me right, someone didn't address me right, someone didn't take care of me properly, someone used me improperly..." Consequently, a person who always sees him or herself as the victim becomes the perpetual victim because violence brings more violence. For instance, a coup d'etat of a government will only increase the chance of another violent overthrow in the future. There will be attacks similar to those created by the initial perpetrators.

In terms of slaughterhouses, the killing of millions and millions of animals will only increase the likelihood of war because, karmically, violence leads to more violence. People do not see the parallel between the slaughtering of animals and the constant war and violence. People do not see the violence involved in harsh thoughts, harsh words, harsh entertainment, harsh relationships, or harsh leadership. They do not see the evil of violence associated with sectarianism and fanaticism. They do not see the violence associated with certain diseases that develop from unhealthy mindsets. Negative mindsets can literally make the cells act violently against each other to the point that they attack. Needless to say, we live in a very violent world.

General Douglas MacArthur went to the heart of the issue in a radio address on September 2, 1945 following the surrender of the Japanese:

> Men since the beginning of time have sought peace. Various methods through the ages have been attempted to devise an international process to prevent or settle disputes between nations. From the very start, workable methods were found in so far as individual citizens were concerned, but the mechanics

of an instrumentality of larger international scope have never been successful.

Military alliances, balances of power, leagues of nations, all in turn failed, leaving the only path to be by way of the crucible of war. The utter destructiveness of war now blocks out this alternative. We have had our last chance. If we will not devise some greater and more equitable system, our Armageddon will be at our door. The problem basically is theological and involves a spiritual recrudescence, an improvement of human character that will synchronize with our almost matchless advances in science, art, literature, and all material and cultural developments of the past two thousand years. It must be of the spirit if we are to save the flesh.

Our duty as spiritual warriors is not to engage in conventional physical warfare, but to attack the violence by waging peace and compassion. Yes, we are called to war, and each day we have to determine what we have done on the battlefield. Did we act as cowards by hiding and allowing others to fight the battle? Did we stand by and watch millions and even billions get wounded and meet total devastation? Or do we hear the clarion call to take up or continue the battle of spiritual warriorship? Beloved, examine every day you live to see if you are adding to the violence or helping to create a world of auspiciousness by waging love and peace. The spiritual warriors' ranks are increasing, but not fast enough. Let us increase our influence on this planet.

Epilogue

His Holiness Bhakti Tirtha Swami, the author of this creative book, has been my associate for many years now. I particularly recall the many counseling sessions I had with him when I was the Director-General of the Ghana Prisons Service. He had also on several occasions addressed senior officers of Ghana on several issues such as leadership, prison reform, violence, nation building, our image, and consciousness. Those were impressive and fulfilling sessions.

The daily fear and insecurity in our present world manifests in terrorism, fanaticism, civil wars, ethnic cleansing, suicide bombing, and many other forms of violence. There has been an escalation in violence across the world after the events of September 11, 2001. The levels of poverty, hunger, bad governance, and corruption in many third world countries have set the stage for violence as a means of survival for desperate people. Violence is a product of intolerance and greed. Simply arresting and sending people to prison does not in any way address the causes of violence. Huge prison populations create their own problems, and there are no signs of remorse on the part of perpetrators of crime, which does not promote restorative justice, reconciliation, and healing. Genocides which result from differences in race, tribe, and religion, and bomb attacks, suicide bombings, and diseases which emanate from wars, put the figures of people dying daily at frightening heights. There is depression, frustration, gloom, and anxiety among a large number of people due to the growing mistrust in the world.

We must find an antidote to the tension and ever increasing violence and misery in the world. Many nations pay lip service to the human rights of people but create situations where the basic human needs of survival hardly exist due to manipulation, cheating, and exploitation. Priority expenditure in the world is now on war, violence, and acquisition of instruments to destroy humanity, and not on poverty alleviation or the needs of the majority of the people in the world.

His Holiness B.T. Swami engaged us in new approaches to saving this world from self-destruction. Peace, compassion, selflessness, and sanity are what can save the world. Love is the strongest single weapon for the people. War is always evil, and we cannot justify some wars as "just" wars. Violence leads to more violence. Receiving fulfillment of peace from a spiritual context and avoiding materialism is the way forward. Increase in consciousness is the solution to stopping hate and violence.

The quest for peace and justice in the world is not the responsibility of a few individuals. We must all wage a war for love and peace. The world needs serious reconciliation and forgiveness. The culture of aggression and retaliation against race, religion, tribe, or gender should not be allowed to destroy this beautiful creation of God. Love, justice, and peace should now be the battle cry. We can effect the needed change any time we want. It is a choice between fear and love, violence and peace. This book is an excellent guideline for waging Peace and Love.

—Richard Kuuire
    Former Director-General of Ghana Prisons Service
    Advisor to the Honorable Minister of Interior

Notes

[1] Lisa Miller, "Why We Need Heaven," *Newsweek* (August 12, 2002): 45-51.

[2] Ibid, 50.

[3] All purports from the *Bhagavad-gita* and *Srimad-Bhagavatam* are quoted from A. C. Bhaktivedanta Swami Prabhupada's translations and commentaries on these Vedic scriptures. See full citations in the Bibliography.

[4] Srila Saccidananda Bhaktivinoda Thakura, "Stages and Varieties of Faith," *Sri Krsna-kathamrta* (No. 5): 17.

[5] Geo Widengren, *Muhammad, The Apostle of God, and His Ascension* (Uppsala, 1995): 108.

[6] Ranchor Prime, *Prince of Dharma: The Illustrated Life of the Buddha* (Novato, California: Mandala Media, 2002): xiii.

[7] John Cleveland Cothran, "The Inescapable Conclusion," *Evidence of God in an Expanding Universe*, ed. John Monsma (New York: G.P. Putnam's Sons, 1958), 41-42.

[8] Geo Widengren, *Muhammad, The Apostle of God, and His Ascension* (Uppsala, 1995): 107-108.

[9] Srimad-Bhagavatam 1.8.5, purport

[10] "6,000,000,000 Consumption Machines." *International Wildlife*, September/October 1999.

[11] Ibid.

[12] Ibid.

[13] Margo Okazawa-Rey and Kirk Gwyn, "Maximum Security," Social Justice 27, no. 3 (2000): 120.

[14] World Health Organization, *The World Health Report 2001: Mental Health: New Understanding, New Hope* (Geneva, 2001).

[15] Shannon Mcmanimon and Rachel Stohl, "Use of children as soldiers," Foreign Policy in Focus (1 November 2001): 1.

[16] "Iraq tops the agenda." The Washington Times, 20 January 2003, A14.

[17] Sara Nomberg-Przytyk, Auschwitz: True Tales from a Grotesque Land, trans. Roslyn Hirsch, eds. Eli Pfefferkorn and David H. Hirsch (Chapel Hill, NC: University of North Carolina Press, 1985).

[18] Iris Chang, The Rape of Nanking: The Forgotten Holocaust of World War II, 1st ed. (New York: Basic Books, 1997): 82.

[19] Callum MacDonald, "Chapter 11 The Nanking Massacre of December 1937 and Japanese Policy in China," The Massacre in History, eds. Mark Levene and Penny Roberts (New York: Berghahn Books, 1999): 223-241.

[20] Yuki Tanaka, Hidden Horrors Japanese War Crimes in World War II, 3rd ed. (Boulder, CO: Westview Press, 1998): 103.

[21] Ibid, 76.

22 Krishna Dharma, *Mahabharata: The Greatest Spiritual Epic of All Time* (Badger, CA: Torchlight Publishing, 1999): 828.

23 James Parton, Eminent Women of the Age: Being Narratives of the Lives and Deeds of the Most Prominent Women of the Present Generation (Hartford, CT: S.M. Betts & Company, 1869).

24 Lerone Bennett, "Free for Christmas," Ebony (December 1994): 52+.

25 Mary Craig, *Blessed Maximilian Kolbe: Priest Hero of a Death Camp* (London: Catholic Truth Society, 1973).

26 Ibid.

27 Eva Fogelman and Valerie Lewis Wiener, "The Few, the Brave, the Noble; Only a Handful of People Helped Victims of Nazi Oppression. What Made Them Act When Others Turned Away?" Psychology Today (August 1985): 60+.

28 Charles P. Vaclavik, *The Vegetarianism of Jesus Christ* (California: Kaweah Publishing Co., 1986).

29 Paul Pearsall, Ph.D., *The Heart's Code*, New York: Broadway Books, 1998.

30 Juliet Gellatley, *The Silent Ark* (London: Thorsons, 1996).

31 David Feinstein, "Subtle Energy: Psychology's Missing Link," *IONS Noetic Sciences Review* 64 (June-August 2003): 21.

32 Juliet Gellatley, *The Silent Ark*.

33 Micheal A. Cremo, *Divine Nature* (Los Angeles: Bhaktivedanta Book Trust, 1995).

34 Ibid, 16.

35 Ibid, 17.

36 Ibid, ix.

37 Michael Baigent and Richard Leigh, *The Dead Sea Scrolls Deception* (London: Arrow Books, 1998): 340.

[38] Howard Bloom, *The Global Brain: The Evolution of Mass Mind from the Big Bang to the 21st Century* (New York: John Wiley & Sons Inc., 2001): 93.

[39] These ten signs are taken from J. Bradley Keena's essay entitled, "Ten Signs of a Culture's End" as found on the following website: http://www.rense.com/politics4/tensigns.htm

[40] Brendan I. Koerner, "Porn Dot Com: A Lust for Profits," *U.S. News and World Report* (March 27, 2000): 36-38, 40, 42, 44.

[41] John Leland, "Millennium Madness," *Newsweek* (November 1, 1999): 70.

[42] Kenneth L. Woodward, "The Way the World Ends," *Newsweek* (November 1, 1999): 68-73.

[43] John Fetto, "A Royal Flush," *American Demographics* (September 2002): 72.

Glossary

Acarya: A spiritual master who teaches by his own example, and who sets the proper religious example for all human beings.

Adhibautika: Misery caused by other living beings.

Adhidaivika: Misery or natural disturbances caused by the demigods.

Adhikara: The qualification or ability to understand spiritual matters due to previous spiritual activities.

Adhunika-vada: To apply spiritual precepts practically in consideration of modernity.

Adhyatmika: Miseries arising from one's own body and mind.

Ahankara: False ego, by which the soul misidentifies with the material body.

Aparadha: An offense.

Arca-vigraha: An authorized form of God manifested through material elements, as in a painting or statue of Krishna worshiped in a temple or home; actually present in this form, the Lord accepts worship from His devotees.

Asura: One who is envious of God, and is averse to the supremacy and service of the Supreme Lord; demon.

Atma: The self (refers sometimes to the body, sometimes to the soul, and sometimes to the senses).

Brahmajyoti: The impersonal bodily effulgence emanating from the transcendental body of the Supreme Lord Krishna, which constitutes the brilliant illumination of the spiritual sky.

Brahmana: A member of the most intelligent class of men, according to the four Vedic occupational divisions of society.

Dasya-rasa: The servitor relationship with the Lord.

Desa-kala-patra: Time, place, and the performer.

Deva: A demigod or saintly person.

Dhama-aparadha: Offenses against the holy places.

Gosvami: A person who has his senses under full control; the title of a person in the renounced order of life, sannyasa.

Guru: Spiritual master.

Guru-aparadha: Offenses against the spiritual master.

Kama: Lust.

Karma: The law of material cause and effect.

Kirtana: Glorification of the Supreme Lord; the devotional process of chanting.

Ksatriya: The martial-spirited, administrative class of Vedic society who protect society from danger.

Madhurya-rasa: The spiritual relationship in conjugal love which the Supreme Lord and His devotee reciprocate as lovers.

Maha-tattva: The total material energy.

Mana-seva: Service performed within the mind.

Mantra: A pure sound vibration that delivers the mind from its material inclinations and illusions when repeated over and over. A transcendental sound or Vedic hymn, prayer, or chant.

Maya: The external energy of the Supreme Lord, which covers the conditioned soul and does not allow him to understand the Supreme Personality of Godhead.

Nama-aparadha: An offense against the holy name of the Lord.

Nirvana: Freedom from material existence.

Prana: Life air.

Sac-cid-ananda-vigraha: The Lord's transcendental form, which is eternal and full of knowledge and bliss.

Sadhana: Systematic practices aimed at spiritual perfection, especially Deity worship and chanting the holy name of the Lord.

Sakhya-rasa: The spiritual mellow of friendship; one of the nine principal limbs of devotional service.

Samadhi: Total absorption and trance of the mind and senses in consciousness of the Supreme Godhead and service to Him.

Sambandha: The transcendental sentiment of relationship.

Samsara: The cycle of repeated birth and death in the material world.

Samskara: One of the Vedic reformatory rituals performed by a person from the time of conception until death for purifying a human being.

Santa-rasa: The relationship with Supreme Lord in neutrality.

Seva-aparadha: Offenses in devotional service.

Siddhi: Mystic powers achievable by practice of yoga.

Smarta-brahmana: A brahmana interested more in the external performance of the rules and rituals of the Vedas than in attaining Lord Krishna, the goal of the Vedas.

Sravana: The devotional process of hearing about the Supreme Lord.

Vaisnava-aparadha: An offense against a devotee of the Lord.

Vatsalya-rasa: The relationship with Krishna as His parent.

Yajna: Sacrifice.

Yoga: Spiritual discipline to link oneself with the Supreme.

Yogi: A transcendentalist who practices one of the many authorized forms of yoga, or processes of spiritual purification.

Bibliography

The Holy Bible. Translated by George M. Lamsa. Philadelphia: A. J. Holman Company, 1957.

The Glorious Qur'an. Translated by Muhammad M. Pickthall. N.p.: The Islamic Call Society, n.d.

LaFree, Gary. Losing Legitimacy: Street Crime and the Decline of Social Institutions in America. Boulder, CO: Westview Press, 1998.

Pert, Candace Ph.D. *Molecules of Emotion: Why You Feel the Way You Feel*. New York: Scribner, 1997.

Prabhupada, A. C. Bhaktivedanta Swami. *Bhagavad-gita As It Is*. Los Angeles: Bhaktivedanta Book Trust, 1983.

———. *Srimad-Bhagavatam*. 18 vols. Los Angeles: Bhaktivedanta Book Trust, 1987.

.

Index

About the Author

Bhakti Tirtha Swami was born John E. Favors in a pious, God-fearing family. As a child evangelist, he appeared regularly on television, and as a young man, he was a leader in Dr. Martin Luther King, Jr.'s civil rights movement. At Princeton University, he became president of the student council and also served as chairman of the Third World Coalition. Although his main degree is in psychology, he has received accolades in many other fields, including politics, African studies, and international law.

Bhakti Tirtha Swami's books are used as reference texts in universities and leadership organizations throughout the world. Many of his books have been printed in English, German, French, Spanish, Portuguese, Macedonian, Croatian, Russian, Hebrew, Slovenian, Balinese, and Italian.

His Holiness has served as Assistant Coordinator for penal reform programs in the State of New Jersey, Office of the Public

Defender, and as a director of several drug abuse clinics in the United States. In addition, he has been a special consultant for Educational Testing Services in the U.S.A. and has managed campaigns for politicians. Bhakti Tirtha Swami gained international recognition as a representative of the Bhaktivedanta Book Trust, particularly for his outstanding work with scholars in the former communist countries of Eastern Europe.

Bhakti Tirtha Swami directly oversees projects in the United States (particularly Washington D.C., Potomac, Maryland, Detroit, Pennsylvania, West Virginia), West Africa, South Africa, Switzerland, France, Croatia, and Bosnia. He also serves as the director of the American Federation of Vaisnava Colleges and Schools.

In the United States, Bhakti Tirtha Swami is the founder and director of the Institute for Applied Spiritual Technology, director of the International Committee for Urban Spiritual Development and one of the international coordinators of the Seventh Pan African Congress. Reflecting his wide range of interests, he is also a member of the Institute for Noetic Sciences, the Center for Defense Information, the United Nations Association for America, the National Peace Institute Foundation, the World Future Society, and the Global Forum of Spiritual and Parliamentary Leaders.

A specialist in international relations and conflict resolution, Bhakti Tirtha Swami constantly travels around the world and has become a spiritual consultant to many high-ranking members of the United Nations, to various celebrities, and to several chiefs, kings, and high court justices. In 1990 His Holiness was coronated as a high chief in Warri, Nigeria in recognition of his outstanding work in Africa and the world. In recent years, he has met several times with then-President Nelson Mandela of South Africa to share visions and strategies for world peace.

In addition to encouraging self-sufficiency through the development of schools, clinics, farm projects, and cottage industries, Bhakti Tirtha Swami conducts seminars and workshops on principle-centered leadership, spiritual development, interpersonal relationships, stress and time management, and other pertinent topics. He is also widely acknowledged as a viable participant in the resolution of global conflict.

Leadership for an Age of Higher Consciousness I

Administration from a Metaphysical Perspective

by B.T. Swami
(Swami Krishnapada)

$23.00 hardbound ISBN #1-885414-02-1
$14.95 softbound ISBN #1-885414-05-6
320 pages, 2nd edition

"An example in the truest sense of global principle-centered leadership, Swami Krishnapada manages to take consciousness-raising to its highest platform of self-realized actuality in humanizing the workplace. My experience in working with all of the nations of the world convinces me that such a book is the corporate leadership guide for the coming millennium."

The Honorable Pierre Adossama
Director, Labor Relations (Retired)
International Labor Organization
United Nations

The Leader In You

Leadership in any capacity has taken on such awesome proportions that even the best leaders must find innovative and creative ways to deal with today's complex situations. *Leadership for an Age of Higher Consciousness: Administration from a Metaphysical Perspective* is a ground breaking self-help manual written for those who seek to develop a more penetrating perspective and greater effectiveness in the leadership process. This book is relevant for heads of government, organizations and families, and for anyone seeking greater insight into self-leadership.

Leadership for an Age of Higher Consciousness II

Ancient Wisdom For Modern Times

Become An Authentic Leader

by B.T. Swami
(Swami Krishnapada)

$23.00 hardbound ISBN #1-885414-11-0
$14.95 softbound ISBN #1-885414-12-9
209 pages

"Good leadership is not just a matter of making things happen; it is a matter of making essential things happen, making important and productive things happen, and helping people feel good about what is happening. Leaders need to have a vision, but they also need to know how to convince others that their vision can manifest, and how to empower them to participate in the mission of bringing the vision about."

—*Excerpt from Leadership for an Age of Higher Consciousness, Vol. 2*

In this sequel to his internationally acclaimed *Leadership for an Age of Higher Consciousness: Administration from a Metaphysical Perspective*, His Holiness Bhakti-Tirtha Swami Krishnapada explores the greatness of two famous leaders from the Vedic tradition of ancient India.

Addressing the leader within each of us, B.T. Swami shows us that the greatest leaders see themselves as servants first, they place integrity and character before personal gain, and they know how to tap into the help that is available from both the earthly and spiritual realms. True servant leaders are animated visionaries who cultivate divine power to transform diverse individuals with scattered goals into communities with a unified, sacred mission.

by B.T. Swami
(Swami Krishnapada)

$12.95 softbound ISBN #1-885414-01-3
200 pages, 2nd edition

"As we rapidly approach the new
millennium, more and more people
are searching for spiritual answers
to the meaning and purpose of life.
The search, of course, begins with
Self, and Swami Krishnapada's
book, *Spiritual Warrior*, provides a
practical companion for the journey of the initiate. I am honored to
recommend it."

Gordon-Michael Scallion
Futurist; Editor,
Earth Changes Report
Matrix Institute, Inc.

Spiritual Warrior I

Uncovering Spiritual Truths in Psychic Phenomena

Ancient Mysteries Revealed!

Get ready for a roller-coaster
ride into the intriguing realm
of ancient mysteries! It is rare
to find the subjects in this book
handled in such a piercing and
straightforward way.
*Spiritual Warrior: Uncovering
Spiritual Truths in Psychic
Phenomena* focuses on the
spiritual essence of many topics
that have bewildered scholars
and scientists for generations,
such as extraterrestrials, the
pyramids and psychic intrusion.
A fresh perspective is revealed,
inviting the reader to expand
the boundaries of the mind and
experience a true and lasting
connection with the inner self.

Spiritual Warrior II

Transforming Lust into Love

New!
2nd edition with expanded text.

by B.T. Swami
(Swami Krishnapada)

$12.95 softbound ISBN #1-885414-20-X
296 pages

"*Spiritual Warrior II: Transforming Lust into Love* is a book to savor and treasure, a book that needs to be read and reread because of its spiritual potency and priceless value for everyday living….I am currently on my second and even third reading of certain chapters of this divinely inspired offering…. Everyone needs a copy of this book."

—Terry Cole-Whittaker. D.D.
Author of *What You Think of Me Is None of My Business*

Opening Your Heart

Today's world is suffering from an overdose of lust, while people everywhere are starving for love. In *Spiritual Warrior II*, Bhakti-Tirtha Swami offers profound insight into the critical issues of the body, mind, and spirit that touch us all. Tough questions are addressed, such as: What is love? Where does lust come from? How can sexuality become a constructive force? How can we have better relationships? Provided with insightful answers stemming from a broad, compassionate perspective deeply grounded in spirituality, we are shown how to live from the heart, loving ourselves, one another and God.

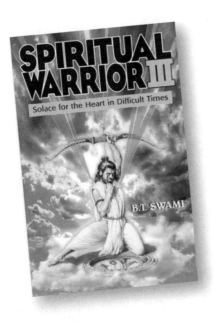

by B.T. Swami
(Swami Krishnapada)

$14.95 softbound ISBN #1-885414-17-X
304 pages

"*Spiritual Warrior V* is not only an inspiration for a new aspirant on the spiritual journey, but it is a manual for all experienced people of higher consciousness."

—Gyanendra Mahapatra, M.D.
(Former Vice-chancellor of Vedic University in Noida India)

Spiritual Warrior V

Making the Mind Your Best Friend

Access The Warrior Within

Building on the *Spiritual Warrior* series, *Making the Mind Your Best Friend* explores advanced spiritual weapons for our battles with apathy and depression. Short-term goals, gratitude, enthusiasm, and mindfulness help us maintain our fighting spirit, while directed imagination helps us involve the rebellious mind in constructing a healthy future.

Spiritual Warrior VI

Beyond Fanaticism, Terrorism, and War: Discover the Peace Solution

Embracing Faith, Defeating Fanaticism

The amount of violence currently pervading the planet has people wondering what we can do as individuals to make a difference. Bhakti-Tirtha Swami examines the causes and effects of war, terrorism, fanaticism, and sectarianism. Along the way he lovingly reminds us that each of us has major influence over whatever happens on this planet. The more that we understand what we can attain through righteousness and purity, the more we will want to move away from ignorance and confusion by running towards the higher goals. Let us get involved in raising consciousness as we move on and march as spiritual warriors committed to producing a better planet.

by B.T. Swami
(Swami Krishnapada)

$14.95 softbound ISBN #1-885414-18-8
336 pages

"The quest for peace and justice in the world is not the responsibility of a few individuals…. We can effect the needed change any time we want. It is a choice between fear and love, violence and peace. This book is an excellent guideline for waging peace and love. His Holiness B.T. Swami engages us in new approaches to saving this world from self-destruction."

—Richard Kuuire, Former Director-General of Ghana Prisons Service, Advisor to the Honorable Minister of Interior

The Beggar I

Meditations and Prayers on the Supreme Lord

Serenity in the Lord

Deeply penetrating reflections in the form of a personal dialogue with God remind the reader of the necessity to dedicate time to spiritual growth along with secular pursuits. Written in an easily readable, non-sectarian style, this book explores such topics as patience, tolerance, humility, compassion and determination. The author presents these subjects not as quaint musings from another age but as necessary tools for maintaining sanity in a far-from-normal world full of conflict and stress.

by B.T. Swami
(Swami Krishnapada)

$11.95 softbound ISBN #1-885414-00-5
160 pages

"Now, my dear Lord, I am completely confused. I have tried to attract You, but I see I have nothing to attract You with. I am a pretender. I want Your kingdom, without You. I am a criminal who has tried to plead innocent, and now I have nowhere to hide, no presentations to make. What am I to do, dear Lord?

"Then I heard the Lord say: 'You have always been, and always will be, dear to Me, but you do not believe it. Therefore, you separate us by being an enemy to yourself. Come on, My child, and experience what it is to be fully dear to Me.'"

Excerpt from *The Beggar*

The Beggar III

False Ego: The Greatest
Enemy of the Spiritual Leader

Release Your True Self

by B.T. Swami
(Swami Krishnapada)

$12.95 softbound ISBN #1-885414-10-2
215 pages

"Bhakti-Tirtha Swami's books are all written to facilitate us in keeping our highest Self in charge of our lives as we move toward our greatest potential and highest good. *The Beggar III* is his latest contribution to helping us do the often-difficult inner work of understanding that our life force is our God force. Typical of all true leaders, he teaches by loving, living example."

John T. Chissell, M.D.
Author: *Pyramids of Power*

"...Selflessness is the ingredient most lacking in today's world, because people misunderstand the purpose and principle behind this wonderful science. Genuine selflessness is not thinking less of yourself, but thinking of yourself less.

"My mentor continued: 'Selflessness doesn't mean to give up pursuing adventurous goals, but rather to attach ourselves to transcendental goals. Actual selflessness means we must genuinely access humility and submissiveness. This can be very scary, because we normally identify humility and submissiveness with low self-esteem.'"

—*excerpts from The Beggar III*

The Beggar IV

Die Before Dying

by B.T. Swami
(Swami Krishnapada)

$12.95 softbound ISBN #1-885414-22-6
184 pages

Death is to Remove Everything False and Secondary

This newest offering of prayers and meditations written by Bhakti-Tirtha Swami began after he was diagnosed with advanced cancer. Through these illuminating meditations we participate in the process he calls "die before dying." It is easy to take so many opportunities for granted, even life itself. However, when we no longer have such opportunities, we are often forced to reflect more on how we have benefited from past situations. Just as there is life, there is death. Someone or something takes birth, grows, stays for some time, deteriorates, and then dies. Therefore, it is important to say and do whatever is best for all now because once the body is gone, the soul departs for its next encounter.

"We must allow every day of our lives to represent healthy closure now! When we live for love, this is most natural because all of our associations will be quality associations in which we share our compassion, determination, and realizations, and receive the same from others. This is the technology of how to celebrate life now and live with proper preparation and detachment, so that we will master the science of dying before dying so as to connect with the soul and its home—the spiritual world. After all, death is to remove everything false and secondary. I am that lowly beggar who is desperately trying to die before dying."

—excerpts from The Beggar IV

Reflections on Sacred Teachings

Volume One: Sri Siksastaka

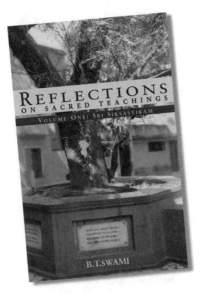

by B.T. Swami
(Swami Krishnapada)

$14.95, softbound ISBN #1-885414-13-7
260 pages

"O Govinda! Feeling Your separation, I am considering a moment to be like twelve years or more. Tears are flowing from my eyes like torrents of rain and I am feeling all vacant in the world in Your absence."

Explore Timeless Wisdom

"Lord Caitanya Mahaprabhu instructed His disciples to write books on the science of Krishna, a task which those who follow Him have continued to carry out down to the present day. The elaborations and expositions on the philosophy taught by Lord Caitanya are in fact most voluminous, exacting and consistent due to the system of disciplic succession. Although Lord Caitanya was widely renowned as a scholar in His youth, He left only eight verses, called *Siksastaka*. These eight verses clearly reveal His mission and precepts."

– A.C. Bhaktivedanta
Swami Prabhupada

Nearly five hundred years after Lord Caitanya Mahaprabhu walked among us, the *Sri Siksastaka* verses continue to lead all Vaisnavas ever deeper into the science and experience of pure, spontaneous and enveloping love of God.

His Holiness Bhakti-Tirtha Swami explores these verses from a contemporary perspective and helps modern devotees derive strength and realization from this timeless message, while reminding us of the important role we must play in carrying Lord Caitanya's legacy to future generations.

—*excerpts from Reflections on Sacred Teachings. Sri Siksastaka*

Reflections on Sacred Teachings

Volume Two: Madhurya-Kadambini

The Sweetness of Devotion

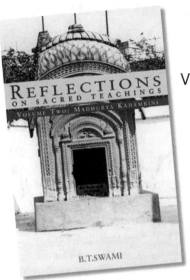

by B.T. Swami
(Swami Krishnapada)

$14.95, softbound ISBN #1-885414-14-5
244 pages

"Srila Visvanatha Cakravarti has given us a detailed analysis of the obstructions to our individual and collective devotional service. He has also given us a sublime outline of the stages of progress up to *prema*. Now the challenge is before each of us to fully use what he has given us. How blessed we all are to receive this opportunity through the blueprints given by such great *acaryas*, to facilitate us in returning back to the realm of pure, enchanting, enduring and animated love."

The Bhakti Trilogy is one of the great works of Visvanatha Cakravarti and his first presentation is the *Madhurya-Kadambini*. The word *kadambini* means a long bank of clouds that are showering *madhurya*, the sweetness of devotion. These clouds manifest over the environment to shower the *madhurya* and extinguish the blazing forest fire of material attraction and attachments. His Holiness Bhakti-Tirtha Swami explores these verses as a way of reminding the reader how such mentors and their teachings, although ancient, are as relevant now as they were in the past. Let the *madhurya*, the sweetness of devotion, shower us all as we take shelter of Srila Visvanatha Cakravarti Thakura's unlimited mercy.

—*excerpts from Reflections on Sacred Teachings: Madhurya-Kadambini*

Reflections on Sacred Teachings

Volume Three: Harinama Cintamani

The Holy Name Is The Key

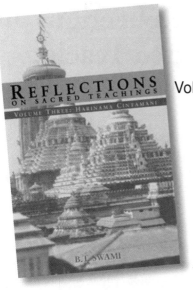

by B.T. Swami
(Swami Krishnapada)

$14.95, softbound ISBN #1-885414-15-3
308 pages

"In previous ages, a person could reach perfection through meditation, temple worship or *yajnas* but in Kali-yuga, we cannot even perform one of the nine-fold activities nicely. Although just one of these nine activities can result in full love of Godhead, we engage in all nine and still have problems. Fortunately Srila Haridasa reveals the holy name as a source of hope in spite of the constant challenges in this Kali-yuga."

—excerpts from Reflections on Sacred Teachings: Harinama Cintamani

"*Sri Harinama Cintamani* is the extraordinary conversation between the Supreme Lord Sri Caitanya Mahaprabhu and His devotee Srila Haridasa Thakura on the potency and efficacy of the holy name. His Holiness Bhakti-Tirtha Swami, a devout spiritual teacher in the Vaisnava line, leads us through the *Sri Harinama Cintamani* step-by-step, and enables us to hold onto the key of the holy name, unlocking the mysteries of our own pure and effulgent qualities. Srila Haridasa explains that the holy name will reach out—in spite of all the barriers and formalities—to the person who grabs and holds onto it.

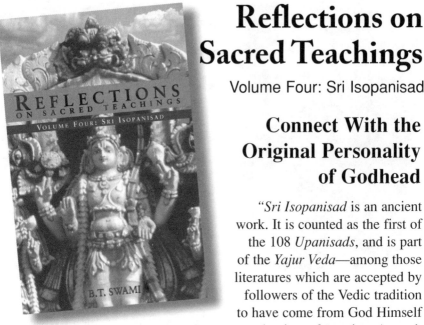

Reflections on Sacred Teachings

Volume Five:
Srila Bhaktisiddhanta's
Sixty-four Principles
for Community

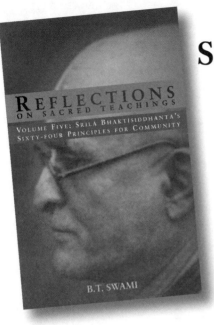

Building Healthy Communities

Srila Bhaktisiddhanta Sarasvati Thakura has given sixty-four principles for the Vaisnava community as compiled by His Holiness Bharati Maharaja. We want to beg Krishna to allow us to fully understand these great sixty-four teachings. Most importantly, we want to pray for the ability to use them as guides in strengthening our communities. Let us imbibe these principles so that we can help establish the type of communities envisioned by Srila Bhaktisiddhanta and our own Vaisnava spiritual master Srila Prabhupada: Communities that treat the heart rather than just the temporary body. Let us create communities that are living examples of these sixty-four principles.

by B.T. Swami
(Swami Krishnapada)

$12.95, softbound ISBN #1-885414-21-8

"Srila Bhaktisiddhanta Sarasvati Thakura founded his Gaudiya Matha on sixty-four principles, which outline a perfect and complete foundation for a spiritual society. His Holiness Bhakti-Tirtha Maharaja has molded his life according to these sixty-four principles. Therefore, he is able to expertly guide the world towards the ultimate goal of life, not only by elaborating on them, but also by leading with his personal example."

—Bhakti Caru Maharaja
International GBC and ISKCON Guru

Order Form

Item	Quant	Costs	Item	Quant	Costs
Leadership for an Age of Higher Consciousness, Vol. 1 (2nd ed.)	hard $23.00 x ___ = $ _____ soft $14.95 x ___ = $ _____		The Beggar, Vol. 1	soft $11.95 x ___ = $ _____	
Leadership for an Age of Higher Consciousness, Vol. 2	hard $23.00 x ___ = $ _____ soft $14.95 x ___ = $ _____		The Beggar, Vol. 1 audio tapes	6 tapes $28.00 x ___ = $ _____	
Spiritual Warrior, Vol. 1	soft $12.95 x ___ = $ _____		The Beggar, Vol. 2	soft $11.95 x ___ = $ _____	
Spiritual Warrior, Vol. 2 (2nd ed.)	soft $14.95 x ___ = $ _____		The Beggar, Vol. 3	soft $12.95 x ___ = $ _____	
Spiritual Warrior, Vol. 2 tapes and CDs (1st ed.)	10 tapes $45.00 x ___ = $ _____ 9 CDs $60.00 x ___ = $ _____		The Beggar, Vol. 4	soft $12.95 x ___ = $ _____	
Spiritual Warrior, Vol. 3	hard $23.00 x ___ = $ _____ soft $14.95 x ___ = $ _____		Reflections on Sacred Teachings, Vol. 1	soft $14.95 x ___ = $ _____	
Spiritual Warrior, Vol. 4	soft $14.95 x ___ = $ _____		Reflections on Sacred Teachings, Vol. 2	soft $14.95 x ___ = $ _____	
Spiritual Warrior, Vol. 5	soft $14.95 x ___ = $ _____		Reflections on Sacred Teachings, Vol. 3	soft $14.95 x ___ = $ _____	
Spiritual Warrior, Vol. 6	soft $14.95 x ___ = $ _____		Reflections on Sacred Teachings, Vol. 4	soft $14.95 x ___ = $ _____	
			Reflections on Sacred Teachings, Vol. 5	soft $12.95 x ___ = $ _____	

Subtotal	
Shipping & Handling	
Total	

◯ I'd like more information on other books, CDs, audiotapes and videotapes from HNP.

Name: _____

Address: _____

City: _____ State: _____ Zip: _____

Daytime Phone: _____ Evening Phone: _____

Email Address: _____

Shipping and handling: **USA:** $5.00 for first book and $1.75 for each additional book. Air mail per book (USA only): $5.00. **Outside of the USA:** $8.00 for first book and $4.00 for each additional book. Surface shipping may take 3-4 weeks. Foreign orders: please allow 6-8 weeks for delivery.

Internet: www.ifast.net/hnp
Mail: Hari-Nama Press, PO Box 76451, Washington DC 20013